DUCK AND COVER:
A Memoir of My 1960's Brooklyn

By Rosemary Neri Villanella

D1264243

Duck And Cover: A Memoir of My 1960's Brooklyn
by Rosemary Neri Villanella

Printed in the United States of America.
Edited by Xulon Press.

ISBN 9781498499736

"The Tennessee Waltz" is quoted from a 1950 recording by Redd Stewart and Pee Wee King, 1947

www.xulonpress.com

Table of Contents

Prologue

Before it was the borough of Park Slope Parents vs. Williamsburg Hipsters, Brooklyn was regarded as a lesser suburb of Manhattan and, unlike tonier Long Island, Westchester, or Connecticut, it only cost fifteen cents to get there. Before I was born, my parents looked at homes in Levittown, a planned community with a special attraction for World War II veterans who wanted to buy new homes. After driving an hour to get there, however, and finding it offered nothing more than our home borough (but with higher property taxes and houses that all looked alike), they turned right around and never looked for a home outside Brooklyn again.

"Why would you ever choose to travel such a long time to get to work every day when we have parks, stores, and good schools right here?" My mother would say whenever she heard about anyone planning to leave Brooklyn for Long Island.

The clincher for them was we could walk to everything we needed in our own neighborhood; not having to drive in a car to get groceries was especially important to my mother who didn't learn to drive until my sister and I were much older.

"We have the best of everything here and we even used to be our own city before we allowed them to demote us to a borough," my father would say proudly whenever I'd ask him to tell me about why we lived in Brooklyn.

"We even had our own baseball team for a long time," he'd add wistfully.

Although I never lived here when it had been a city unto itself, I do remember when we had the Brooklyn Dodgers, the Brooklyn Naval Shipyard, and more churches and synagogues per square mile than any other city on earth, or so it said in our history textbooks.

The families who lived in or moved to Brooklyn after World War II were, by and large, the children of immigrants whose families had left the now-cool neighborhoods called "TriBeCa" (the Triangle Below Canal St.) and "NoLita" (North of Little Italy), but which they knew only as The Lower East Side. These neighborhoods were often their first stop in the United States, but they didn't stay long. Many of those families ran to Brooklyn from the mean concrete and tar streets of Manhattan as soon as they could save enough money to do so.

They loved their borough, their home neighborhood, and their country—in that order.

If they wanted to return to Manhattan to see old friends who hadn't made it across the Brooklyn Bridge yet, the subway fare was low and the cars were clean and safe to ride. In fact, as if to prove its status as the most livable of the five boroughs, signs in our local subway stop on I

Avenue U didn't read:
To Manhattan ——————-
——————-To Coney Island

They read:
To City——————-
——————-From City

Most Brooklynites didn't go back to the "City" too often, though, because everything they could ever want was found in their home borough.

The neighborhoods hadn't yet become diversified, but Brooklyn was always a multicultural melting pot. Although each ethnic group hyphenated its name and added American after the hyphen, they retained the flavor, food, and traditions of the places from which their parents or grandparents had come. There were Irish, Germans, and Greeks in Bay Ridge; Italians in Bensonhurst and Gravesend; black people from the Caribbean and the South in Fort Greene, Bedford-Stuyvesant, Downtown Brooklyn, and

Coney Island; Scandinavians in Sunset Park; Jewish people of many ethnic backgrounds in Brighton Beach and Flatbush, and so on.

In the 1950s and 60s, you could walk from one neighborhood to the next and experience many different foods and ethnic stores without ever leaving Brooklyn, and we did. As a child, I loved the special butter cookies from Olsen's Bakery in Sunset Park and the handmade knishes from Schatzkin's in Coney Island just as much as the Sicilian (we called it "square") pizza from our neighborhood Italian bread store at lunchtime.

We even learned in elementary school that my particular neighborhood, Gravesend, had been originally settled by the Dutch, the first ethnic group to arrive before the English established themselves in New York in the 1600s. The Lady Moody House was mentioned in our fourth grade textbook about the history of New York and as students we were filled with pride when the text said it still stood not far from PS 95, my old elementary school. While the house is still there, it, like Brooklyn, is different, but, in some ways, still the same.

I decided to write this memoir almost two decades ago when my daughter returned from a summer program studying Italian in Padova, Italy. While there, she lived not in a dorm, but with an Italian professor from the local university and her son in their apartment. When she returned, she told me that in that small Italian

city not far from Venice, people still sat outside in the evening and everyone got to know
each other —both locals and visitors—from sitting, strolling, and talking in the piazzas after
dinner when the heat of the day waned. She
said she finally understood a little bit of what it
had been like for me and my sister, growing up
in Brooklyn and playing outside until bedtime
in the summer.

She told me of her experiences in Padova a
bit wistfully and I realized then that it was my
job to let my children and grandchildren know
life in our city wasn't always the same as it is
experienced today. Studying history is vital, but
first you must know your personal history, and
Brooklyn is a large part of my family's personal
chronicle. I knew I'd be remiss as a mom and a
nana if I didn't try to share that story with my
family and, hopefully, with you.

If you, like an incredible twenty-five percent
of all Americans, can trace any part of your
roots to Brooklyn...if you live in Brooklyn now...
are thinking of moving here...or if you've only
heard of Brooklyn and want to know what it
was like then:

"*Andiamo!*" — Let's go!
We'll travel back there together, just you and I.
"*Comminciamo!*" — Let's begin!
And *Buon viaggio!* — I hope you enjoy
the trip!
Rosemary Neri Villanella
April 8, 2016

Chapter 1

Babysitting The Naked Baseball Player

In the summer of 1960, the Fifties weren't over yet in Brooklyn. Although our parents warned us repeatedly about the bad things that could happen to us on the streets, living in Brooklyn, especially my neighborhood, wrapped me in a feeling of safety that I took for granted then. The neighborhood my family lived in was a big step up from the Lower East Side tenements where most of our Italian-American grandparents had lived when they first came to the United States from southern Italy and Sicily. Most fathers worked, most mothers stayed home, and kids did what they still do today: played and tried to avoid chores, responsibilities, and homework, not necessarily in that order. Although this trifecta of avoidance has evolved into a lifestyle for many in subsequent generations, especially among a lot of millennials, most of my generation was expected to pull some of our own weight financially by high school, if not before. This was especially true in the working class neighborhoods of the borough, which more resembled the bedroom communities of the surrounding suburbs outside of New York City than they do today.

The mother of one of my school friends was known to repeatedly respond to any of her son's requests for money with the words: "Got hair under your arms?"

Too humiliated to respond, he could only stand in his kitchen, silently mortified. She continued virtually without a pause: "Time to get a job and earn your own money."

The whole scenario wore him down pretty quickly and he got a job delivering prescriptions for a local druggist, although we were a little shocked by the graphic nature of her phraseology, almost all my friends experienced the same kind of sentiment from our parents, especially with regard to asking them for money after the age of twelve. This lack of funds began to interfere with our real lives, especially in the summer. My girlfriends and I tried to solve this dilemma by babysitting, which we did mostly at night, so that we could have our days free and still earn some money to buy things without asking our parents.

In my neighborhood, Gravesend, we were all outside as much as the weather permitted, which in summer was most of the day. Although the houses on West 5th Street, the block of my grandfather's house where we lived then, were set close together and most shared driveways, (which we called alleyways) narrow passages that led to tiny garages, they held many places for us to play. The front stoops, the alleyways, and even the street itself were all regarded as the ideal sites for all the street games of a Brooklyn summer.

The cement walls of the houses rising up on either side of the alleyways were perfect for War, or as some kids called it, Russia: the two words being almost equivalent to us. Despite its ominous, Cold-War-inspired name, War was usually played by girls. To play you needed only another kid and a pink, rubber Spalding ball, known in common parlance as a "Spaldeen," which cost fifteen cents. Whoever won the choose was allowed to be "America" and went first. You played by bouncing the ball against the wall from one to twenty times, each time repeating whatever maneuver had been agreed upon to fit that number and involving intricate series of bounces, claps, and spins with the ball. If you missed, the other country was up. It was usually assumed the better player would be "America" and would inevitably win, since we all knew the "Commies" were losers and would never beat us, especially those of us from Brooklyn.

The sidewalk in front of the houses was perfect for games of Boxball, which was a more gentle form of city tennis played with neither a court nor a racquet. The game required both skill and a steady arm to return the ball into the opponent's box (which was delineated by the lines in the cement which formed the boxes in the sidewalk) with the flat of your bare hand without hitting it too hard so it went out of bounds, or too softly so it remained inside your own box. You couldn't be too wild with the ball, either, or it would go into the street. Real skill and self-control were required, so even boys and grownups played Boxball. My father was good at it, probably because of his two outstanding qualities: patience and gentleness.

My favorite games were Stickball (named after the broom handles that were originally used as bats when my father's generation played in the same streets of this neighborhood) and Punchball, both of which were more like my father's favorite—baseball—but could be played with no equipment at all except for the inevitable "Spaldeen." We played these games in the street if the schoolyard was too crowded. My father remembered when Stickball had been played in the vast, empty lots of Gravesend before World War II; but there weren't so many lots left by my youth, so we all raced to the schoolyard to get the space for the game staked out before the older kids from the junior high school took it over. You couldn't win a fight with them for the space, so if they were already there, it was a street game that day. Street or schoolyard, we loved this neighborhood version of baseball; we played for the sheer joy of the game, and, in doing so, were allowed to learn for ourselves about losing and winning.

By 1960, when I was almost thirteen, few of my friends still played Stickball or even Punchball. By almost thirteen, we were all supposed to be more interested in boys, hair, and makeup. I was, but I still loved to watch any games played and secretly longed to play again myself, but this wasn't something you admitted at thirteen. It was a secret "babyish" vice, like playing with dolls, that you kept to yourself if you wanted to survive as an adolescent in my neighborhood. Only in the summer, when my family went away to the Twin Lakes house in Narrowsburgh, New York for our annual two weeks of barefoot summer vacation, did I play on the team of summer kids there. At the Twin Lakes house, none of the visiting city kids (mostly from New York City and Philadelphia) were afraid to regress and become a "hick"; on vacation we were all bound together by the temporary nature of our circumstances and knew we would part when our vacation was over. No one from the different neighborhoods we each called home would know about our collective secret and we would never tell about our summertime reversion to a younger stage of childhood.

At home in Brooklyn, I had become less adept at avoiding responsibility than I was at avoiding the label of "baby." In the almost four years since my grandmother had died, I had become responsible for watching my younger sister, Alice (who was almost four years my junior), whenever my mother was at work. This meant taking her home at lunchtime from school and eating with her alone in our kitchen, since almost no one ate lunch in school until you went to junior high in seventh grade.

I had started babysitting but not yet changing diapers, with my friend Marissa, who lived a few houses up the block from us. Marissa had it worse than I did, with both a younger sister and a younger brother. I had heard my mother tell my father that the little brother and third child, Markie, who was two and a half, had been a "surprise." I vaguely suspected what that meant, but knew better than to ask about it, since even I knew babies, and their appearance, surprise or not, was related to one of my mothers' forbidden topics for discussion: sex. Once, when I was eight and sitting in the kitchen doing my homework and looking up words in the dictionary, I asked my mother what the nun at religious instruction meant when she told us that all Catholics were baptized, but Jewish boys were circumcised.

"What did you say?" She asked me back, her head spinning in my direction and away from the potatoes she was peeling with a quickness that jolted me.

What had I said? I hesitated, swallowed, then answered.

"Last Wednesday at religious instruction Sister Veronica said Jewish people have the rite of circumcision the way we have baptism, and I wondered what that was."

"I know what baptism means," I added, hoping to placate her although I didn't understand why.

"I'm surprised a nun would use a word like that with you. Where did you really hear about this?"

"From Sister Veronica," I answered slowly.

She kept looking at me like I had pulled my skirt up in public.

"If you don't believe me, why don't you write her a note?" I answered in what I hoped was a reasonable defense.

"Don't get snotty with me," she said, still looking angry.

Then she walked over to the table, brought her face closer to mine, lowered her voice and almost whispered: "It's when they cut off the end of a man's thing!"

That was all she said.

"What thing?" I blurted out, completely baffled by this time and trying to figure out what was going on.

"You know," was all she said. Having no brothers, I didn't. But I did know enough to let it drop there.

She went back to her potatoes, looked at my confused face and, reassured I told the truth said more softly: "They do it to all Jewish boys when they're eight days old. Even Jesus had it done."

I nodded my head up and down like I understood and went back to my work, but I was lost. If it was so terrible to ask about, then why had it been done to Jesus? And if it wasn't so terrible, why had she gotten so angry? The answer must have to do with sex.

The next word to define for my homework did not begin with the letter "c", but that's where I turned to in the dictionary, casually and carefully so she wouldn't notice anything unusual. Keeping my notebook over the dictionary like a shield, I read. It said, "to cut off all or part of the foreskin." She hadn't lied about the cutting part. Now I was off to "f". That one said "the fold of skin covering the tip of the male sex organ." I had been right; I immediately understood, not what it all meant (Marissa explained that to me later, after having watched her mother change her brother's diapers right after he had been born, she'd asked and been told about the whole procedure), but why she'd gotten so angry with me. I guess old Sister Veronica didn't think too many of us kids from the public schools would head straight for the dictionary and incur our mothers' wrath for our inquis-itiveness. I went back to my real homework, feeling that I had won a small, secret victory in my quest to learn everything I could about Things My Mother Wouldn't Talk About, espe-cially sex. I also knew I was really glad I wasn't an eight-day-old boy.

Markie may not have been planned, but he was a little angel to me. Not only did Marissa explain all about circumcision to me, because she had to know about it to help her mother change his diapers as a newborn, but I loved holding him when he got bigger and even helping to take care of him myself. I had always envied those friends who had a new baby cousin to fuss over and hold, and since I was eleven when he was born, Marissa's mother trusted me to help take care of him along with her. Together, we gradually became the pro-verbial and much-desired, reliable, trustworthy pre-teen mother's helpers. Marissa didn't get paid when she took care of him alone so we always tried to get her mother to trust us for longer periods of time as he got older and past the infant stage. This wasn't too hard because Mrs. Collaro was often forced to divide her time between Marissa, her sister, and the baby, as well as doing all the housework, cleaning, and shopping. No one we knew had a cleaning lady or a maid; heck, it hadn't even worked out for the Riccardo family on "I Love Lucy"!

Mr. Collaro was one of the only men on the block who had a white-collar job. Most of the other men, including my father, who worked at the Brooklyn Navy Yard, wore work shirts and pants and carried their lunch as they went to and from work on the "N" subway line, which was called the "Sea Beach Line" in those days. Even without his shirt and tie, Mr. Collaro was also one of the handsomest men on the block. I remember thinking, when the first James Bond movie, "Dr. No", came out a few years later and I went to see it, that he looked like an Italian- American version of Sean Connery. He was dark, with thick, wavy hair that he wore parted and combed away from his face. His hair was groomed with enough Vitalis to make it shine, but not so much that it looked greasy. Everyone loved him. His real name was Giacomo (Italian for James) but everyone called him Jackie. I think I had my first crush on my friend Marissa's father just because of his looks, but because he was also funny and unfailingly kind to me, just as he was to Marissa and her sister.

He used to call me "bookworm," a name that would have been deadly if any of my other friends had heard it; but when he said it, there was affection and respect in his voice. Unlike the boys my age, he made me feel that being both smart and a girl was a wonderful thing. He always asked me about my marks, and when I was the only sixth grader chosen from

PS 95 to attend junior high school in a special program run by Hunter College High School in Manhattan, he was the only one who urged me to go.

"A smart girl like you should go to the city for junior high school," he said to me.

Marissa's mother disagreed.

"Don't tell her that, Jackie," she'd admonish him when he asked me about junior high. "Her mother is probably worried about her traveling alone on the subway, like I'd be. She's smart enough to do well right here at our local junior high, anyway."

He wouldn't answer, just wink at Marissa and me conspiratorially and say: "How about if you and Marissa don't have hot dates for tonight, you two girls watch Markie so I can take his mother to the movies? For pay, of course."

Of course we said our movie star dates could wait while we watched Markie. I'd have done it for nothing as a favor to Mr. and Mrs. Collaro.

One late Saturday summer afternoon in 1960 while walking back from confession, the kids on the block were organizing a stickball game. Mrs. Collaro waved and called out to us from the second floor window as we approached Marissa's house.

"Girls! Marissa!" she called out, waving excitedly as soon as she caught sight of us. We ran to the front stoop to see what she wanted.

"Marissa, listen. Run and ask Rosemary's mother if she can stay for dinner and then the two of you can babysit Markie for pay. Daddy and I were invited out with his boss at the last minute tonight," she said, sounding stressed.

Marissa looked annoyed.

"But we were going to the movies! You promised we could go! Rosemary even got permission from her mother!" she protested.

"Don't argue with me in the street! Just come up here!" The window shut fast.

We went inside the front door and up the stairs, Marissa saying, "Dammit!" Under her breath the whole time. I knew she was angry.

"Thank God you don't have a baby brother!" was all she said to me.

I said nothing. I wasn't as disappointed as she because I knew that her parents would be out late and we could stay up late and watch Gunsmoke and The Late Show (which I was never allowed to do at home), and talk after her brother had gone to sleep. Maybe we'd even sneak a peek at her mother's copy of *Peyton Place*—the forbidden book of that era that we read for sex education, *not* story—like we had done a few times in the past. Anyway, if my mother let me do it, I'd be staying up later than I would have if we'd just gone out to the movies. We'd also get paid. We could still go to the movies another night.

As soon as we got upstairs, Markie came running out to greet us.

"Hi sister," he said to Marissa.

He turned to me. "I got new PJ's," he smiled shyly at me.

"Hi Markie," I said. "You been a good boy today? How about a hug?"

"No!" He said. "First Donald Duck talk."

I started to hug him anyway, and he screamed: "No!" and started to hit me, not hard, just light two-year-old smacks.

"Markie!" Mrs. Collaro said sternly. "No hitting! What did I tell you?"

He pushed out his lower lip and stared at me.

"I'm sorry," I said. "It was my fault for teasing him."

Then I bent down and quack-talked in his ear. He laughed and hugged me and I picked him up. I loved to take care of him. Markie-boy, as he was known to his older sisters when he didn't drive them crazy, was two-and-a-half years old, two-and-a-half feet tall, and not quite that wide, but pudgy. He had an angelic face and large grey-blue eyes, framed by the darkest, longest lashes I had ever seen on anybody, male or female. He was chubby because he loved to eat everything. I had known him to polish off a big, blue plastic Tupperware bowl full of his favorite snack, cornflakes and milk, before bed, but after dinner and dessert. He liked grown up foods and would eat calamari salad the way other kids ate peanut butter and jelly sandwiches, which he would also consume with delight. He only drank a bottle when he was tired and couldn't be consoled any other way. Sometimes, when he slept peacefully and I'd check on him during a night of babysitting, I wished he was *my* little brother.

"I'd love to stay and play, but I have to go home and ask my mommy if I can come back and stay with you tonight," I told him. "Be a good boy and I'll try to be right back."

"No!" he screamed. "Don't go home!"

"Call instead," Mrs. Collaro said, handing me the phone.

"By the way," she said to Marissa as I dialed my home phone number, "Your sister is staying downstairs with Aunt Patty tonight. Your father and I didn't think it was fair for you to have to watch her, too. Okay?"

Marissa's scowl lifted a little bit. "What about the movies?" she asked.

"I promise you can still go and your father will even drive you to the Kingsway if you just sit for me tonight. I really need your help."

"Okay," Marissa finally relented.

The Kingsway was a fancy and expensive first-rate movie theater that was now affordable because of the money we earned.

"But this is a real promise, no backing out."

"Cross my heart," Mrs. Collaro said. "I don't want to spoil your fun, but his boss has orchestra seats for a Broadway play and the other couple dropped out at the last minute. It's important for your father's job that we say yes. We have to leave soon, so please help out."

"Okay, I understand," Marissa said, looking somewhat less sullen.

"Thank God this was my regular day to have my hair done," her mother muttered, almost to herself, the matter decided to her great relief.

I waited through six rings for someone to pick up the telephone and was almost going to hang up and walk home when I heard my father's voice say, "Hello?"

Fate was with me. It wasn't my mother.

"Hi Dad, it's me. I'm back from confession and I'm calling from Marissa's house. Her parents have to go out unexpectedly and they asked me to babysit Markie with Marissa tonight because they're going to be out late. Please let me do it, say it's okay," I begged.

"Wait a minute, Rosemary," he said. "I thought you were going to the movies with Marissa tonight. Your mother and I already agreed to that."

"I know, but Mr. Collaro's boss called at the last minute and they have to go. It's important for his job, so we're going to go to the movies another night this week."

"Well, are you watching her sister, too?"

"No, she's going to her aunt downstairs. We're even going to eat dinner here. Please let me do it, Daddy. I can really use the money."

"If her aunt's going to be home all night, I guess it's all right with me."

Then the usual dreaded response: "Let me check with your mother."

I crossed my fingers and mouthed the words "my mother" to Marissa, who had been listening to everything.

My father returned to the phone and said, "Your mother isn't crazy about the idea of your being out late. She says you can only stay until midnight and then I'll walk over and pick you up. That's late enough. You know you have to get up for ten o'clock Mass tomorrow."

"Thanks Dad. I'll see you at midnight. Knock on the storm door but don't ring the bell so it won't wake Markie up. Her aunt will leave the second door open and the screen door locked so we'll hear you. And Dad—"

"What else, Rosemary?"

"I love you!" I said, knowing better than to argue with one of my mother's edicts. I was glad that she had said yes at all. She must have been in a good mood to let me eat dinner here, too, I thought.

I hung up the phone with a smile.

"I can babysit, but only until midnight when my father will come to get me. Is that okay?" I said to Mrs. Collaro, who looked relieved.

"Of course it is," she said. "I want Marissa to go to bed then anyway. We'll be out later than that, but her aunt is here if she needs anything after you leave."

"All right, now what do we need to do now?" she said. "Maryanne, you go get your pajamas, toothbrush, and underwear and bring them down to Aunt Patty. You're eating dinner down there with her."

She turned to us.

"You girls get the water running in the sink and we'll give Markie-boy his bath before I get dressed. There are cold cuts and fresh mozzarella salad with tomatoes in the fridge, and there's a loaf of fresh Italian bread that I bought on my way home from the beauty parlor, too. Is that good enough for dinner?"

"That's fine, Mom," Marissa answered. "Let's get Markie and give him his bath."

It was absolutely fine with us. We loved the *mortadella* with slices of pistachios in it, Genoa salami, and imported ham and cheeses that her mother had purchased from a fancy Italian American *salumeria* (literally, the store that sells salami) that my parents thought was too expensive. Our mouths watered at the thought of the fresh, round golf balls of homemade mozzarella marinating in a bath that consisted of green olive oil, red wine vinegar, onions, and spices as well as the tomato chunks from their grandfather's garden, which we would spoon onto the ends of the bread. This would accompany big, dinner-sized sandwiches that would make up our meal.

We went through the dining room and into the living room, whose windows overlooked West 5th Street. Markie had pushed a hassock over to the closed window, had climbed up on it and tried to reach past the window guard to the latch that opened it.

"Markie!" Marissa screamed. "Get down from there! You know you're not allowed by the windows unless there's a grown up with you!"

"You're not a grown up!" Markie said, still reaching for the latch.

"I'm closer than you are, you little brat boy!"

"I'm *not* a brat boy!" he screamed. He hated to be called names.

"Markie," I said, walking over to him. "Would you like to look out of the window with Donald Duck?"

He nodded a yes and I sat down next to him and duck-talked into his ear.

"Donald says you have to be a good boy if you want to play with us when Mommy and Daddy go bye-bye tonight. Okay?"

He hugged me tightly, nodding.

"Okay Ho-mary," he said.

"Let's look out the window at the big boys together," I said.

"Your sister will go and get your sink bath ready."

I motioned to Marissa that I would take care of him myself while she prepared the water and his bath stuff and pajamas.

The Stickball game was still in progress, but the players had moved down the block toward Avenue T, chased away by old Mrs. Ferucci, who hated Stickball because it threatened her newly installed storm windows. As usual, she had yelled at them in Italian, gesturing vigorously as she hollered from her stoop across the narrow street. Eventually she had succeeded in harassing them enough to get them to move somewhere else or risk losing their ball because she had put the evil eye on them. Although most of the kids had been born in Brooklyn, we all believed to some degree or other in the *malocchio*, or evil eye, that could be put on you by someone out of jealousy or meanness, and no one wanted to risk it with her. She had actually been born in Sicily, wore only black, and we all partially believed she could curse us, or the ball, if we crossed her.

Markie and I were still able to see the game fairly well from the window by turning our heads right, and we watched for a few minutes together and then Markie said: "Ho-mary, I wanna be a baseball player."

"You'll be a great one if you keep on practicing," I said. "My dad says that's the key to the whole game."

"I want to *pract-ice*!" he said.

"Maybe I'll throw the ball to you another day. We'll have our own baseball practice."

"*Pract-ice*!" he replied, delighted with the new word.

Then his sister called: "Markie, sink bath time! Come on!"

He jumped off the hassock and, while I made sure the window was locked, he ran into the bathroom yelling: "Pee-pee! Pee-pee first!"

"Good boy!" Mrs. Collaro said.

Then she told me, "I've been trying to teach him to use the bathroom. My girls were toilet trained around this age and he finally seems a little interested since his father showed him how a big boy does it."

I blushed, picturing the scene, but not wanting to.

When we got to the bathroom, Markie had pulled off his diaper and all of his clothes and, wearing only little plastic sandals was proudly peeing against the wall of the bathroom, and then the floor of the bathroom, everywhere except into the toilet bowl, singing, "Pee-pee all day long" as he did it.

"Markie!" yelled Marissa. "That's not where Daddy showed you to make pee-pee! Stop doing that!"

He obliged, holding the same part of his anatomy that I had once been so curious about with both hands for protection. Marissa grabbed his arm.

"In the toilet bowl, nowhere else!" She said sternly.

"No!" He screamed back at her. "All over, all day!"

"Boys who do pee-pee all over can't play baseball because they're still babies! Big boys do it in the bowl," she said.

He ran out of the bathroom, and Mrs. Collaro ran in. "What did he do, wet on the floor?" she asked.

"On the floor, the walls, everywhere he could except the bowl," Marissa answered.

"Oh God, I'll never get dressed in time now, and I don't even know if I should leave him with you girls now." She sounded tired and defeated.

"We'll take good care of him," I said. "He's just acting up because he knows you're going out. He'll be fine with us after you go. He's always a good boy for us. I'll help clean this mess up."

"No, it's okay," Mrs. Collaro said to my relief. "You give him his bath and I'll clean this mess up and then get dressed. Go ahead, girls."

She reached under the sink, put on her pink rubber gloves, and got to work.

We went into the kitchen to give him his bath, but he wasn't there. Marissa and I looked at each other and then ran silently around the apartment looking for him. No Markie. When we got back to the kitchen, we noticed the door leading to the stairs was open. We raced down, not saying anything to each other. The front door, that I had promised to leave open for my father later, was open as well. I looked from it to my friend.

"Don't go nuts on me." I told Marissa.

"Quick, say a prayer to St. Anthony and we'll find him."

"God, where did he go?" She said, panic in her voice as we raced through the door, down the five steps of the stoop, and out of the front gate.

"He was just here. He couldn't have gone too far. You go toward Avenue U and I'll go toward Avenue T. Meet back here as soon as you find him," I said.

"Hope to God we do. My mother will kill me and then drop dead herself if we don't."

I hardly heard her as I walked toward Avenue T, looking into every stoop area and behind garbage cans, where he loved to hide when we played with him, all the time praying: "Please, God, let him be okay and help us find him."

As intent as I was on my search, I couldn't ignore old Mrs. Ferrucci, who screamed something in Italian at me from across the street and gestured with her hand to catch my eye.

"*Lui gioca cogli schiffosi!*" she yelled over to me, gesturing with her hand in my direction.

I didn't speak much Italian then and didn't understand anything she said, except that *schiffosi* was what my father called the tough kids who hung out on corners and smoked cigarettes instead of getting jobs. Was she saying the tough kids had grabbed Markie?

"Oh God," I prayed again. "Please let him be okay!"

Then I looked where she pointed and saw the Stickball players up the block, laughing and smacking each other playfully on the arms and I knew everything was all right. Mrs. Ferucci might think these kids were *schiffosi*, but I knew most of them and they were good kids.

I ran down the sidewalk and saw Markie, still naked except for his jelly sandals, with one of the Stickball players, standing in the middle of West 5th Street. He was holding a Stickball bat and the other kid had his arms around him, helping him to hold and swing the stick the way an older brother would teach you how to do it. I was too happy to be embarrassed.

I called out: "Markie!" and waved to him.

The other players laughed at me and called out things like: "Loose something?" and "Can't you afford clothes for the kid?" but it didn't bother me. By this time, Marissa had caught up to me and now ran past me to get Markie, pulling the stick away and scooping him up in her arms.

He screamed in indignation as she struggled with him: "*Pract-is, pract-is!* No bath!"

We both got hold of him and it seemed that the whole neighborhood watched the show as we both half-dragged and half-carried him back down the block toward his front stoop. Some of the kids who'd let him play ball had followed us down the middle of the street, laughing and calling out: "Let the kid play! He's gonna be a slugger someday!" And even, "Go Markie-boy! Way to get ejected from a game!"

Even old Mrs. Ferucci crossed the street, leaving her stoop free to be vandalized, her new windows broken, and the roses in her front garden unprotected from pickers as she hollered *"Disgrazia!"* and *"Che vergogna!"* at us, which I recognized to mean "What a disgrace!" and "Shame!" because it was one of the only things I'd ever heard my father's mother (who lived with us) say in response to something she read in the newspaper. Shame was what I felt as the neighborhood parade followed us to the stoop, giving one last cheer of, "Go Markie!" as we dragged him up the front steps and inside the vestibule, letting the storm door slam behind us.

I felt responsible and hugged him as he sat on the clean tile floor of the vestibule, sobbing so hard that I thought he would never catch his breath. He hit me hard at first, and then let me pick him up and carry him on my back up the flight of stairs to the apartment door. Mrs. Collaro didn't even yell, just stood with a dripping toilet bowl brush in her hand, framed by that door. Maryanne was behind her, peeking around her as I trudged up the steps with Marissa at my back, hands ready, to make sure we didn't fall backward from the uneven weight of his body. When we got to the top step, she took Markie from me gently and held him for a minute as he made little mouse sounds, which I recognized as meaning that his breathing slowly returned to normal and he whimpered for his mother now that all the excitement had died down. In a few minutes she put him down and offered him a usually discouraged bottle of milk, cold from the refrigerator, which he drank, holding it in one hand, while rubbing on the edge of her housedress between the fingers of his other hand.

I had a sick feeling in my stomach and now felt more like throwing up than eating cold cuts. I felt terrible because I thought watching the kids playing out the front window had given him the idea to run outside, and I admitted as much to Mrs. Collaro. I knew if a parade of kids and neighborhood people had appeared at my mother's front door, I wouldn't get out of the house again until I got married, if then. So Marissa and I waited for her to kill us.

Finally, she said: "Marissa, you should have watched him better; you know that, don't you?"

Marissa nodded silently, her anger gone and tears beginning to gather in her eyes.

"And Rosemary, I thought you were much more responsible than this."

I felt myself start to fill up with tears of shame as she continued, looking into my eyes as she talked: "You know how much Markie loves you and looks up to you."

The tears burst through and flowed down my face and I began to sob, as Markie had done, unable to hold back all the feelings that had rolled over me in the last two minutes and I was unable to speak.

She shrugged her shoulders and squeezed mine with her free hand, continuing: "Well, at least I was still home and didn't have to hear about this from any cops. I hope the worst is over for tonight. Your father and I will be home as soon as the play is over." Then she turned to Maryanne.

"Go get your stuff; you're going down to your aunt. Now."

"You're letting them watch him after all that?" Maryanne asked in her I'm-the-good-one-now voice.

"Don't get snotty with me, just do what you're told and go! Your aunt's waiting," her mother answered in her don't-push-your-luck voice.

So Maryanne went with a surreptitious backward lick of her tongue at us as she slipped out the door and descended the steps.

"Don't forget to take your rubber sheet for when you wet the bed!" Marissa called after her. Mrs. Collaro gave her a watch-your-step look, took Markie's hand and gave it to me, sighed and turned to go back to the bathroom to finish cleaning it up and then put on her makeup and get dressed.

It was only after he squeezed my fingers hard and pointed to the puddle left on the floor from the toilet bowl brush that I stopped crying myself and realized my blouse felt wet.

"Pee-pee, again," Markie said and laughed, pointing to the huge wet spot on my back that had appeared on my best white, sleeve-less blouse that I had worn to confession what now felt like hours ago. I felt moisture dripping down into my underwear and shorts, which were both pretty wet, too.

"Markie, is that what I think it is? Did you make pee-pee on Rosemary?" Marissa asked.

He looked serious for a minute, then giggled and ran to the bathroom, where his mother was finishing up her cleaning, and let it rip right into the toilet bowl: a real gusher this time.

Mrs. Collaro said, "That's a good boy, Markie. You be good for the girls tonight and go take your bath now."

He came into the kitchen dragging his special duck towel after him and smiling at us.

We ran some more hot water into the deep sink and lifted him up and put him in with the bubbles and his bath toys. The Collaro's had the fanciest kitchen on the block, with a deep double-basin turquoise sink that matched the rest of the room and was still big enough to accommodate Markie. Covered in non-stinging soap bubbles and laughing again, he looked like a Christmas cherub—one who had peed on my back, that is.

Then Marissa's eyes met mine and all at once, as many other times in the past, we saw the humor in it all and both of us started to laugh at the same time, unable to control or stop ourselves. Before we knew it, tears once again coursed down our faces and we had as hard a time catching our breath as we formerly had had catching Markie. I felt sopping wet and hot and didn't care, as I gave myself completely to the laughter. It felt especially good, after everything that had happened to us that afternoon to forget it all and laugh until our ribs ached.

Markie didn't pay any attention to us. He just splashed with his toys in the sink, which I saw now barely accommodated him, and sang, "Pee-pee all day long."

Amen to that! I thought.

Chapter 2

Brooklyn, Sicily, Italy

We hadn't always lived in Gravesend. My first small memories of the sights, sounds and smells of my life had their roots in another place and time, in the railroad apartment that we lived in for the first eight years of my life that was in another part of Brooklyn, on 57th Street near Fort Hamilton Parkway. When we moved to an apartment that took up the whole first floor of my grandfather's house on West 5th Street near Avenue U in March of 1955, our family felt we had taken another step up, but as excited and happy as my parents were, I missed the old place.

I had an especially hard time leaving our old parlor, or "front room" that was the best room in the apartment, with two large windows onto the street that, to my young eyes, framed our view of the north end of the block so it became a moving painting, especially in the heat of summer when the curtains were pulled back to catch a breeze. Whenever the green, room-darkening shades were pulled down in the evening, or in preparation for my afternoon nap, I felt robbed of the drama that happened on the street—as if the curtain were being prematurely pulled down on the stage while the actors still recited their lines. I missed the parade of life on that block that moved before me like I was on an observation deck. I loved sitting in that room with my maternal grandmother, Granma Mary, after my father left for his 4:00pm-12:00am shift in the Brooklyn Navy Yard, and before my mother returned home from work in the years before television. It was hard to grow out of the comfort of the first years of my life when the ends of my world were measured by the distance you could see from left to right through those windows.

That view had changed abruptly when we became one of the first families on 57th Street to buy one of those big Emerson television sets the size of a small desk in its large, dark wood cabinet. It had a rectangular screen, which was tiny in proportion to the size of the cabinetry; the screen was a light avocado color when the set was turned off. It was probably the finest piece of cabinetry we owned and I remember running my small fingers along it to feel the smoothness of the wood and smelling it the way people still smell new cars. The little screen, about as big as a first-generation computer monitor, had rounded corners and the quality of what we saw on it was grainy and unclear until my father got permission from the landlady to install an antenna on the roof.

The arrival of the set meant the focus of my preschool days was now divided between the view outside and that magic screen, which transported me to "Ding Dong School" where kindly and patient Miss Frances helped me to learn the alphabet and my numbers. Hers was the only kindergarten I ever attended because my mother's boss wouldn't allow her to use her vacation time in fifteen minute increments each morning so she could take me to kindergarten at the local public school while my father caught up on his night's sleep after his shift at the Navy Yard and my grandma was busy with my baby sister. I didn't even know about this academic deprivation and certainly didn't care as long as I had that magic screen that had the power to bring the world I longed to see outside the windows into my house. Miss Frances' kindness influenced my perception of what real school would be like and my expectations were high.

I also loved "Winky Dink and Me", which was probably the first interactive television show for kids. It featured a thick, green plastic sheet, purchased by the adults, which you wiped with a "magic" cloth, so it clung to the TV screen, held on by static electricity. The main character had all sorts of adventures and the children lucky enough to have a magic screen could draw in (with crayons) the thing that was missing on the TV screen picture, thus participating in the episode. That was the "and me" part of the show because you were part of the story; there was even a cloth to erase the crayon so you could draw on it again. Since it combined two of the things I liked to do best—coloring and watching TV—the show was a hit with me. Like most of my contemporaries, I was hooked on TV at a young age.

In the late afternoon of winter days, when I awoke from my nap to a darkening sky, I was greeted by the face and voice of Kate Smith, now known primarily to Yankee fans. Her show was on Monday to Friday from 4:00 to 5:00pm and Granma and I watched it every weekday together. The show always included her famous version of "God Bless America", which still brings back to me feelings of warmth and of being safe at home with Granma as it grew dark. When we moved away to West 5th Street, I never watched the show again, but her voice and image stayed with me into my adult life. Whenever her voice is broadcast at Yankee games and I'm at the stadium, or following the game on TV or radio, she's singing not just a song, but homage: to our country, our city, and to the necessary loss of the enveloping comfort I found while I unknowingly missed out on kindergarten.

* * *

Spirelli are pieces of pasta formed in the shape of a corkscrew; they hold onto the sauce better and are still one of my favorites, but even as a child they confused me. I wanted a simple beginning, middle, and ending to both my stories and my dinner, but the *spirelli* denied me that. Held in your hand, each piece of pasta looks simple: just a twisted dried piece of semolina, durum wheat, and eggs, molded into a shape like a corkscrew and cut into a one and a quarter inch length, but up closer, they're both fascinating and frustrating. Tracing their shape with my finger to see where the line between beginning and ending was, I was often reprimanded for playing with my food, but the desire for the missing pieces of who I was did not begin and end in my dinner plate. I longed for the stories of who and what had come before me, but couldn't show it lest the tiny pieces I'd managed to put together by my silence when the adults were talking might be the only ones I'd ever hear.

In the schoolyard of PS 95 in Gravesend, the question of "What are you?" which encompassed "Who are you?" in those innocent days, took on a different meaning. While waiting your turn on line to jump in as we played jump rope with the long ropes jealously guarded and stingily shared by the older girls, this question was often phrased, "You're *Barese*, aren't you?"

which meant your ancestors had lived in the Adriatic coastal city of Bari, Italy in the poor and all but forgotten province of Puglia.

The answer would often be: "No, *Napoletana,*" which meant your people were from the poor, but proud region surrounding Naples, on the western coast of Italy.

To each of these girls, I would reply my grandfather (my father's father) from *Porto Empedocle* just south of Agrigento on the southernmost coast of Sicily, would have called them Northerners.

Although most non-Italians would accept the name of the country that your ancestors came from as a specific enough description of your ethnicity, Italian-Americans were never, and still are not, so easily satisfied. They need to know at least the region, if not the very village, that your people called home. No place was too tiny to be included in this answer, and almost everyone had *paisani*, fellow countrymen, who would smile at the mention of the name of the most obscure little town that they or their ancestors had left behind when they came to *L'America.*

This is at least partly due to the fact that Italy's *"Risorgimento"* or reunification had begun in the 1860's and was not completed until 1870. Before that time, the country had still been divided almost feudally into separate regions with a loose city-state configuration. Austria, France, and Spain held dominion over the different parts of the nation until Giuseppe Garibaldi, ably assisted by his wife, Anita, led his troops, the *Camici Rossi*, or red shirts, to rally the nation into a united whole for the first time since the fall of the Roman Empire. But old ways of living continued and persist to this day, which is why there is so much variety in Italian cuisine (with each region or even town preparing its unique dish differently from its neighbors) but also in the Italian language, with different dialects and accents in different parts of the country. The proud island of Sicily, while still a part of Italy, takes pride in its completely different language, which my grandfather knew, although he also spoke generic Italian.

The Sicilians, perhaps the proudest of all the Italian peoples, still maintain their unique language, cuisine, poetry, and artworks are the best of the best that Italy has to offer. Having emigrated in great numbers to the United States, the Sicilian Americans, my grandfather among them, only became more convinced of the superiority of their mother culture the longer they were in exile from it, while simultaneously embracing their identity as Americans. It's a complicated situation. In the late 1980's, during my first visit to Italy, a Roman guide told me that I should ease up on accenting my "t's" so heavily when I pronounced words in Italian, or people would think I was a Northerner. I laughed at her remark because

I had never been taught Italian or Sicilian at home, but began to study it at JHS 228, where my Italian teacher taught us the intricate rules of grammar and had praised my pronunciation. She must have been a Northerner, and my parents, who wanted me to learn "proper" Italian, hadn't realized they distanced me from my roots a little bit by not allowing me to learn the dialect of my grandparents at home. Maybe that's why I identify so strongly with the Sicilian part of my heritage and nature: complicated, like the *spirelli*.

The biggest problem with my Sicilian grandfather was that you never knew just how much of what he told you to believe. There's a quintessentially Sicilian logic to the fact that the part of the story of his emigration from Sicily to Galveston, Texas to New York City that I found the hardest to believe was the part that actually happened. It's also the easiest part of the story to document; the rest I know only from hearsay, from my fly-on-the-wall listening to my parents' conversations and the rare times my mother felt like talking about his personal history at all.

Grandpa Giuseppe Neri had been born in *Porto Empedocle*, a town in the southern province of Agrigento, Sicily on February 9, 1879. *Porto Empedocle* is about as far south as you can go and still be in Italy. The cities of Tunis and Tripoli, directly across the water, on the northern coast of Africa, are less distant from

Sicily than Rome, or even Naples, which lie to the north on the Italian mainland itself. Sicily exceeds Greece itself in the number of ancient ruins of Hellenic origin that are scattered throughout the island.

Grandpa's hometown had gotten its name from the local legend that its resident Greek philosopher, Empedocles, committed suicide by jumping into the volcano at Mt. Etna near the city of Catania on the island's eastern coast. Greece and Africa are also evident in some of the faces of the Sicilian people who are regarded with a disdain bordering on racism by many of their compatriots in the area north of Rome. This ugly, fraternal racism, along with a lack of economic opportunities, was enough to cause many southerners who wanted the chance of a better life to cross the sea and come to America, as my Grandpa Neri did.

Sicily has been referred to by the author Connie DeCaro as *The Trampled Paradise* in her book of the same name because of the numbers of different ethnic and political groups that have marched across the island, desiring to conquer its rich land and subdue its people, with failure after bloodshed the single eventual outcome. My high school Italian teacher, Mr. Munisteri, used to tell us that many true Sicilians have blue eyes and red hair like their Viking forbears who came from much farther north in Scandinavia.

In leaving his home, Grandpa Neri escaped the battle of south versus north, which continues to be fought on the economic battlefield of Italy to this day. In fact, on a trip to Naples in 1998, I felt compelled to purchase a plaster statue which shows *Pulcinello*, the symbol of that proud city, sitting with his right hand held high above his shoulder, poised for a spanking, and a man lying face-down across his lap, his pants pulled down to reveal his bare buttocks as he awaits a blow from that hand. If you have been in an authentic 1960's era pizzeria in New York City, you have probably seen a statue of *Pulcinello* with a dish of spaghetti in his hand; he is the symbol of Naples, where Pizza Margherita (what we get when we order a regular pizza) was invented.

The man being readied for his punishment is Antonio Bossi, the original leader of the Northern League, an Italian political party that suggested Italy be divided into two nations, with the area south of Rome to be called *Padonia*. Printed in elegant letters on Bossi's buttocks, immediately under *Pulcinello's* threatening hand, are the words: *"Legga Nord"*, or Northern League. One statue is worth a thousand words.

Life in *Porto Empedocle* during the time my grandfather came of age was highly structured, with many rules governing the behavior of respectable men and women, with these rules probably more numerous than the available jobs. Despite these economic hardships (or perhaps because of them), almost everyone was concerned with these social rules and the consequences for breaking them, since they were often enforced at best by the threat of ostracism, and at worst, by the threat of violence. Grandfather left Sicily and headed for the United States in a hurry in 1898 (100 years before I visited Sicily for the first time) because he'd been out walking, and maybe more, with an unmarried lady of his village without a chaperone. He had broken one of the major social taboos that dictated he was either to become engaged to her or had declared his insanity with regard to his own well-being. Being neither insane nor ready to marry, he decided a rapid change of scenery was the solution to his problem, so he left Sicily. From what I know of his character, I sometimes think he saw this occurrence as an omen from fate that he should seek his future in the United States. So he took the honeymoon trip without the bride—whose own fate was never spoken about, although I have my suspicions.

He arrived in New York in steerage class and went through the immigration process at Ellis Island, where his first name, Giuseppe, was translated on his immigration papers into its English equivalent: Joseph. Unlike many of his compatriots, however, New York was not his destination of choice. While he didn't miss the constrictions and regimentation of life in Sicily, he did miss the climate, so he sought out its American equivalent and found the city of Galveston, Texas. Physically, Galveston is as far south in Texas as *Porto Empedocle* is in Sicily, a city situated far south in the Gulf of Mexico. I don't know how he got to Galveston, but I do know he liked it there. It was almost as far south as you could go and still be in the United States, but the rules there were different and you had a more equal chance to make something of yourself. So he began working toward the dream of owning a restaurant by washing dishes in someone else's when another woman entered the picture.

No one, except my mother in a rare moment of candor, has ever said much about her. Her existence was actually a secret to the rest of the family, perhaps even to my paternal grandmother, Rosina. I always had the feeling that, no matter what he may have felt for her in years gone by, the memory of his relationship with this woman had become a potentially embarrassing fact that he wanted buried, along with the wreckage of his finally achieved restaurant, under the debris from the hurricane that had taken it all away from him on September 8, 1900 when he was twenty-one years old. We never found out how he escaped; only that he succeeded in getting away in time and went north to New York City.

Perhaps some of the silence was kept out of respect for my grandmother, Rosina, my father's mother, whom my grandfather married years later in New York. All I did hear from my own mother was she was pretty sure that he had been married once before, in Texas, but his wife had died before he left for New York after the hurricane wiped him out in 1900. I have a strong feeling that this unknown woman helped him achieve the goal of the restaurant, either by giving him money, or by introducing him to people who helped him. She was supposed to have been beautiful. My mother told me that once, while cleaning out a drawer after my Grandmother Rosina died, she found an old photograph of my grandfather with a woman, probably that first woman. She said when she saw the photo, my grandfather took it from her with no explanation, visibly upset, and she never saw the photo again. I can believe a beautiful woman could have loved my grandfather, who stood over six feet tall, was not conventionally handsome, but had a compelling quality about him and, even into his eighties, possessed a sense of purpose that would have made his younger self attractive to women and was more important than vapid good looks. He had a lot of charm and told a terrific story, as well as being in possession of the inner strength to leave his native country and start his life over not once, but twice in that new country.

He also had a quality that was well hidden by his affable exterior: a coldness at his core that enabled him to pick himself up and begin his life again and again with no visible concern for those left behind. In the years to come, I would be a witness to his repetition of this pattern yet a third time, but as a child, I was unaware of this darker side. I would often sit at the dinner table listening to his stories about his life in Galveston; he delighted in making us laugh at his stories about his horse, which he swore had developed a taste for macaroni and would only eat his oats if they were mixed with the leftover spaghetti from the customers' plates. He said that his horse had a persistent red stain on his muzzle and was always easy to identify. He would act out scenes of feeding the horse and adding the spaghetti to the oats and speaking to him in Sicilian while he ate and my grandfather patted his back.

Although I was a little skeptical, even at eight years old, of the specific facts of the story, I greatly enjoyed it as well as the appreciation my grandfather had for his heritage—one that was not shared by the larger culture outside of our neighborhood. Virtually the only Italian-American characters I saw depicted on TV were either Al Capone-type criminal figures on The Untouchables, or the buffoon-like stereotypes of Mrs. Manicotti on The Honeymooners or Bacciagalupo on The Abbott and Costello Show. None of these people had ever taught a horse to appreciate Italian cuisine like my grandfather had, and even fewer of them knew anything more sophisticated than the dish the horse loved. But my grandfather made even his deceptively simple pasta dishes into something more unique than the horse or the culinary uncultured could ever imagine. Grandpa Neri was gone by 1996 when I saw the movie "Big Night", but it reminded me a bit of him and his strong conviction that Italian food was one of the finest of the world's cuisines. Unlike the characters in the film, though, he didn't give up.

During the years that we lived with him on West 5th Street, I saw him eat many varieties of macaroni, which had not yet evolved into the gourmet pasta that it is today. Although it was often topped with his excellent version of the traditional southern Italian red sauce made from tomatoes, his pasta was more often topped with a variety of ingredients such as broccoli rabe, the deliciously bitter greens that are on the menu of any self-respecting *trattoria* today, or *aglio olio,* the deceptively simple but demanding sautéed garlic and oil. Once, when he was short on ingredients, he even served *Occhi di Lupo* (literally "wolf's eyes"): fat, large tubes of macaroni topped with a chopped up hardboiled egg and some parsley. For my grandfather, macaroni, in any shape and with any variety of accompanying sauce, was always referred to almost religiously as *"la gloriosa",* the food of foods. It was this food that he wanted to share so much with others and make his living from, enjoying both preparing and serving it.

He had succeeded in living out this dream for at least a little while; he told us that he had fed many people in Galveston, who would come to his restaurant and enjoy the food he made for them. But his dream ended abruptly with the hurricane that hit the city on September 8, 1900. That storm washed away the dreams of many others along with the lives of over 6,000 of his fellow residents, who were caught unaware because the local newspaper weather prediction of the day before the storm was for fair weather with "fresh, possible brisk northerly winds on the coast." The next morning, when the residents were warned a tropical storm on the Gulf of Mexico had changed directions and was headed straight for them, they refused to be overly frightened by the kind of storm that they had survived before. Many people drowned because they went down to the beach to see the sight of the storm approaching, not knowing, by the time it had passed, late in the evening, many lives would be lost or changed forever.

I don't know if, as my mother said, he lost his mysterious first wife/lover as well as his dream of the restaurant in that hurricane, but I do now that my grandfather decided to return to New York City to start over instead of remaining in Galveston. He left his second southern city on the coast and returned to the north to start his life over once again. He never again had his own restaurant, but held many different jobs after returning to New

York City, working as a machinist and later as an organizer for the machinists' union. In his later years, he changed careers again and became a successful insurance salesman for Metropolitan Life, selling to others the insurance policies that might have kept his dream of a restaurant alive if he had known about their existence earlier in his life.

He met my Grandmother Rosina in New York City after he returned. She too had come from *Porto Empedocle,* where she was born on October 7, 1880, and sought a different, better life in the United States. When they met, she lived with her brother and his wife and worked in a dress factory. She had come to United States as an adult after making the unusual decision to leave the Sicilian convent where she studied after a number of years, but before taking her final vows as a nun. Perhaps it was this common experience of not having followed the rules of life set out for them in Sicily that drew them to each other, or perhaps they had known each other in *Porto Empedocle.* Maybe she had been the mysterious woman he hadn't been ready to marry that forced him to do so or leave—hence the convent for her? Some family questions have no clear answers. Not knowing any of the details of their courtship, I can only speculate, but one thing is certain, after finding each other, they wasted no time.

They were married in a Catholic wedding ceremony at the Church of the Transfiguration on Mott street in New York City on November 5, 1916, a little more than a month after my grandmother's thirty-seventh birthday; she was considered to be quite an older bride by the standards of those days, when many women were grandmothers at the same age. At thirty-seven, my grandfather was also considered a mature bridegroom, if this was his first marriage. Their marriage certificate stated, "Before performing the marriage ceremony, the officiating priest ... should first ascertain whether the parties have the legal right to marry... Where the marriage is celebrated by a priest or minister the ceremony shall be according to the forms and customs of the Church or society to which he belongs." Either my grandfather lied about a first wife, she had died, or they were never married at all. This question about the woman is just another part of the puzzle that is a big part of what I know of his life, unknown and hidden from me, as I look for all the answers about him. It makes me wonder if he told Grandma Rosina the truth; if he had, she might have married him anyway.

Her options were limited and they had a great deal in common that would serve them well in facing the new life they were about to create together. On the other hand, if he hadn't told her, why did he keep the photograph? It sticks inside my head; a question that will never be answered.

Their life together went on, regardless of the past, and when their first child, Salvatore, was born a year later, this question was either resolved or forgotten in the day-to-day. By the time that my father, Vincent, their second son, was born on March 27, 1919, in their apartment at 63 Mott Street, they had already looked across the river to Brooklyn, where they eventually moved. In Gravesend, Brooklyn they had a new home, new neighbors, and would become a new family making a fresh, if late, start in their adopted country where people looked always to the future and often forgot about the past as much as possible.

* * *

Granma Mary, my mother's mother, was only with me for the first eight years of my life, but her effect on me was far greater than that of others I've known much longer. She was born in the United States, also on the Lower East Side of New York City, on December 10, 1894, but she went back to Italy with her parents for a few years as a young child. Her people were from Potenza, the landlocked capitol city of Basilicata, an economically poor region a few hour's drive southeast of Naples. Matera, a smaller city of the province, is better known throughout the world because of its *sassi,* abandoned cave-houses, and routinely attracts more tourists than Potenza. The memoir, *Christ*

Stopped at Eboli by Carlo Levi describes in detail the poverty of daily life in a small town of the region during the 1930's. Even though Americans had begun to suffer their way through the Great Depression, there was a difference between the poverty in Italy and poverty in America. So, the property in Potenza was sold and the family returned to New York; because of this, Granma spoke English with no trace of an Italian accent, and she was literate and fluent in both languages.

After their return to the United States, Granma and her older sister lost both parents in quick succession. They were lucky enough to be sent to live at the Catholic orphanage founded by Mother Frances Cabrini in Dobbs Ferry, New York, which was on the site of a formerly exclusive private girl's school. Granma often spoke to me about her life there, which was as far from a Dickensian orphanage tale as it could be. Although they grieved for their parents, the nuns were good to her and her sister and she loved the life in the country, being outside and running and climbing the trees on the grounds with the other Italian American orphans who were a special part of Mother Cabrini's ministry.

Granma said a favorite pastime of the children was to distract the nun in charge while another child climbed as high as possible in a tree on the grounds. According to family lore, Granma once hurt her arm falling from one of the trees on a day that Saint Frances Xavier Cabrini herself visited the orphanage that she founded. Instead of berating her for her naughtiness, Mother Cabrini helped her up and eased her crying by hugging her and kissing the arm, which Granma said never bothered her again after it quickly healed. As a child, I thought my own mother and Granma called her "Mother Cabrini" because she founded an order of nuns, but also she acted like a mother to the orphans. Only later did I discover this unique Italian- American saint of the Catholic Church and the ministries she instituted were continued in the US by the Missionary Sisters of the Sacred Heart of Jesus, the order of nuns she founded in Italy in 1881.

Saint Frances Cabrini was herself an immigrant from Italy, who, with fellow Missionary Sisters, founded a free school and ministered to the poor Italian immigrants on New York City's Lower East Side who faced both poverty and discrimination. From March of 1889 until her death on December 22, 1917, she founded schools in New York City and upstate New York and in New Orleans, as well as hospitals in New York, Chicago, and Seattle. The orphanages she founded in New York, Colorado, and Seattle also ministered to the many immigrant children of these communities who were educated and provided for because of her work. She also founded a private school for daughters of well-to-do Italian families, Sacred Heart Villa, and utilized the tuition and other monies from that school to subsidize the free schools. At her death, it was said of her that she had established sixty-seven ministries of the Institute of the Missionary Sisters of the Sacred Heart—one for every year of her life. My grandmother, and ultimately my entire family, and countless others, benefitted from her life's work, a wonderful legacy.

Granma's older sister eventually left the orphanage to marry Rocco Pellettieri, my maternal grandfather, who was born in the United States in 1878. His family was also from Potenza and it was considered a good match. He worked as an assistant at the Ward Baking Company and as a barber's assistant before opening his own coffee store on the Lower East Side of New York City in Mother Cabrini's territory. It was planned that Granma Mary would leave the orphanage to live with them and help her sister with any babies as soon as her education was completed. Unfortunately, her sister died soon after their marriage without having had any children. So, after a mourning period, and following the accepted tradition of the time, Rocco came to the orphanage and asked Mary to be his second wife and she accepted. They married and moved to an apartment at 41-51 Kenmare Street, near his store. They soon had two children, my Uncle Domenico, who was born in 1919, and my mother, Margaret, born in July 1923, only two days shy of Mother Cabrini's birth date.

Initially, Grandpa Rocco was able to make a nice life for their family due to his hard work. All the sepia-toned photos from their children's early years show Granma Mary stylishly dressed in silk outfits with her hair beautifully finger waved and styled. My mother often told me proudly that these early photos were taken in a photographer's studio, a sign of upward mobility among the Italian American immigrant community. My uncle's First Communion photo shows him staring reluctantly at the camera, wearing a blue wool suit with short pants and sporting the large, white bow on his left arm that was the traditional outfit for the commemoration of the First Communion Day for boys. My mother is shown in the same series of photos looking seriously at the camera, her Buster Brown haircut softened by a ribbon; she, too, has a silk dress with a large bow at her waist.

For me, these photos are precious beyond the fact that they portray my Grandpa Rocco, whom I never knew, and my uncle and my Granma, both of whom I miss to this day. In their formal, stylized way, these photos, along with my Granma Mary's wedding photo, portray the last time that the Pellettieri family was ever to be this economically comfortable and self-assured until after World War II. In 1929, one year after my mother remembers the lighting fixtures in their building being changed from gas to electricity, my Grandfather Rocco died of a massive heart attack and everything changed for them, and in some inevitable way, for me as well.

* * *

If Grandpa Rocco had lived, they would all have all lived through the Great Depression together and survived it as a family. They might not have spent the next ten years of my mother's life moving around Brooklyn, where they had moved a few months before my grandfather's death, from one apartment to another, trying to find a more affordable rent for a family now headed by a widow on a limited income. My mother might not have left Bay Ridge High School six months shy of graduation to help supplement the family income by working full-time at the factory where she had previously worked only after school, until she managed to find a better job as a typist. She might have been able to find a good job as a secretary right out of school, had she gotten her diploma.

Then, if Grandpa Rocco had lived, he might not even have allowed her to go to the Friday Night Social Evening at Our Lady of Mount Carmel Church, on 65th Street in Brooklyn, where she met my father and they fell in love while dancing to Frank Sinatra records under the watchful eyes of the church chaperones.

They might never have met and I might never have been born to watch Kate Smith and play jump rope in the schoolyard of PS 95. The speculation that I might owe my own existence to the death of my maternal grandfather never crossed my mind while waiting for my turn in jump rope that day in the schoolyard, but it does occur to me now and then as an adult, and I am as puzzled by the thought now as I would have been frightened by it then.

The best I can do with the dilemma that thought presents me with is to shrug my shoulders at it, ascribe some of my darker and convoluted speculations to my Sicilian roots and the *spirelle* within my mind, and just jump back into my life—the same way I jumped in when it was my turn many years ago in that schoolyard in Gravesend, Brooklyn.

Chapter 3

Lemon Ice and Lightning Bugs

In New York City before air conditioning, summer was lived mostly outside, especially if you were young; the summer of 1960 was no exception in Gravesend, Brooklyn. Few people were aware of pedophiles, street crime was low in my neighborhood, and almost no one knew the dangers of excessive exposure to the sun. Beginning right after breakfast, Marissa and I would spend a lot of time doing what we referred to as "calling for" each other or for other friends so we could decide what we would do that day. Multitasking—the behavior, not the word—was well known to us however, because we tried to accomplish this while simultaneously trying to elude our younger siblings. Getting out to enjoy the freedom we sorely lacked while confined indoors wasn't easy given the fact that, at nearly thirteen years of age, neither of us had our mothers' permission to venture much further than the other side of the street or down the block before lunch time. Permission to do more than this was rarely granted and therefore, highly prized.

"Calling for" a friend almost always meant going to the house in person and knocking on the door or ringing the bell. The telephone was only rarely used in this process if your mother was home, because the object was to get out of the house and away from you mother before she realized she hadn't given you any chores or told you to take your brother or sister out with you. Nonchalant speed was the essence of this tricky escape maneuver. The quicker I got dressed, washed, breakfasted, and out of the house, calling out in a light, nonchalant manner as I went, "I'm going to call for Marissa; I'll see you at lunchtime," the better my chances of actually escaping.

Silence in response to this declaration of intent was the secret to our summertime freedom and words, any words other than, "Okay, have fun," from our mothers in reply were as welcome as a judge's imposition of a heavy prison sentence to a first offender guilty only of a misdemeanor.

The fate of an entire summer morning was in limbo during that moment of hesitation before bounding down the first step and out the side door and into the alley. The rule was you *had* to wait for a reply. Not waiting to see if your mother had heard you and knew you were going out was as bad as actually sneaking out without permission: a felony crime in my house, where the existence of thousands of crazies on the street lying in wait to snatch and murder twelve year old girls was absolutely accepted twenty years before the national crime rate rose sufficiently to justify any such parental fears.

"I don't care what your friends are allowed to do. You have to let us know whenever you go out. Even if it's into the alleyway to play ball."

Both of our parents had repeated this so often to my sister and me -especially our mother- as to make the Litany of the Saints at Benediction appear like shorthand by comparison.

To avoid this, I would wait until my mother was in another room, dusting, changing sheets, or airing out a room, to declare my intention to go out in a loud, confident voice. As I rushed to the side door, my ears would be straining to hear what The Voice would say while praying to St. Anthony that she didn't call me back. Receiving no negative reply to my morning's declaration of independence was as satisfying to me as being given money for ice cream or lemon ice twice in the same day had been a year or two before.

"Wait a minute, young lady. Don't disappear. I might need you to go to the store for me." These were the kind of words I dreaded nearly as much as: "Don't forget to take your sister with you. She'll be ready sooner if you comb and braid her hair now."

Those words, dispassionately uttered by The Voice, were the equivalent of the pronouncement of a death sentence on any possibility of fun the morning had previously held. We might as well have been in school for all the good the sunshine and freedom from teachers and homework meant to us when we had to do anything, even go to the store, with one or more younger sisters in tow. If only one of us was burdened with this responsibility, it was inevitable that the other little sister would almost immediately find out through some sort of creepy, radar-like ESP that passed between them and show up and demand to come with us too.

Maryann, Marissa's little sister, was a year younger than my sister Alice and they didn't often play together unless Marissa or I had to take one of them with us. The fact that they didn't like each other or get along that well was forgotten in their mutual desire to tag along after us. They even disagreed and squabbled while they were with us.

"Just to break our chops, that's why they do it," Marissa would say. "They don't even play together unless we have to take them with us."

Marissa's mother hated it when she used that expression, so, whenever we'd be forced to walk to the bakery for bread or the pork store for cold cuts with our two sisters tagging along on an otherwise beautiful summer morning, Marissa would almost chant the words like our own personal mantra of pain: "Breaking our chops, breaking our chops...that's all they're good for."

She'd complain even louder as our sisters would linger, staring at the front window of Taverna's 5 & 10 on Avenue U a few stores down from DeMarco Bakery, where we all bought our bread. If we had any change left over after the bread was bought, our sisters would inevitably run east along Avenue U in the opposite direction from our block, West 5th Street, and toward Van Sicklen Street and the 5 & 10. We'd try to pull them away after they'd run the few feet and glued themselves to the front window, but they would not budge. They'd strain their necks to see the newest issue of the *Little Lulu* comic or a new doll that they would salivate over and then look longingly at the mechanical rides in front of the store and beg us to use up the change we had left so they could have a ride.

"Please, just one," they'd beg, climbing on a horse or car in front of us before we could do anything to stop them.

There were few fates more humiliating for a twelve-and-a-half year old Gravesend girl than to be seen squeezing her almost nine year old sister into a ride meant for a five year old on the public sidewalk, unless you doubled the humiliation factor by two. We'd once actually tried to get both of them onto one little horse so we could at least save one of the nickels we had left to get a lemon ice that we'd share later when we got rid of them for the afternoon. Although they'd both complained they'd done as we'd asked and gotten on the horse together, knowing well that we'd have kept our promise to tell on them for running away from us if they didn't comply.

Getting in trouble for running away from an older sister watching you was as close to a hanging offense as you could commit in their world. Even our younger sisters listened to us most of the time if we threatened them with "I'm telling," especially in the presence of a witness, which Marissa and I would be for each other if it came to that.

This was the downside for them of tagging along with us and we enjoyed seeing them climb the steps up to the horse and argue about who got to sit in front and put their feet into the stirrups, squashed together on the tiny saddle. My sister won and I put the nickel into the slot and the horse jerked up and down, awkwardly mimicking a carousel ride, and making our sisters look as ridiculous as a miniature version of Laurel and Hardy—skinny Alice taking the Stan Laurel part with chubby Maryann as Oliver Hardy. Marissa and I laughed out loud. At one point, the owner of the store came out and told them they were too big to be on the ride and he'd make their parents pay for it if it broke. At this, Marissa and I backed away slowly until we were in front of the store next door, never minding that it was Bella's Corset Shop, the kind of store we'd never linger in front of.

When the ride ended, our sisters got off and walked over to us, ready to cry.

"Now we're telling on you," Maryann said, tears in the corner of her eyes.

"Go ahead," said Marissa. "I'll tell Mommy that you run on the rides whenever we have to take you with us to the bakery. I'll tell her that you run away from us every time, too," she threatened back, her voice getting shrill. Now the owner of the 5 & 10 looked at all of us.

"Look," I said, lowering my voice and leaning into them, focusing on Maryann. "It's just that you're getting too old to go on that ride and the owner is a real grouch. If he didn't see you, we were going to tell you when you got off that you can't go on the horse any more anyway. It's for little kids like Markie-boy, not for you and Alice, okay? You don't want your friends to make fun of you, do you? If they saw you on the horse, you'd hear about it all summer and they'll make fun of you all over the school in September."

My sister nodded, understanding, and stared at Maryann.

"She's right," she said. Then she whispered into Maryann's ear.

They both smiled at each other and Maryann said, "You're right, Rosemary. We won't ask to go on the horse again and we promise not to run away again, if—"

"If what?" Marissa said.

"If we get lemon ice next time," my sister, Alice answered, looking right at me with a smirk.

Of all the requests she could have made, I found this one to be the most annoying and gave her a look meant to intimidate, my own version of my mother's "Stop-in-your-tracks-and-don't-say-another-word" one that she reserved for the rare times when she wanted to maintain control of us in public without uttering a word. It never failed with me, but either Alice, as a second child, had a greater immunity to it, or else I just wasn't able to carry it off.

"Come on, sis," she said. "A small one. One little lemon ice each next time and we'll be good for you, right Maryann?"

Maryann nodded, looking somewhat more warily at her own sister than Alice had at me.

For some reason, even though on some level I knew I was being taken, I would always try to make peace with my sister at a certain point, usually after I had punished her enough for the torture of having to take her with me in the first place.

I looked at Marissa and could see her grey eyes getting even more opaque with anger, so I furtively crossed my fingers and winked at her and said it was a deal, both of us knowing the crossed fingers undid my promise as if I hadn't given it in the first place. The anger left her eyes as she returned the wink, grabbed Maryann's hand, and we all started for home.

"Let's hurry up now," I said to Marissa, grabbing my sister's hand to cross Avenue U. "We want to get the rolls home before they cool off or your mother will complain we took old ones."

One of the reasons for sending us out for bread sometimes more than once a day was to get the bread as freshly baked as possible. In the winter, you couldn't expect to get it home piping hot, but in the summer, your mother expected to be able to cut into the loaf and still feel the heat inside or you would be accused of letting them give you the old bread that was left over from the morning and not the fresh, noon batch. More than once, I had been told I was not to accept any bread unless I saw the baker come out from the back area where the ovens were and refill the bins with the fresh loaves and rolls. I was never to accept any bread that had been sitting in the bins unless it was the end of the day, when the "beggars can't be choosers" rule applied. That rule did not apply to lemon ice, however.

The reason that Marissa and I were usually so anxious to get home for lunch was that after we had eaten and were allowed outside again, it was usually time for the first lemon ice of the day, especially if it was hot. We looked forward to our summer lemon ices the way many of our fathers looked forward to their first cigarette of the day after breakfast, if they had waited that long to smoke it. For those of us who were lucky enough to grow up near a pastry store run by Italian Americans, what we referred to as lemon ice was as much a part of the summer as a bedroom air conditioner is now. Lemon ice was what it was called regardless of the flavor you chose, thus, "get me a chocolate lemon ice" was perfectly understandable to us, with the simple but delicious lemon flavor was referred to as a "regular" lemon ice. I think you had to have been born in Brooklyn during my time to understand it, but we understood because it was a part of our everyday language then.

At Ciccone's Pastry Shop, which was on Avenue U near the corner of West 6th Street, right next to Ricci's Pharmacy, our local drugstore, they made the ices fresh every day. The flavors were varied, depending on what the owner felt inspired to make. Lemon and chocolate were usually available every day, but you took a chance if you got your mouth ready for pistachio, my favorite, with its bright green color and tiny pieces of pistachios. Or burnt almond, my father's choice, with a creamy consistency, tiny pieces of almonds, and the unmistakable flavor of an ice-cold macaroon cookie, and arrived to find it was sold out already.

The ices were as carefully made as the pastries were, by hand, in small batches in the back of the store. They had real lemon peel and juice or dark cocoa or pieces of pistachio or almond and almond extract added to the sweetened and flavored ice with what tasted like a bit of liqueur or cream, depending on the flavor being prepared. These icy confections bore as much resemblance to the store bought frozen "Italian ices" now available in grocery freezers as a tofu burger does to real beef. My father would have called them "cardboard" ices, a phrase he used to refer to any packaged and falsely labeled "fresh" product from cake to bread to cookies that he felt should only be purchased on the day they were prepared, from people who knew what they were doing and (more important to him) cared enough to do it with pride.

Marissa and I were anxious to get our first lemon ices of the day so we could enjoy them, but also to savor the knowledge of what flavors were available that day, which we might or might not share with people who asked us. We had begun to learn knowledge was power and also began to decide what to do with the little power we possessed. For instance, if my stuck-up next door neighbor, Anna Russo (whose aunt by marriage had taught her some words in French instead of Italian because she thought it was, by Anna's description, "classier") asked us if they had any chocolate when she saw us licking our ices, the answer would be, "All gone!" even if we knew they had just taken out a fresh new container while we were there.

The knowledge that we had even temporarily made her feel disappointed made us feel better because Anna, who was fourteen and well developed for her age, always tried to make us feel like stupid babies, and she usually succeeded. She loved to tell dirty jokes that she knew we didn't understand, just to see us squirm and laugh uncomfortably, preferably when a lot of her friends whom we didn't know were around. Then she'd ask us to explain the joke to those friends, who always were dumber or not as good looking as Anna, but who followed her around like slaves. Even though we loved her grandmother, Mrs. Rinaldi, we hated Anna and might have spit in her lemon ice if she ever asked us to get her one. She probably knew that and never asked us for that particular favor, so "no more chocolate" was the closest we got to any revenge. On the other hand, if little Markie-boy asked me if they had more lemon ice or even for a lick of mine, the answer was always, "Yes, of course!"

That first trip to get lemon ice also prepared us for the evening rush after dinner. When the sun finally went down and most families had finished their dinner and the adults sat on their stoops while their children got their last licks at playing, a lot of people craved a cold lemon ice to cool them down before bed. The owners of the pastry shop knew this and stayed open late in July and August to accommodate the customers who didn't buy as much pastry in the hot weather, but loved their lemon ices. On these hot nights, Marissa and I would walk up and down both sides of the block closest to Avenue U and announce to any of our neighbors we found sitting on their stoops: "We're going for lemon ices; do you want us to bring you back some?"

Sometimes the neighbors said no, but the usual response was for any little kids who heard our offer to beg their mothers for a final treat of the day, and we could take an order for a maximum of six ices: that was how many could be fit into the sleeve made of the hollowed out box that the paper cups for the ices came in. When we made a big order at Ciccone's, they'd give you the box like a shell filled with a row of ices as a courtesy because although you and a friend could carry the ices three at a time, cradled in both hands, they wouldn't travel well around the corner on a hot night. The ices would develop a layer of flavored icy syrup around the semi-solid ice no matter how quickly you walked with them because of the heat of your hands in the summer. So Marissa and I would make several trips on an evening, traveling back and forth, delivering our boxes of ices from seven o'clock until nine o'clock when the pastry store closed.

Although we didn't ask for it, most of the neighbors we brought ices to rewarded us with a nickel or two for the convenience of having the ices brought to them only slightly melted. We enjoyed having a few extra nickels to spend, but that wasn't all of it. I remember the satisfaction I felt while watching those people, young and old, licking those ices and feeling that delectably flavored coolness fill their mouths and slide down their throats while they enjoyed what my father liked to call the "liquid air conditioning" effect that they produced. In fact, if you weren't careful when eating a lemon ice and went too fast, you might actually freeze the roof of your mouth.

The little kids were the best ones to watch. They would lick and then suck the ices out of the paper cup as they ate and, as the level of the ice in the cup went down, they would push the edges of the white, folded paper together so that more ice squeezed out, the cup got flatter, and the smile surrounded by the mess on their faces got bigger. When they had extracted as much as they could (and usually if their mothers weren't watching), they would often put the whole, soggy cup into their mouths and chew it until it was nothing but a papery mess. Then it was usually spit out, sometimes at the kid standing next to them and doing the same thing—a sure signal to their mothers that it was time to go inside for the night and get ready for bed. Most of the neighbors appreciated those lemon ices as much as Marissa and I did. They knew we were fast and honest and that we ran back as quickly as possible without dropping our cargo, which wasn't as easy as it sounds.

Sometimes, older and tougher boys, who hung out in the schoolyard of PS 95 at night, would show up on their bikes for their own ices and then follow us along the block of Avenue U to the corner of West 5th Street, bothering and teasing us as we tried to race back, sometimes sweeping one hand in front of us as they pedaled slowly and threatened to take all our ices or throw them onto the sidewalk, or take our money. These were the boys who were only a year or two older than us, but never studied or did homework. In the summer, they hung out at a candy store on McDonald Avenue, the street that ran under the elevated subway line where it was dark even during the day. They smoked cigarettes and made dirty remarks about any girl over the age of eight who passed by, which we never did. Our parents didn't like us walking in the shade of the "El" as it was called, and none of the stores our families frequented were on that block anyway, so we had no trouble keeping away from those boys most of the time.

If they showed up early when we were going for lemon ice, we'd either decide to call it a night right then (knowing they wouldn't follow us onto our block with our fathers there waiting for us) or else we'd ask Mrs. Rinaldi, who lived next door to me, if she wanted to have her bulldog walked and take him with us to get the ices. He was the sweetest bulldog I've ever known, but those stupid tough boys didn't know that. They didn't know he ran away in fear of an aggressive cat owned, of course, by Anna Russo, Mrs. Rinaldi's granddaughter, and he liked to lick the drips off our fingers while he wagged his tail after we got back from delivering the ices. They always left us alone if they saw us with Mrs. Rinaldi's dog; they'd get on their broken down bikes, lick their own ices, and return to their candy store or to the deserted schoolyard. Even though it was more difficult with the dog because one of us had to wait outside with him while the other got the order, it was worth it to keep those creeps away.

Her dog was our friend and protector and we often let him lick out the paper container that held the ices after it was emptied out, but we never let Mrs. Rinaldi see us letting him do that.

While she felt it was just fine to let him eat a dinner of leftover spaghetti, she didn't think a dog should have sweets, so we always hid our crime from her. The experience of using that sweet dog's ferocious appearance to keep the creeps away taught me the value of what my father had always referred to as "brains over brawn," which had finally gone from an abstract idea in my mind to a concrete course of action. When Mrs. Rinaldi told her grandson, Fat Richie, what good neighbors we were for walking the dog, Marissa and I smiled and nudged each other a little surreptitiously.

After our lemon ice, most of the younger kids had gone in for the night, we were often allowed to stay out as long as we remained on someone's stoop nearby and our parents knew where we were. No wandering around was allowed after ten o'clock, an hour when most of us had to be in bed in the winter to prepare for school the next day. If my father was on the later shift at the Brooklyn Navy Yard the next day, he would stay outside too, and on one of those evenings, he taught me to catch lightning bugs. He told me that the correct name for the insect was "firefly," and encouraged me to look it up in the dictionary. *Funk and Wagnalls* said it was "a night-flying beetle emitting a phosphorescent light from an abdominal organ." That fascinated me, and the idea that a living being could produce its own light stuck in my mind because one of the ways you knew the sun was going down in summer was when you could see the lightning bugs.

When I was little, my father had told me that their glow was harmless and this knowledge later reassured me after I read a biography of Marie Curie, who died of radiation poisoning due to her experiments with radium. I had once seen a watch with a radium dial that glowed in the dark and it both fascinated and repelled me. The idea that a little bug could glow in the dark without being harmful to itself or to human beings felt especially comforting during that era of the Cold War, when we were old enough to be afraid of nuclear war and its consequences.

We used to joke about the "Take Cover" drills that many of us had participated in as first or second graders, where the teacher would stop the lesson, look at the class seriously, and say the words, "Take Cover!" in a loud voice and we would have to duck under our desks and tuck ourselves into a ball. As older kids, we would say they taught us the first two steps:

1) Duck

2) Cover

...but left out the last step:

3) Kiss your ass goodbye!

We would all remember this dark attempt at humor as we were hunched in a ball, absurdly waiting for the explosion and the mushroom cloud, like a character in a surreal cartoon.

Being a part of the "Duck and Cover" generation made us all frightened whenever we thought about what it truly meant, so the idea of these tiny, glowing bugs not harming themselves or anyone with their light endeared them even more to me. I lived on a mostly concrete block in the borough of Brooklyn and frequently heard the expression "Nuke 'em till they glow," mindlessly used by kids whose thoughts never went beyond those words to what it would be like afterward. My own habit of constant reading had made my personal fear of radiation take root in the back of my mind where I had consigned it to a small but important space; the lightning bugs were my own antidote to some of the fears that my little bit of knowledge had produced in me. Like a toddler who had insisted on running ahead of its mother, and then turned around to be sure she was still behind him watching, I wanted the knowledge, but also wanted some consolation from the fear it produced.

One night after I'd helped wash the dinner dishes and before we went on our lemon ice rounds, my father told me that he'd made me something to help me catch a lightning bug, a thing I had wanted to do for a while. He said I had to promise to let it go after an hour or so because it shouldn't live in a jar and needed to be outside. I immediately agreed, delighted to get a gift from my father that had to do with an interest of mine, and he handed me an old mayonnaise jar, washed clean and with a few holes punched in the metal screw-on top.

He then gave me some instructions: "Wait until it's really dark and you can see them clearly. Put the jar on the ground with the lid off but right near it. Then, take your hands and rub them together to make them hot, and hold one of them out cupped, like you were going to hold water in it."

He gestured, making his own hand into the shape he had indicated.

"Then, stay still and wait until one of them comes close and put your hand up quickly under it and cover it with the other hand, like you were holding an egg, gently.

"Leave enough room in your hand for the bug to move around. It will tickle, but don't open your hand until you bring it over the jar. Take away your bottom hand when you're right over the jar and it will fly in, if you're lucky. It takes a lot of patience, and you might have to try a lot of times before you catch one, but it's worth it."

I started to try that same night. In between trips for lemon ice, I'd try to stand still and do what he'd told me, but the one time I managed to catch one, I couldn't stand the tickling feeling and let it go. When it was almost time to go in for the night, my father offered to go with me to the quieter and darker part of the block that had lots of trees, closer to Avenue T, and help me.

He warned me though: "You'll have to let it go soon because it's late now and we'll have to go in soon, okay?"

That was fine; catching one was good enough for me. We walked two thirds of the way down the block, past Marissa's house where there were more single-family houses and lots of the neighbors were away on vacation, so it was much more quiet than on our end of West 5th Street. We found a good spot under a tree where the leaves formed a shelter from the streetlights above us and we caught one within what felt like only minutes. My father had to take it from my cupped hands gently and get it into the jar because I still couldn't stand the tickling sensation, but I didn't slip and let it go; I had finally caught a lightning bug with some help from my father.

I remember watching it blink its light on and off inside the jar and felt both exhilarated and sad at the same time. I didn't like the feeling that I limited the bug's freedom when it wasn't harmful to me and had given me pleasure by being alive and glowing in the dark summer night, but I was also proud to have had the patience to catch one with my father's help. He saw my thoughts on my face and smiled and said it was okay with him if I wanted to go and show it to my friends, as long as I let it go soon. I ran up the block toward our house with the jar to show my friends who were still outside, but, as I passed Marissa's stoop, I saw nobody on the stoop.

As I got closer to my own stoop, I saw Marissa and her sister Maryann, as well as my sister Alice, and even Anna were all still outside. They, as well as a group of about four other kids, were all on the stoop next door, looking into the open front windows of the Rinaldi's first-floor apartment where Fat Richie lived. They were all clustered around the three big windows that opened into Richie's parents' living room, peering in as though spying on someone in the bathroom and silently shoving each other to get a better view.

Anna, who was Fat Richie's older cousin, was obviously the ringleader and she waved to me to be quiet as I approached the steps to go up to join them. I put the jar down carefully at the side of the bottom step and silently climbed the five steps to see inside. Anna shoved Maryann over to make room for me and Marissa didn't even get mad; she was too busy covering her mouth with her hands to smother her own laughter.

I peered into the window and, at first, I couldn't see anything except the glow of the television screen, where two thickly muscled men in black trunks wrestled; there were no other lights on. As my eyes adjusted, I saw ten year old Fat Richie Rinaldi sitting in his underwear on the couch in front of the TV set with a dish of pork chops left over from dinner on a snack table in front of him, watching the screen intently as he picked up a chop with his hand, bit it, and swallowed, then called out, waving the chop: "Choke 'im! Go for his neck!"

He stopped to take another bite and then a long swallow from a tall aluminum tumbler, completely unaware half the kids from his side of the block saw him. I learned later that what I had suspected about this incident was true. His own cousin, Anna, had seen him as she headed up the steps of the stoop to get a cold drink from her parents' apartment on the top floor and had stopped and instead gone to call all the kids who were outside to see the show. Realizing my lightning bug paled in comparison to this spectacle, but afraid my mother would come home from Bingo at the church and catch me doing something that definitely crossed the line of acceptable behavior, I choked back my own laughter and backed away as Anna, who could no longer control herself, shouted through the window: "Get him yourself, Fat Richie Pork Chops!

"Fat Richie Pork Chops! Fat Richie Pork Chops!" the rest of the kids peering into the window shouted together, echoing Anna like a comic Greek chorus.

As soon as the words were out of their mouths, he jumped up and upset the flimsy tin TV table, spilling the milk that was left in the tumbler and sending the tumbler itself and the plate with the remnants of the pork chop and the bones onto the floor with it.

He ran to the window and peered out onto the dark front porch screaming, "Who's there? Who's spying on me? I'm gonna come out there and get you!"

As soon as he had left the couch, Anna ran for the front door and raced up the steps inside to her own apartment, and all the kids scrambled down the stoop and scattered, pushing and shoving each other out of the way as they ran. My sister grabbed at me and we both ran next door and into the dark alleyway, to the side door to our house and slammed the door shut. When we were inside, she collapsed with laughter on the floor of the kitchen, hardly able to catch her breath.

When she came up for air she said, "He's even fatter in his BVD's."

At this, I burst into laughter too, remembering the image of Richie waving the pork chop bone at the wrestlers. Laughing tears ran down our faces and muscle spasm pains stabbed at our stomachs when my father walked in through the seldom-used front door with the mayonnaise jar in his hand. I stopped laughing abruptly.

"Rosemary, I think this belongs to you," he said, handing the jar to me.

I took it and waited.

"When I walked back up the block, I saw Marissa and Maryann running into their house and a bunch of kids running across the street. Then Richie from next door came running down his stoop in his underwear and it looked like he was after them," Dad continued, "I looked at his stoop and found the jar so I thought I'd bring it in for you. Maybe it's time to let the lightning bug go free, what do you think?"

"Thanks Daddy. I think that's a good idea. I'm tired, so I'll do it now."

We went out the side door into the dark alley and unscrewed the top of the jar and the lightning bug blinked on and off and rose up, out of the jar and returned to the hundreds of others like it who blinked in the darkness. I lost sight of it and we returned inside.

"Good," my father said. "It's late, so you two go and get washed up and brush your teeth. Your mother should be back from Bingo any minute now." His eyes twinkled as he said, "I think your mother will even say it's hot enough for you to sleep in your underwear; what do you girls think about that?"

At the sound of the magic word, Alice met my eyes and we both started laughing, and so did my father. The tears of laughter continued to flow as I went into the bathroom. I laughed about Richie and would continue to do so every time I thought about it that summer, but I was also just as happy because my father had helped me to catch the lightning bug and then reminded me to let it go.

Chapter 4

Sleeping In

~⟩•··•⟶⟶•◆•·⟶⟶⟨~

$\mathcal{E}$ ven sleep was different when I lived on West
5th Street. In those days, before all-night
cable TV, we measured how grown up we were
by how late we had gone to bed on a Friday or
Saturday night after watching black-and-white
TV. What constituted adult entertainment to us
was that the show was on so late that we kids
had to cajole and whine to be allowed to see it,
even on a weekend night. Since the television
stations all stopped broadcasting in the early
hours of the morning and signed off with the
playing of the national anthem and a shot of
the American flag flying, the claim of, "I stayed
up so late last night that I heard the national
anthem" was answered by, "Yeah, sure, and
then your mommy tucked you in with a bottle
of milk."

If the boaster were someone safe like Fat Richie Pork Chops, we'd all laugh and dismiss the story. If the boaster were Anna (his cousin and my nemesis) asking if her mother knew, her question would be answered by: "Of course not. She was dead asleep, but she let me stay up anyway. Doesn't your mother?"

I would wince at questions like this from Anna and knew better than to challenge anything she said, no matter how outrageous the boast. She alone, of all my friends and acquaintances, had the uncanny ability to target the things I felt the most ashamed of, zero in on them with pointed questions, and expose me for the unsophisticated half-little-girl that I still was, despite all of my reading and thinking. All of the things that I'd learned from books were no help to me when Anna was around.

She was a frightening and intimidating combination of intelligence and meanness, with the latter trait far outweighing the former. Although she was also of southern Italian extraction, with a *Barese* grandfather and a Sicilian grandmother (kind Mrs. Rinaldi, whom we all liked a lot), she had fair coloring. Her hair was what we from Brooklyn called "dirty blonde" and she had bluish green eyes that resembled those on statues of ancient Egyptian cats that I'd seen on a trip to the Museum of Natural History in Manhattan. She loved cats too, while most of us preferred dogs, and I thought this made perfect sense since she was sleek and graceful like a cat, as well, with all of the lack of pre-occupation with the feelings of others that I'd thought of as a feline trait. My father might say her looks had more to do with her genetic heritage from her Sicilian ancestors, whose fair features and hair proved the falsity of the myth of the dark Italian, but I was still struck by her physical and emotional nature, which appeared more catlike than human to me.

Worse than that, however, was the fact that at fourteen, only a little more than a year my chronological senior, Anna could easily pass for sixteen, and often did. She was voluptuous where I was still pretty flat and already resembled the British actress, Diana Dors, who was a close copy of Marilyn Monroe. She also had a quick mind that she liked to use chiefly for her own amusement. Anna loved public humiliations, like the one we had all participated in involving her slower-witted cousin, Richie. Most of the time, she frightened the rest of us into participating in these curbside dramas, which she arranged with no apparent effort. She frightened me and I wasn't alone in feeling that way about her. Marissa couldn't stand her, either, although, since she was already physically developed enough to resemble Sophia Loren, she wasn't as intimidated as I was by Anna's womanly appearance.

Anna went to the local parochial school, Sts. Simon and Jude, and she wore the telltale dark blue plaid skirt and white-bloused uniform as though it were an evening gown. Her skirt was always perfectly pressed, knifelike pleats swaying in formation as she glided leisurely down the block on the way home with her schoolbooks tucked against her side to make room for size 36C breasts, which she thrust forward as though she let them lead her down the block to her door. She never appeared to walk quickly as I usually did, hunched over my own books to hide my own size 30AA training bra that I had pried out of my reluctant mother by making up the story that the gym teacher said it was "safer" for us to participate in basketball if we wore a bra.

"Does the gym teacher think you should take my lipstick and compact to school, too?" my mother had asked sarcastically when I had first brought up the topic of the bra, which she called a brassiere.

"Will that make you look more like the other girls in the class or like the one next door?" she'd said, gesturing with her head toward Anna's house, her hands full of the clean, dry clothes she'd just taken down from the line as we'd talked. My mother couldn't stand Anna, who she felt was spoiled and too advanced for her years.

"Her mother better count on something more than Catholic school to keep that one from getting in trouble, the way she looks and the things she gets away with. I've seen her when she's dressed up to go out with that aunt of hers; she looks at least eighteen. She wears too much makeup for a girl her age."

Then she looked pointedly at me and said: "A man who's up to no good can easily mistake a young girl who looks like that for an older woman. Her mother's not doing her any favors letting her go out looking like that."

Although I secretly agreed with my mother's assessment of Anna, I'd never let her know and would roll my eyes up to heaven as the words, "You've got plenty of time for that later," were pronounced repeatedly to almost all of my requests for anything grown-up. It had taken me weeks of badgering and begging for my mother to allow me to get my first real bra the previous spring, although I'd been menstruating since I was eleven and in the fifth grade, over eighteen months before. Since I had developed breasts a little while afterward, I'd bought myself a bra with the money I'd saved from babysitting. It fit okay around the back, but it had the wrong size cups, since I'd been too embarrassed to ask a saleslady for help, fearing she'd ask me why my mother hadn't accompanied me to make such an important purchase. I'd utilized my home economics skill with a needle and thread and had taken a tuck in the cups instead of filling them with cotton the way a lot of my small-chested friends had.

I figured if I did get caught wearing the bra by my mother (who believed no young girl had any reason to wear a bra before the eighth grade), it was better not to have it filled with anything incriminating so I wouldn't be accused of trying to look older: a grave adolescent sin in my mother's eyes and one that could lead to trouble, which I soon figured out meant sex.

I had first heard about "Becoming a Woman" from some friends at school at the beginning of fifth grade, when I was almost eleven. I had asked Marissa, who although a good eight months younger than me was much more informed about this kind of thing, to tell me what she knew. She hadn't made fun of my lack of knowledge, but rather had just asked her own mother all the questions I'd always longed to be able to ask. One day, while watching "American Bandstand" instead of doing our homework in the finished basement of her house, she repeated the information and advice that her mother had given her.

"My mother said we should call it 'my friend' if I wanted to talk about it any place where boys could be around," She informed me. "She said I could be expecting it to happen any time soon and that I should always wear a skirt, not slacks, when I have it. She's sending away for a booklet that tells you everything about it. It's called *Growing Up and Liking It*."

"Where did your mother get the booklet?" I asked.

"From the Modess or Kotex companies," she explained. "They send it to you for free and I have the address. Do you want to get one, too?"

I hesitated. Of course, I wanted to get one, but what I wanted was for my mother to order it for me and then to sit down with me so we could read it together and have her explain to me all the things that I didn't understand. Marissa was my best friend, but I still couldn't explain that wish to her because of the longing it implied for the kind of mother I didn't have, and she did have. The fact that I asked her to ask her mother the things I wanted to ask mine caused me to feel illogically that somehow, I had caused the situation with my mother to exist, and I felt a huge sense of shame about it for something that I intellectually knew was not my fault.

So I said, "Yes, but I think my mother would get mad if I got something like that in the mail without permission from her and she found out about it."

She looked at me with a puzzled expression, so I continued, "Remember the trouble that I got into about the circumcision question?"

She blushed and she nodded her head twice quickly and looked at the television set instead of me. We watched the dancers and listened to the music for a few minutes and then she said, "I know. I could order two and say that one is for my sister in the letter we send. Then we could read them together and I'll ask my mother about anything we don't understand. Okay?"

It was a plan worthy of my necessarily devious mind. "That would be great," was all I said.

We both ripped a page from our notebooks and wrote individual letters. I gave mine to Marissa a little hesitantly.

"Are you sure your mother won't get angry that you're ordering another one for me at the same time?"

"Of course not," she said, taking it and folding it so it would fit into an envelope with her own letter. Then she stopped.

"What if she wants to get permission from your mother to order them?"

"My mother would kill me if she found out that I went to your mother to find this stuff out. Forget about it. I'll just read your booklet."

So we ripped up the letter and went back to our long division to the beat of the music, looking up from our work whenever one of our favorite "regulars" was spotlighted on the dance floor with her boyfriend doing the latest dance step.

I forgot all about the incident until Marissa ran up to me before school a couple of weeks later with a big smile on her face and said: "Guess what happened, Rosemary?"

"Don't tell me that your mother's having another baby," I said.

"Would I be smiling at that? That would make me a permanent babysitter until I was eighteen and I'd never have a date! I shouldn't tell you for saying something so mean to me."

She looked genuinely hurt and I felt bad for teasing her.

"I'm sorry I said that. Tell me what happened. Please?"

"Remember when we were going to order the booklet but you got scared that my mother would let your mother know about it?"

"Yeah, of course I remember," I replied warily, still a little frightened by the whole subject.

"Well, I got the one I ordered and guess what happened? I got two!"

"What do you mean?"

"I opened the envelope and there were two booklets, not one. They sent an extra one by mistake. Now you can have one too and we can read them together just like we wanted to do. Isn't that great? I can still ask my mother questions and you'll get all the answers just like me. We can still find out about anything we don't understand together, just like sisters. We can start reading them at lunchtime."

With that, she pulled out the booklets from her notebook where she'd stashed them and handed one to me.

"We'd better wait until after school," I said. "I don't want to get caught by the teacher in class with this and have her complain to my mother. She'd really kill me then."

"Okay, after school. We'll say we have to study spelling together and quiz each other on the words. Come over around 3:30 and leave your sister home."

That's just what I did. We opened the booklets together and found out that while we were at school, babysitting, and even sleeping, a lot of stuff went on inside us. I didn't like the idea that this occurred while I had no knowledge that it was even happening, and I had certainly never consented to it. It was like my body had a secret life of its own and I wasn't even aware of it; it just went along preparing me to become a woman whether I wanted it to happen or not. It made me feel strange, like I wasn't in charge of myself anymore and didn't even have control over my own body.

The pictures in the booklet showing sanitary pads and the belts they were worn with frightened me too, but not because of what they were—even though, to me, they looked like secret torture instruments hidden under your clothes. What scared me was I knew I'd have to eventually go to my mother and ask her for this equipment or go to the drugstore and buy it for myself. Although I had my babysitting and lemon ice money, I'd rather die than go into Ricci's Pharmacy and ask Mr. Ricci or one of the boys who worked there for any of that stuff. How could my mother or any other grown woman do that and not die of shame?

Even the name of the booklet, *Growing Up and Liking It*, made me uncomfortable, like they had tried to convince me of something. I might not have any choice over whether I would grow up or not, but I still would be the only one to decide whether or not I'd like it. So far, it stunk. It was like they wrote the stupid booklet to convince you how great it was to buy their stupid equipment—as if we had any choice about it.

I looked up from the booklet to see Marissa didn't look too happy to be growing up either and that made me feel better.

"This doesn't sound like fun to me," I said. "The stuff about the eggs ripening and going down the fallopian tubes can make you sick if you think about it happening inside of you."

She nodded in agreement and said, "I keep thinking about the way my uncle Gino likes to eat his eggs runny. He dips his toast into the yolk and sometimes there's this slimy white part that's not cooked enough and it pools, and he slops that up with the toast with ketchup dripping off all of it."

"Now you're making me sick," I said. "If that's part of how your body has to mature to have a baby, I'm sorry I know about it. I still think the worst part is the pads and the other stuff you have to wear and the embarrassment of buying it."

She nodded, signaling her agreement again.

"How do you think our mothers have the nerve to do that? Maybe they wait until Mrs. Ricci or another woman is behind the counter and they ask her for the stuff."

Now I nodded. "That makes sense. That's what I'd do if I absolutely had to buy it myself."

"Me too," said Marissa, "but I'm asking my mother to get it for me and keep it in the house so I'll be ready."

She saw my face and quickly said, "I'll share mine with you if you need me to, don't worry."

"But what if I get it first?" I said. "I'm older than you."

"I could still get it first. My mother got it when she was eleven and a half. Maybe you won't get it until you're twelve and a half and then you'll be fine."

"I don't think I want to read any more today, okay?"

"Me either," said Marissa. "Let's go outside and play War until it gets dark. We don't have too much time left."

She was right.

I got my period before Marissa did and she was as amazed as I was when I told her that my mother had been nice about it, and even had a belt and some pads ready for me to use.

Although the accompanying cramps were horrible, I surprised myself by feeling proud that my sneaky body did what it was supposed to do; I was content to know everything inside me silently functioned as it should, preparing me to become a mother myself, someday. Maybe.

After I got my first period, I began to crave sleep in a way that I had never remembered before. Not being allowed to stay up late and watch TV, even on Friday or Saturday nights, was still frustrating, but I had gotten around that somewhat by babysitting in the evenings on the weekend. If I found myself at home on a weekend night, I'd read under the covers of my bed with a flashlight until I either fell asleep or stopped hearing noises from the hallway outside the door of the bedroom that I shared with my sister. Before I got my period, I'd had this thing about being the last one in the family to go to bed on Friday night, so I'd roll over and sleep later on Saturday morning and could honestly say, if questioned by Anna, that I was the last one up the night before and that I'd slept in until ten or eleven am

That was before I'd developed a whole new relationship with sleep due to the power of the hormones that brought about many other changes in my body and my mind. I found that right before my period, when my skin would usually sprout a new ugly pimple in a spot where it was impossible to hide it with Clearasil, I would feel jazzed up and not want a lot of sleep. I finished a lot of books under the covers on those days every month. Yet, when my period finally came, usually in a burst of painful cramps and often accompanied by a headache, I'd want to do nothing so much as cuddle up in bed, doused with aspirin and tea. When the cramps subsided, I'd go on a marathon binge of sleeping. Twelve hour stretches and more were not uncommon for me then. What surprised me about all of this was my mother's tolerance of all this sleeping in on my part. She never scolded me for it, but would usually ask me kindly, "How are you feeling, Rosemary? Are the cramps better? Would you like a nice big breakfast or just a cup of tea? Go back to bed if you need to; I'll bring it to you if you want me to."

I found her understanding of and toleration for my need for sleep and TLC something new in our relationship and wasn't sure why it happened and why she was being so nice to me. For someone who was so reluctant to discuss the physical changes I was going through, as well as their implications in my everyday life, she appeared accepting of the fact that these changes had happened to me.

Looking back now, as the mother of an adult daughter myself, I can see my own mother was probably of two minds about it all: On the one hand she was pleased (and probably relieved) that I grew and matured normally. On the other, she was probably frightened of the implications of my physical sexual maturity, knowing it preceded the necessary emotional and intellectual maturity needed to handle it by a number of years. That fact of life hasn't changed in the generation that spanned my first period and my daughter's; the child's physical and sexual maturity almost always occurs before the parent is emotionally ready for it, even if that parent is prepared intellectually.

As a young woman, the message that I got from my mother's dual reaction to my first period was: It's normal (even good and desirable) to go through this because you want to be able to have a baby someday in the distant future; just don't talk about it. It was confusing to have my mother exhibit concern and kindness over the physical symptoms related to my menstrual cycle, while knowing I would quickly provoke her anger if I asked her any of the myriad of questions I had about the changes that occurred to me. As an adult, I sometimes wonder how Granma Mary must have dealt with my own mother's first period and even about what things were like when my grandmother developed into a young woman as an immigrant in a strange country with a sick mother of her own. In retrospect, and compared to her own circumstances, my own angst about getting my period was a little trivial and even a bit self-indulgent.

I do know whatever Granma Mary told my mother when she became a woman, she didn't get the information from Anna, who could make you feel ashamed for breathing.

A little while after the spying-on-Fat-Richie incident, Anna's mother had to take her little sister Addie (who unfortunately resembled both her short, stocky father and her grandmother's bulldog) to an eye specialist in Manhattan to consult about surgery on her left eye, which even we kids had noticed was what we called "going crossed." Addie was so funny looking that we all wondered how she managed to stay sane with Anna for an older sister. No one ever made fun of her looks because we all felt having her sister around her all the time was as much punishment as any younger kid should have to endure. Besides, she was a good-natured kid and never tortured us like our own sisters did, so we were kind to her. Even the adults liked her and I remember her being one of the kids on the block who was always given the extra cookie or the extra five cents from the change when she did a favor and ran an errand for someone. Maybe everyone liked her as a reaction to her sister, but whatever it was, even my mother thought she was a good kid.

In fact, when my mother heard about the possible surgery for Addie, she promptly and uncharacteristically got involved. She volunteered to take Anna out with us to the beach for the day so her mother wouldn't have to worry about both children but could "focus on Addie's eye," as she said with a twinkle in her own when she informed my sister and me of the disconcerting fact that Anna would accompany all of us to the beach.

* * *

Manhattan Beach had opened to the public only a season or two before; and when we went to the beach for swimming, it was our destination, as Coney Island was for enjoying fireworks. It's a tiny beach, consisting of only two bays, but was by far the nicest beach to be found in Brooklyn. Manhattan Beach shares the eastern most part of the same south shoreline as Coney Island and Brighton Beach, but my mother always said Manhattan Beach felt like another world; a private one to which only a few people had access.

It had, in fact, been a private beach, open only to those who were able to afford a house there, in that tiny, affluent neighborhood just south of Sheepshead Bay where the streets were dotted with large trees and the houses didn't look like they did in Gravesend. Most of the residences there were small, gem-like structures made of brick and stucco that looked like smaller versions of the photos of the houses of the stars in the movie magazines all my friends liked to read. Many of the homes were done in what my father told me was "Tudor" style, with leaded and stained glass windows and were built with a type of brick called tapestry brick that came in different textures and shades, giving them a different look from any of the homes I was used to seeing in my own neighborhood.

The public school that the kids of Manhattan Beach attended didn't look like any public school I had ever seen inside New York City either. It didn't have a number on its facade, just the words, "The Manhattan Beach School" carved into the stonework atop its front entrance. Its PS number (PS 195) must have been in a more inconspicuous spot because I never noticed it. It looked like a small elementary school in a well-off suburb—another world to us. That school made me think about the scene from *A Tree Grows In Brooklyn* where Francie Nolan finds another school a long walk from her house and persuades her father to write a letter so that she can go to school there instead of to the local one. Although I had no similar problem with the quality of PS 95, where I had gone to elementary school, I longed to be a part of the world that Manhattan Beach symbolized for me: a more gracious and refined place to live where people dressed and spoke differently than we did. I realized at the same time that it was a place where I probably would not have felt comfortable living, but I only dreamt about it anyway, so I let my thoughts go on inside my head.

Unlike the other two famous Brooklyn beaches, Brighton and Coney Island, Manhattan Beach was not easily accessible by public transportation, and I guess that was part of the reason it seemed so exclusive; it was hard to get there. Anyone going by subway either had to walk from the Sheepshead Bay stop of the Brighton subway line, probably a mile away, or had to pay another fare and get onto the B-1 bus that stopped in front of the subway station and ride it to the entrance to the beach. Once there, you then had to walk on a broad concrete walkway past the children's park and handball courts to the beach beyond. One of the big attractions for my mother were the separate public locker rooms for men and women, with showers and changing cubicles that were both clean and usable. There was also a snack stand where bored high school kids who needed to work in the summer sold what I remember as delicious hot dogs. For us it was about the best place you could find yourself on a hot summer day in Brooklyn in 1960, and we managed to get there for a fifteen-cent bus ride.

When the radio predicted a hot sunny day during the week in the summer my mother would often get my sister and me up early, pack our towels and lunch and other stuff and hurry us out of the house. We would walk down West 6th Street from Avenue U to Avenue X and catch the still-not-crowded B-1 bus there before ten am, when the heat of the day was still bearable, for the forty-minute ride to Manhattan Beach. Although she was over eight years old, my mother would try to get my skinny, younger looking sister to slip by the driver so she could save the extra fifteen cents from her fare to spend on an extra ice cream later. Alice got the extra ice cream if she played along and it worked and we avoided the third fare. Kids under six were permitted to ride free on all public transportation in New York City and anyone who rode the buses in my part of Brooklyn felt it was their civic duty to stretch this rule as far as it could go–which, depending on the driver of the bus, often stretched it far enough to let my sister and a lot of other kids slip through the gap. An interesting phenomenon in otherwise law-abiding, taxpaying citizens of my borough was their delight in bending this particular rule, which I had seen done routinely all of my life. People didn't routinely try to beat the fare themselves, but I think it was paying that extra fifteen cents for children who couldn't read a lot of the signs by themselves that bothered the mothers.

Most of the city buses weren't air-conditioned. Once inside and sitting on the molded plastic seats, the outside air that blew on us as the bus moved felt hotter than the air inside; but this almost-visible hot breeze was preferable to the choking feeling of the lack of air from a closed window with the sun radiating through it that was its only alternative. As we rode down Avenue X after making the long walk straight down West 6th Street from Avenue U, we consoled ourselves during the trip imagining the cool breezes that awaited us at our destination. Through the congestion of Sheepshead

Bay Road and around the bay, past the tiny Catholic Church of St. Margaret Mary (that always looked abandoned compared to our own bustling parish) until the playground at the edge of Manhattan Beach came into view, we sweated and waited for our arrival at the beach. My sister would inevitably be on her feet and heading for the door as soon as she saw the church, even though my mother liked to wait for the next stop, which let you off right in front of the bath house and locker rooms. The locker rooms were what made me dread having Anna with us that day.

Part of the appeal of Manhattan Beach was, after spending the day at the beach, you could shower and go home clean and without sand, and most mothers took advantage of this. Before going home, most mothers with younger kids showered with them in their bathing suits and got them dressed to go home, then they put them right outside of the changing cubicle so they could dress themselves in relative privacy. Some modest adults (and all the teenagers I knew) even got a friend or an older child to hold a towel across the entry to the cubicle, which didn't have a door, guaranteeing them more privacy than the basic cement block structure of the bathhouse permitted. This ritual with the towel was usually accompanied with an admonition to the children to stay put and be sure to hold the towel up and: "*Don't* get full of sand again!"

111

So of course, the first thing the kids did was push the towel duty onto a younger kid and run back to the shower rooms where they tried to get a good look at all the equipment the older and less modest women (who showered without towels) had that they didn't. Of course, I had done it, too, but would never admit it. So has my sister, Alice, who was still too young to be concerned about bras or periods or any of the stuff that made a summer day at the beach a little less fun than it used to be. I knew with all that naked female flesh around (no matter that most of it was either too old or too fat to be anything but disgusting) Anna would find a new "secret" to torture me with—something about sex that I didn't know, but that if I admitted to not knowing, would be all over the neighborhood the next day. When my mother told me that Anna was coming along I felt so betrayed and apprehensive that I felt like volunteering to help Anna's mother take Addie to the doctor on the hot subway.

When Anna showed up at the side door that opened onto the alley we shared with our neighbors, the Rinaldi's, she wore that look of feigned innocence that confirmed my fears about the day ahead. She said, "Good morning" to my mother so politely that I was glad I'd already gulped my breakfast of cornflakes and milk down a few minutes before. My mother asked her if she had brought her lunch and she answered, "No, Mrs. N, but my mother gave me money to buy it at the beach." She held out two dollars to show my mother.

"Would you hold it for me?"

Sickening. More of her innocent little girl act. Only real little kids asked their friend's mother to hold their money for them. Even Alice kept some of her own money in a little change purse that she stuffed into the toe of her sock and hid in her sneaker at the beach. Although, I could see from her eyes that my mother didn't buy the act completely, thank God.

"Well, I can if you want, but I think you should go to Avenue U with Rosemary and buy yourself some lunch before we leave. You don't want to eat the greasy junk they serve there, and you'll have money left over for ice cream if you buy your lunch now.

"But what can I get for one dollar?" She asked so pitifully that I wanted to puke all over her.

"I have to keep some money for carfare, too."

Like my mother didn't know that.

"Go get a small roll at DeMarco's for a nickel and then get a quarter pound of ham at the *salumeria*. That should leave you with enough change for the bus. I'll hold your other dollar for ice cream and you'll still have change to give your mother tonight when we get back. Go now so we won't be too late getting started."

My mother looked at me meaningfully and I knew the day had truly begun. So I went with Anna, acting like I was pleased she was coming with us. If she smelled my fear, I knew it would be all over even before we got on the bus.

"Your mother is smart to think of that idea about lunch. Now I'll have enough left over for a couple of ice creams. There's a cute guy who works at the snack stand and I'll be able to flirt with him more than once now. That'll be fun. Wanna come with me?"

She looked at me sideways out of those cat eyes and I nodded my head in agreement. I smiled, hoping she didn't have any serious stuff in mind and wouldn't do it where my mother could see it.

The rolls had just come out at the bakery and it was so hot in there that the sidewalk felt cool in comparison when we came back out and went across the street to buy the ham. The *salumeria* was on the corner of West 6th Street and was quiet at that time of the morning; the housewives would be in later at lunchtime to buy the salami, *sopressata, prosciutto*, cheeses, and cold salads that were made fresh every day. On the weekend, the backyards of the neighborhood would be redolent with the smell of freshly made *cervellata* sausage, which was thin and flavored with cheese and parsley, made into a big coil by the sausage maker and secured into a large wheel with wooden skewers. For me, the smell of a hamburger sizzling on a charcoal grill always comes in a distant second to the smell of that sausage cooking on a grill with peppers and onions. It perfumes the air outside all around the grill and it shouts "summer" at me and brings me instantly back in time.

After Anna and I got the ham, we returned to my house as quickly as we could. My mother made Anna's bread and ham into a sandwich and added mustard and tomato as she requested. While waiting to go, Anna told me that there was a kind of mustard called Dijon that was much better than any American mustard; her aunt had let her taste it once when using it to prepare a special potato dish for her.

"You know, in French, a potato is called a *pomme de terre.* Want to guess what that means?" she asked me.

"French fry?" said Alice, wanting to be a part of the discussion.

"No stupid, that's *pommes frites.*"

Alice's face fell at the reply. She both feared and looked up to Anna.

"Don't call her stupid just because she doesn't know French," I said. "She's only eight."

"And you're her big sister who's going to protect her from the Big Bad Wolf and you don't even know what I'm saying yourself. It could even be something dirty—better cover her innocent ears," she said and laughed out loud.

My mother finished making the lunch, came in, and stared at Anna, frowning at her laughter. "It's nice to see you're all having fun, but we have to go if we're going to get a seat on the bus."

She handed each of us a beach bag to carry as she spoke and then hustled us out of the side door, pulling it shut and locking it. I walked ahead with my sister as Anna pretended to help my mother by trying to take her large cooler bag from her as she put the keys back into her purse. I took that opportunity to whisper to my sister.

"Look, sis, if you want to stay out of trouble go play by yourself in the water today and stay *away* from Anna. Understand?"

For once, she listened, nodding her head up and down and not saying anything.

My mother and Anna caught up with us and we all walked briskly down Van Sicklen Street to Avenue X that day, taking the longer walk that would put us at the bus stop where fewer people got on. As we got there, we could see two buses traveling toward us only a short distance apart.

"Good thing we didn't waste time; we're in luck today," my mother said. "There probably won't be another bus along for a long time now since these two are coming together."

We moved toward the second bus and got seats in the back as my mother dropped the fare in for all of us, including Alice. Maybe she had started to feel having Anna along risked enough trouble for one day. *No going back now*, I thought. If I'd had a seatbelt I would have fastened it. Instead, I sat with my sister on the double seat that faced the inside of the bus and left the window seat next to my mother for Anna as the bus pulled out from the stop.

The rest of the trip was uneventful. Anna looked out of the window and only occasionally smiled at both of us like a cat who was fed and contented—for now anyway. When we pulled in front of the stop near the main entrance and got off, I tried to work out what to do if I felt uncomfortable around Anna later, so I said to my mother, "If Alice gets bored and wants to go on the swings, I'll walk with her and stay with her later. I know she doesn't have a friend to play with today."

"Thank you," my mother said. "That's a good idea."

As we walked along, the first bus, which had been in front of us at the beginning of the trip but had made the longer stop at the subway station to pick up people, pulled up behind our bus and discharged a load of passengers behind us as we walked ahead toward the sand. I heard a loud voice calling, "Anna, *Anna, wait! Wait for me!*"

We all turned around in time to see a petite, curly-haired girl wearing short shorts over her bathing suit bottom and nothing over the bikini top. She carried only a towel and a bottle of baby oil mixed with iodine for tanning and waved as she ran toward us.

"Lucky you found us so soon," Anna said, smiling and turning toward us. "This is my friend, Annemarie. She goes to Sts. Simon

& Jude School with me." She turned toward Annemarie.

"This is Rosemary and her little sister, Alice. This is Mrs. Neri, their mother."

"Hi," was all Annemarie said, giving us a sly, sideways glance. Then she giggled.

My mother nodded at her. She didn't look too happy, but for once I had nothing to do with that. We all walked down the broad, concrete walkway that led to the sand. That is, Anna and Annemarie walked together buzzing and talking, while I stayed closer to my mother and my sister. My mother led us down as close to the water as we could get and then as far over to the westernmost part of the bay, near the end of the beach itself, where the houses of those lucky enough to live there were easily visible to our right behind the large boulders that served as breakers for the surf.

This part of the beach was a straight walk down from the playground where the swings were, across the promenade and the sand; she liked to sit there because we could find our way back to her easily if we got bored and wanted to go back there on the swings later in the day. We sat as close as possible to the water so that my mother could keep an eye on my sister and me right from her blanket when we swam. It was also easier to find your way back to the blanket after going for ice cream or to the bathroom when the sand got crowded with people later in the day. We almost always sat in this area when we went to Manhattan Beach. The drawback to sitting there was that it was as far away from the area where most of the teenagers hung out—right in front of the concession stand to the east as you could get. When I was alone with my mother this fact didn't bother me, but I knew it would be a problem today, and it was.

As soon as we pulled out our blanket to spread on the sand and get settled, Annemarie blurted out, "You're not staying here, are you?"

My mother continued to arrange the blanket and unpack the suntan lotion, acting as if she hadn't heard a word.

Annemarie continued: "This is so far from where the kids are! We'll spend the whole day walking back and forth! Let's move closer to the snack stand."

My sister and I looked at each other. Finally, when she was finished arranging the blanket, towels, cooler bag for our lunch, and her own book, my mother said, "Look, I don't know who you are and I don't care where you sit, but I promised her mother (pointing at Anna) that I'd take care of her today and that she'd be with me, and this is where we're sitting. If you want to go over there, then *go*." Without another word, she turned her back to Annemarie, sat down and began rubbing suntan lotion on her arms.

Annemarie made a face at her behind her back so I would see it out of the corner of my eye and then Anna whispered something into her ear and she walked away. Then Anna spread out her own towel and sat down on it while she opened a book with French writing on it and buried her head in it.

I said to my sister, "Hey Alice, want to try the water?"

She nodded and we walked over to the shore and down from our blanket.

We put our feet into the water and it felt warm. Alice turned back and called out, "Mom, can we go in now?"

She nodded and we both splashed our way in for the cooling sensation on our bodies after the heat we'd felt all morning from traveling and from our situation, as well as from the weather. I forgot about Anna and her friend for the moment and allowed myself the luxury of swimming and splashing in the warm July water. After a while, I joined my sister in her favorite water sport: letting the gentle waves break over me in the shallow water at the edge of the shoreline and then carry me out again with the pulling of the next wave. I knew the bottom part of my bathing suit would get filled with sand and I'd have to wriggle around in the water to get it out before I stood up, but I didn't care, and continued to enjoy myself like a little kid while I could.

When we returned to the blanket, Anna was gone. We looked at our mother, asking her about it with our eyes.

"She asked me if it was all right for her to go see her friend and I told her it was okay with me as long as she checked in with me at least once and was back here by three-thirty when it was time to go home. She even took her lunch with her. Are you two hungry yet?"

"You bet," my sister answered immediately, delighted as only a younger child could be with the seeming solution of an annoying problem and the offer of food. I nodded; although I was momentarily relieved at this development, I had learned it was better, when dealing with Anna, to always be suspicious of anything she did that appeared to have a simple explanation. I knew this was only a postponement and there would still be trouble ahead from her and her so-called friend. So I began to eat my lunch with a less optimistic heart than my sister, while thinking there were a lot of disadvantages to being the older sibling.

One of the worst things that you could be called in my neighborhood was a Flat-Leaver, and if Anna had been anyone else, she would certainly have earned the epithet by her behavior. I was so pleased not to have her and Annemarie around that the word didn't enter my mind that day. Instead, I wondered if there was a way to get my mother to let her go home with her friend, alone, and preferably on a different bus. After that happy thought, I enjoyed my sandwich a lot more. Anxiety usually made me lose my appetite, but I began to feel hungry just then.

The day passed as quickly as it usually did when I had fun at the beach.

After lunch, I took my sister to the play-ground and pushed her on the swings, longing to get on one of them myself and pump my legs until I was up high above Anna and Annemarie and all of their plots, but I was a little too old for that and besides, I was afraid they might appear out of nowhere and see me doing it.

Anna had shown up at our blanket only once with Annemarie to check-in with my mother as she had agreed to do; she said she would be staying "around the snack stand" if my mother had to find her for some reason. Then she winked at me and asked me if I wanted to come with them after she had said this, but with her back almost turned to me. I'd whispered to her that my mother made me watch my sister for a while and I'd try to get there later. They both went off in a cloud of giggles with their heads together. When I did go for ice cream with my sister after she got off the swings, they merci-fully weren't around.

So I finished my ice cream and read my Nancy Drew mystery, more content than I'd thought I could be that day. Finally, after another swim, my mother announced we had to pack up and head for the bathhouse to shower before our trip home. As she packed up and pulled out her watch to check the time, Anna walked over to the blanket. She picked up her towel and joined us as casually as if she'd spent the whole day there with us and we all walked over the sand to the locker rooms.

Once we'd showered and changed for the bus ride home, and I started to feel happy that the day was almost over, I spotted Annemarie coming over to the cubicle where my mother was in the process of changing. Anna and Alice and I were outside waiting for her and I held up the towel to give her privacy.

Annemarie said to me, "Did you get to ride on the swings today?"

"No, I just pushed my sister."

"How cute. A bigger jerk pushing a little one."

I called in to my mother that we wanted to get a drink of water and asked if she could do without the towel. When she said it was okay, I dropped it inside on the little bench and grabbed my sister's hand and said we were headed to get a drink of water. Anna and Annemarie followed us as we made our way to the water fountain.

As my sister got a drink, Annemarie sneered at me and said: "I bet you don't even know the Fact of Life, do you?"

"Of course I do," I answered quickly.

"Oh really? Then tell me what this joke I heard today is about if you're so smart, but send your little sister away first if you don't want her to learn this stuff too young."

I pushed Alice toward the cubicle and Annemarie started to tell the joke as my stomach produced an internal ball of flames. All I could remember is the last line: "Lady, the cucumber is hard enough not to get hurt, but please don't squeeze the grapes!"

What I do remember is the way Anna and Annemarie howled with laughter—so loud that the towel-clad women passing by and the little kids in bathing suits or underwear looked at them like they were crazy.

"You don't get it, you don't, admit it!" said Anna, wiping tears of laughter from her eyes.

I pictured in my mind the stone face that Bette Davis had worn at the end of the movie "Marked Woman" when she faced down the mobster who had her face cut with a knife so she'd be scarred for life. I'd seen that movie maybe a dozen times on "Million Dollar Movie" and had kept that look in my mind for a time like this.

I willed my face to look tough like hers, stared at both of them and said: "Don't be so naive," and walked away as they howled even louder.

When I got back to the cubicle, my mother could see from my face that something had happened.

"Where's Anna?" she said.

"By the water fountain with Annemarie."

"Did they bother you too, Alice?" she asked my sister.

"No! Please let's just go home," she said, looking at my face.

As we gathered our things and walked over to the fountain, we saw them, still laughing, but not as loud as they had been before.

My mother gave them The Look as only she could, and said, "Time to go, Anna. I told your mother we'd be home by five o'clock."

"Mrs. Neri, do you mind if I sit with my friend on the bus?" she asked sweetly.

"Not as long as you get off when you're supposed to with me. Here's your carfare and the change for your mother. Give it to her."

"Thank you. And thanks for taking me. I had a great time."

"Let's go before the bus line gets too long," my mother said, increasingly fed up with Anna herself.

I spent part of the trip back listening to Anna and Annemarie laughing together and calling out, "Don't be so naive!" what felt like every few minutes from the last two seats at the back of the bus. At first I was forced to stand near them because we were some of the last people to get on. A few people even shouted at them to shut up a few different times, which they did for a little while, until the bus pulled out of a stop and some riders got off and others replaced them; then it was back to torturing me again. My mother sat with Alice in the row of seats behind the back doors, occasionally glancing at them with an expression that I had never done anything bad enough to merit from her.

Finally, when we arrived at the Brighton Beach subway stop where a lot of people got off, she gestured to me to sit near them when a seat near her opened up, simultaneously gesturing to me and throwing her cooler bag onto the seat to hold it for me. It didn't help a whole lot because I still heard them cackling; at one point they even started singing some song in French, but Annemarie didn't know the words so they went back to what had worked before, and continued throwing my own words back at me.

All I could do was pretend to read my book and ignore them, but inside I thought the next day I would set a record for sleeping in and in all of my dreams I would definitely kill Anna and Annemarie in a variety of different, gruesome ways borrowed from the horror movies I loved to watch. Maybe I'd even tie their necks together into a knot, like they did in cartoons, until their eyes popped out of their heads, like grapes! Nancy Drew was entirely too civilized for those two! They deserved the ending from every gory film ever produced by Hammer Films.

Annemarie got off the stop before we did, giggling all the way out the back door and off to her house on the other side of West 6th Street. By the time we got to our stop, my mother had definitely seen the error of her ways in inviting Anna to the beach with us. If she had bothered to ask me, I would have told her that in the first place, but as usual, she had never bothered to consult with me. Despite her adult status, she had been too naive, but I was sure she was cured of that now.

Chapter 5

Barefoot Time

As early summer turned into mid-July and most of the kids on the block longed for something different to do and somewhere else to do it, I felt lucky knowing my family would soon be leaving Brooklyn to spend two whole weeks in the country. After years of trying to choose the right two weeks (meaning hot, sunny, and as rain-free as possible) for our annual vacation, my parents had decided their best bet was the last week in July and the first week in August.

So every summer, just when the novelty of being out of school began to wear thin and the trips to Manhattan Beach became routine, we left the city for what felt like, to my sister and me, to be an idyllic, mostly shoeless experience at the "Twin Lakes House" near Narrowsburgh, New York.

"How much longer until we go to Twin Lakes?" was a question my sister asked me almost incessantly as she inquired about whether or not I knew what her birthday gift would be every July. As an answer to the second question, I'd always say I didn't know what her gift was, even if I did. To answer the first question, I'd take her to the calendar that was in the kitchen; it was given out at St. Simon and Jude during the Christmas holidays and featured all the religious holidays and saints' days for the liturgical year. It had magnificent pictures that reminded me of the stained glass windows of the church where we went to Mass almost every Sunday of the year. The faces of the Blessed Mother, Jesus, St. Joseph, and all the saints pictured on its pages appeared to possess at once a beauty and a peace that I'd found considerably lacking in myself. As proof of that, and after her inevitable question, I'd take my sister's arm and nearly drag her to that calendar, point to the date we were scheduled to leave, roll my eyes up to those saints in heaven, and say, "Count," to which she'd invariably respond: "Great! Only __ days after my birthday!"

As if I could possibly forget! Her birthday was only two days before our mother's, which was near the feast day of Our Lady of Mount Carmel. Since my sister had been born, my mother had often told us the story of how glad she was that Granma Mary hadn't named her

Carmela in honor of the feast day closest to her birthday (which was a common practice among other Italian Americans of her generation), but had opted instead for Margaret, a derivation on the name of Mary, and a name my Granma had liked better for her second child. My mother had also told me that, as the oldest child, I had been named after both my grandmothers, a traditional custom with which she had felt comfortable. When it was my sister's turn to be named, however, she'd picked a name for her that she "just liked." When I was annoyed at my sister, the second child of a second child, I'd imagine what her life would be like if *she* had been named Carmela, and I had been named a name my mother had "just liked."

After those two birthdays passed, it was always a relief for me to think about the place we called "Twin Lakes," the huge old farmhouse situated near Route 652 in southwestern New York state, only a few miles from the Pennsylvania border. My father had heard about the place years before we had moved to West 5th Street from someone he had worked with at the Brooklyn Navy Yard; we had gone there since before my sister was born. At that time, and for years to come, the first attraction of the place for my parents was its affordability for a family vacation. The biggest attraction for my sister and me, however, was that we were allowed to go around without shoes for a lot of the time that we were there. Unlike my ancestors in Sicily or Southern Italy, going without shoes was a sign of freedom for us and we felt like throwing our shoes out of the window of the car as we pulled up into the red clay driveway leading up to the house on the first day of our vacation, not out of mischief, but to express sheer joy for the freedom we had there.

The Twin Lakes house was run by a family named Cosgrove as a sort of summer boarding house where one dollar plus the child's age per week (in addition to the modest sum charged for adults) entitled the family to two small but clean bedrooms and the use of one of the huge bathrooms in the hallway, which were shared by all the guests on the floor. The bathrooms were older than the one we had at home, but were kept spotlessly clean. That fact didn't stop my mother from taking her can of generic scouring powder (no expensive Ajax for her) with her on vacation and using it before the first bath we took in the tub. I never understood this because we bathed there the whole vacation, but I only saw her clean the tub once, like she wanted to baptize it before we used it and one cleansing was all that was necessary. The modest price also included three huge meals a day, which featured fresh bread, milk, and butter from the working dairy farm on the same land, as well as the kind of food that my father referred to as "real American farm cooking," which was a great compliment from him. It was simple abundant American fare and we enjoyed it three times a day.

Those two vacation weeks were my first real opportunity to try a different kind of cooking, where the only pasta served was the thick, hearty egg noodles that usually accompanied the pot roast. Many of the kids there liked to eat them plain, but I followed my father's instructions and topped them with a dab of homemade gravy, which was served at the tables in thick, white gravy boats, with the steamy heat evaporating off the top surface of the gravy and floating up toward the ceiling until it disappeared into the cooling air of the midsummer's evening. It was the kind of food that would neither have appealed to us nor been easily digested in the steamy warmth of the same evening in Brooklyn, and I could never have imagined us eating it in our kitchen back home.

Yet, there, at the Twin Lakes house, we devoured it as eagerly as the Cosgrove's and their farm workers, who had labored since the sun was up, when they ate their supper before the paying guests were served.

My mother used to tell us that we had such hearty appetites for this heavy food because we were outside in the fresh country air all day long. At first, I accepted this, thinking the air closer to Pennsylvania was cleaner than the air in the city where we lived. Only later did I realize her explanation didn't make sense—we were usually outside all day or at the beach where the air was pretty clean. I finally came to believe we all simply loved the novelty of eating a different kind of food while we were on vacation, and my mother certainly loved not having to cook it. The food was as much a part of the change from our daily lives as being away from Brooklyn was; and although I didn't like French as much as Italian, I think we'd all agreed the phrase, *"Vivre le difference!"* explained it beautifully.

My parents' delight with the moderate price of our annual vacation (which allowed us all a two-week break from our usual routine) was only surpassed by the delight that my sister and I took in the whole experience of feeling like we lived with the Cosgrove family while we were there.

The main house was situated on a hill over-looking the dusty, red dirt road that ran in front of it. All the guestrooms were on the second and third floors. A red clay and pebble footpath meandered from the base of the wooden steps below the front door to the splintery wooden stairs that led down the hill and across the road to the first of the two lakes that gave the house its name.

The closer of the two was the fishing lake, and its integrity was vigilantly guarded by Mr. Higby, the local Game Warden, who made sure no one over the age of sixteen cast a pole into that lake without a fishing license—a costly item that was not included in my parents' budget for our summer vacation. This not-discussed but pervasive fact of our family's economic life explains why my father never did more than bait the hook during all the years that we vacationed there.

Every summer, on our frequent trips to the fishing lake, I was the only one in our family who put a pole into the water. On a good morning, I would haul one or two medium-sized catfish and throw them back in. My delight in catching the fish did not extend itself to the thought of keeping them and eventually eating them or giving them to someone else to clean and eat. The fun of fishing was tied up in my mind with the pleasure of just being on the lake in a rowboat with my father, talking with him and listening to him. It was years before I developed a taste for fresh fish and often, as an adult, I've wished for the opportunity to return to that lake and catch some fish to clean and cook, knowing they were fresh, but simultaneously knowing it wouldn't be the same without my father there with me.

On the first day of our vacation, it became a ritual with me to ask my father if he would fish with me instead of just baiting the hook, and every year he'd look at my mother and then at me, smile and shake his head. Then he'd say since I did such a good job of pulling in the fish by myself, he didn't want to interfere with that. Not until I was about ten years old did I learn from one of the other kids that an adult had to purchase a fishing license or risk a hefty fine from Mr. Higby for illegal fishing. As much as I loved my father and wanted to go out on the weathered wooden dock and into a rowboat with him to fish, I felt cheated by this information that my solo status as the family fisherman had more to do with saving money and our family economics than it did with any talent on my part and that knowledge made it a little less special for me.

Despite my tiny disappointment, I still loved that lake and, as I got older, I asked my father to take me out for a rowboat ride in one of the boats that were available for the guests to use. The boats were all a weathered, splintery grey color with three flat, plank seats: a narrower one in the bow, a wider one in the stern and middle one for the person(s) rowing. First, we'd look for a good boat with a fairly dry bottom and a large old tin coffee can tied to the metal "O" hook that held one of the oars, which was supplied to bail water out of the boat. Then we'd row to the far side of the lake where the water was murky and look for turtles, who might lift their heads out of the water if you hit their shells with a piece of dried bread crust. Sometimes, if it were still, my father would take the oars out of the water and let the boat drift gently on the surface so we could hear the darning needles as they flew by us skimming the surface of the lake over the water lilies that floated on top of the water. If it was hot and he was tired, I often rowed most of the way back. It felt good to row us back and let my father have a chance to relax, and I felt proud to navigate the boat close to the dock and helped tie it up for someone else to use.

The second of the lakes was for swimming. Unless it was unusually hot, we walked there after lunch, wearing our bathing suits under our shorts and carrying our towels rolled under our arms. The swimming lake was down the same red clay road that passed in front of the Twin Lakes house and had a manmade pebbly beach as well as a changing room far more rustic than the one at Manhattan Beach; it was actually no more than a rough little wooden shack without electric light. It was equipped only with a slab of wood nailed onto two smaller pieces of wood that served as a rough bench to sit on—at your own risk for splinters—while you buckled the strap on your sandals (which my mother made us wear while we walked on the road to and from the swimming lake) after changing into your clothes when you finished swimming and had to go back for dinner. There were many times when we were afraid to use the changing shack because a nest of wasps had been found in one or another of the corners of the ceiling. I almost never used the shack unless my mother insisted and then she had to accompany me inside because I had a terrible fear of being stung, which occurred as a result of the only unpleasant experience I ever had during all of my vacations at the Twin Lakes house.

When I was about four and a half years old, and my sister was still a baby, I'd unwittingly run my hand over a huge bee as I slid it along the wooden bannister that ran along the outside steps from the first to the second floors of the main house while we were on our way upstairs after lunch. I can still feel the sensation of the intense pain in my hand that radiated immediately like searing, liquid electricity up the palm and along the underside of my arm; it burned even worse than the weekly vitamin B-12 shots I had been given to treat an anemic condition a year before. I also remember feeling a rush of guilt radiating from my stomach along with the pain in my hand and arm, and thinking I'd stupidly gotten a huge splinter in my hand because I hadn't listened to my mother's warning not to slide my hand along the splintery wood. The two sensations, the burning pain and the guilt, filled me up and burst out of me in a scream.

My mother told me that within a few minutes of the sting, my hand and arm turned a purplish color and I ran a fever that registered over 103. My parents ran to their car with me to rush me to the nearest hospital when Mr. Higby, the Game Warden, came by and, seeing what had happened, told them instead to take me to their room and make me lie down with cold compresses on my head; he must have convinced my usually skeptical parents that he knew what he was doing because they did what he said. Within minutes, he came upstairs, carrying with him a small bucket of mud. He told my parents to let him put it on my hand and then take me to the hospital if it didn't help in a minute or two. My father took me on his lap and Mr. Higby pulled out the stinger with tweezers and shoved my hand into the bucket of mud. It immediately felt so cool and soothing that I stopped crying and closed my eyes and leaned my head on my father's chest.

Within a few minutes, I was asleep, and my parents told me later that my head felt cooler to the touch in just a few minutes and they never did take me to the hospital, but let me sleep it off. That night I slept in bed with my mother, who checked my head frequently to be sure the fever hadn't returned. It never came back that night, and when I woke up the next day, my hand was still sore but that was all, except for the memory of the pain. My mother never made me go into the changing shack when we went to the swimming lake unless I asked her to come with me inside, which she always did whenever I requested.

The manmade beach at the swimming lake was pebbly and you had to walk gingerly over it to get to the water, which was always calm and much clearer than the water in the fishing lake. The swimming lake also boasted a floating dock about fifty feet from the shore that all the kids swam out to as soon as they could dog-paddle well enough to reach it. That dock would always bob up and down as soon as there were more than two or three kids on it, and so it was a source of great amusement to us, constantly threatening to spill you over and into the lake, but never quite doing it. On a hot day, that raft was the focal point of all our water games. We'd have swimming contests from the shore to the raft or the raft to the shore—or as close to the shore as you could get before scraping the bottom, which was covered with the same pebbly rocks that made up the beach. The oldest kid around would get to yell, "Ready, set, go!" to start the race and also would call out the winner's name. There were no prizes for the winner; it was all for fun. When we got bored with racing, there would be diving contests off the side of the raft that faced the deeper water of the lake, doing cannonballs to see who could make the biggest splash.

The little kids were mostly confined to the shallow edge of the beach, wearing their plastic inflated tubes around their waists while their mothers and fathers hovered over them, since there was no lifeguard. The time I spent on the raft in the summers before my sister learned to swim, when I was allowed to be out there away from my parents and sibling, alternately diving, splashing, and swimming in the cool lake water and then lounging in the sun with all the other kids who were liberated from the city for a week or two, were some of the happiest of my summer memories.

Although the summer evenings at the Twin Lakes house were as different from those in Brooklyn as was possible, they were filled with what I thought of as the same feeling of "neighborhood" that I was used to having back home on West 5th Street. After dinner, there was often a bonfire at a cleared area way in the back of the main house in a pit that held the ashes of hundreds of old evenings. The adults and kids alike looked forward to this event and I remember it as one of the few times that I'd seen my mother wearing the one pair of blue jeans that she owned, since everyone sat down on the grassy area around the fire without benefit of the folding aluminum chairs with colored webbing and white stripes that were used on summer evenings on big front stoops in Brooklyn.

Sometimes the kids would sneak back to the bonfire pit after swimming and before dinner to find a few pieces of old charred wood to put in their pockets. After we had finished playing a game of horseshoes and the sun had gone down, but before it was too dark and the bonfire got going, the charred piece of wood would appear and be passed around to rub onto our faces, which our mothers had futilely scrubbed clean before dinner. When it finally had gotten dark and we knew our parents wouldn't protest too much because they, too, had joined in the spirit of the evening, another piece of the charred wood was passed around again and used to paint the faces of our younger siblings. By this time, their faces were usually dirty anyway from the remnants of dinner and the ice cream that preceded a bonfire, so few of the adults protested this action, which was a sort of primal childhood ritual that had no explanation; we simply did it.

Then Mr. Higby would tell us all stories about all the things that he'd seen in his years as a Game Warden and, after the stories, would lead the singing that followed. I can't remember the specifics of even one of the stories he told, but I have an image of him, dressed in khaki pants and brown leather boot shoes, like the ones my father had worn in old army pictures of him from World War II. To my childhood eyes, Mr. Higby's face resembled, more than anyone else's, the face of a thinner Teddy Roosevelt that was mounted on the wall near the auditorium of PS 95 where I had gone to school in Brooklyn. I think for a while I had Mr. Higby mixed up in my mind with TR and I'm sure this happened because of his kindness to me after the bee sting. Because of his knowledge, skill, and kindness, he had assumed near-mythic status to me and rose to be on a par with that feisty President from the portrait at my elementary school.

After the singing, it was time for the final and best event of a bonfire evening. As the last strains of the last song died down, one of the younger Cosgrove men would appear at the edge of the bonfire circle with a bunch of long, pointed sticks and several packages of marshmallows. Kids who were determined to be old enough and responsible enough got a parental nod of approval when the stick was passed to them and they got to spear and roast their own marshmallows, with varying degrees of success. If you didn't let it cool enough, the marshmallow tasted awful, like a regular marshmallow that had been dragged through ashes. If you let it cook too long, it became a lump of melted, sweet mush coated with charcoal that would burn the roof of your mouth as you tried to eat it. Luckily, my father was good at roasting marshmallows and knew exactly how long to let them roast. So, after taking the stick from my hands and carefully piercing the marshmallow with it, I'd take it back and put it into the fire, turning it slowly as he had taught me so no one side got burned too quickly.

While concentrating on this work, I would imagine what it had been like when this was the only way to cook food. When I finally popped the marshmallow into my mouth, whole, and savored the unique flavor of the melted sugar blended with the taste of smoke from the fire, I'd feel grateful to be living exactly when I was. It was wonderful to know after being outside all day and eating marshmallows around a fire, we were headed inside to sleep in our clean, comfortable beds. This thought made me feel so content that I'd usually roast a marshmallow for my sister and give it to her without being told. Usually.

On rainy weekday nights and every Friday and Saturday night, we all dressed up in clean jeans or clam diggers and went out with our parents to the White Owl Tavern, which was down the road near the swimming lake. The White Owl was big and dark and made you feel both at home and grown up when you walked inside. As soon as we entered through the double screen doors, we smelled a scent that my sister and I thought was unique to the place, but which I later discovered was common to all old bars and taverns. Every time we'd pass the one local bar on Avenue U and catch a whiff of that smell, my sister and I would be reminded of The White Owl and would wish it were summer and we were back at Twin Lakes. Although no one in my family ever went inside that place on Avenue U, and my parents made negative remarks about the "bar flies" who hung around there and wasted their lives and money, we still couldn't help loving that smell. It was a secret my sister and I shared: we loved a thing connected in some way to the kind of life of which our parents disapproved. It was an affirmation of our ability to see things differently from our parents because of our shared experiences as siblings and it bonded us together.

Years later, as a student at Brooklyn College, I entered the local college pub, The Glenwood Rest, with my date (and future husband), inhaled, and immediately blurted out how much I loved that smell. He looked at me in a questioning way I hadn't seen before as he waved to our friends who were already seated at a table and said, "But, that's just the smell of beer—stale beer."

I was instantly humiliated at the implication of what I'd just said, and explained the origin of my affection for that particular smell and he understood, having himself a more highly developed olfactory sensitivity than I would ever hope to achieve. The incident didn't diminish my love for the smell, however. To this day, one whiff of stale beer and I feel simultaneously young and secure with my spirits immediately lifted, no matter how bad I may have felt before inhaling.

The White Owl had lots of attractions for us besides the smell of stale beer. It had the usual long bar that served its beer and other alcohol for the adults, but it also had a smaller bar, built on a far wall perpendicular to the one for the adults, which was reserved for the sale of ice cream and snacks like potato chips and caramel popcorn. You could get a one-scoop ice cream cone for five cents and two scoops for a dime. Ice cream sodas with real whipped cream and a cherry on top were fifteen cents, and they could also make you an order of French fries for ten cents or a cherry coke for a nickel.

There was always plenty of fun for kids as well. The bar and its surrounding cluster of little old wooden tables (where the kids would sit so that they weren't too close to where the liquor was sold) gave way to a large open area for dancing to the juke box (where a nickel bought three songs) or, on special nights, to the live band that played only square dance and country music. The back of the tavern boasted a real bowling lane—the kind where you had to reset the pins by hand—as well as four or five pinball machines that had the likenesses of Roy Rogers and Dale Evans, or Zorro or the Cisco Kid. Some of the older kids were so good at playing pinball that it was an evening's entertainment just to watch them see how far they could go on one nickel, stretching it out into extra games for the points they accumulated by having the metal ball that was released at the beginning of the game repeatedly hit against the metal buttons that earned the points before it inevitably disappeared into the black hole at the end of the tunnel that finished the game.

A few of the older kids who were only a few years away from turning eighteen (the legal drinking age then) and being able to order a beer from the grownup bar, were so good at the game that they could play for what felt like hours on a quarter's worth of nickels. They were usually touchy about letting you watch them play, insisting you stood far away from the machine so that you wouldn't accidentally lean on the machine and spoil their game. We thought it was worth it, though, just to be able to see them manipulate the game. Whenever I heard the song "Pinball Wizard" from the rock opera *Tommy*, I would think about the nameless older kids I had watched during the many summer nights I spent at The White Owl.

Some of what my sister and I liked best about being there with our parents was the fact that we were with them, but we really weren't. We had the freedom to wander a little, just like we did on our block at home. This made us feel that while there, just like at home in Brooklyn, our parents had their group consisting of other adults like them who wanted to escape the city for a couple of weeks during the summer with their kids. Also, while at The White Owl our parents' mouths weren't constantly filled with the "no's," "cant's," and "don'ts" that constantly plagued us back home. It appeared to us that it was more than being on vacation, though; it was as though we had a chance to see them as they had been together before we were born, especially when they laughed together and drank a beer or two, but most especially when they danced together.

Other kids we knew were ashamed to see their parents dancing together, even doing one of those corny square dances where they do-see-doed like we did in school when the whole school danced outside to celebrate Flag Day, but my sister and I liked it. If I happened to be outside trying to catch lightning bugs (they had them at Twin Lakes too) with some kids and the dancing started, she'd come to find me and we'd watch together, looking in through the outside of the rear screen door, where we had the best view, as our father swung our mother around to the beat of the square dance caller's commands. We were ashamed about a lot of things having to do with our parents, and that number inevitably grew when we became teenagers, but seeing them dance together was never one of them.

Whenever they danced together, my mother's face wasn't that of mommy, but rather belonged to Margaret, a young woman, dancing and enjoying herself with her young man. Daddy certainly wasn't my father at those times, either, but became Vinny, the young man who had met her at a Friday night dance sponsored by her parish church. Those were the days when she had worn clear, red lipstick and styled her hair in an upswept chignon piled on top of her head, like Bette Davis in Now Voyager; I knew because I had seen the old photos of the way they both looked in that seemingly distant time before World War II when they did what they referred to as "keeping company."

My father was the guy who saw her that night and hadn't been discouraged when she said she had to leave with her girlfriends at ten o'clock, but had simply returned the next Saturday night early enough to have time for a few more dances with her before her coach turned into a pumpkin. We'd begged them both to tell us the story of how they had met many times over so we knew exactly how to cast the parts of the younger "thems," who would magically reappear for us a few times a year when the band at The White Owl played amid the smell of beer and ice cream sodas. We thought in our hearts, my sister and I, the band played especially for them (and for us) at those times.

Whenever we'd hear the band play the beginning strains of "The Tennessee Waltz," my sister and I would be so happy for the duration of the song that we'd sometimes slide our arms around each other's waists and sway back and forth, watching through the mesh of the rear screen door while our parents danced and Patti Page sang:

> I was dancing with my darlin' to the Tennessee Waltz
> When an old friend I happened to see
> Introduced her to my loved one and while they were dancing
> My friend stole my sweetheart from me.
>
> I remember the night and the Tennessee Waltz
> Now I know just how much I have lost
> Yes I lost my little darlin' the night they were playing
> The beautiful Tennessee Waltz.

Sometimes that song brought tears to our eyes, although we didn't cry for a lost love, but because, even then, we knew we couldn't spend the rest of our days living in summer nights, watching our parents dance, and being friends as well as sisters. The only bad thing about going on vacation to the Twin Lakes house was the fact that, from our first hours there, we knew it had to end, and exactly when that would happen. Even at six or seven years old, you're old enough to know vacation time, like party time or summertime itself, is a finite quantity and passes much more quickly than school time or dentist time.

At the Twin Lakes house, the official end of one vacation week, and the start of another, was Saturday afternoon. All the families who left that week were acknowledged with a round of applause at dinner on the Friday evening of their last full day there. It was the signal to exchange addresses with the kids you liked so you could promise to write to each other over the long year that intruded on your friendship until the next year's summer vacation. This time was also my first object lesson in endings and in some way it prepared me to accept the inevitability of loss in my life.

On the Saturday afternoon of the end of the first week of vacation, as soon as breakfast was over, the bell that usually called everyone in for dinner would be rung again for a different reason. Then everyone would say goodbye to the families leaving that day, giving them a formal sendoff before they had to load up their cars and pull out of the dusty driveway to begin their trip back home. A lot of the children of the families who returned to Twin Lakes year after year would always stick around after breakfast on Saturday to take part in this ritual. Afterward, I would always feel some sadness mixed with the usual excitement that preceded a Saturday afternoon of swimming. When we went upstairs to change for swimming my sister and I would bother our mother with immediate requests to see whichever friends had left "sometime" when we got back to the city. When we were younger, we'd accept her standard reply of "We'll see."

It was my mother's stock response to any and all of our unexpected and unwelcome requests, which was usually given as she urged us out of our clothes and into our bathing suits so we wouldn't waste any more time getting to the swimming lake. When we were younger the newness of blowing up a new red or blue plastic swimming ring or discovering a "last week treat," as my father called it, of a new tin pail and shovel were usually enough to distract us on our walk to the swimming lake. As we grew older, however, a different phenomenon occurred.

My sister would ask my mother to see whatever friend had just left with her family and would then fight with her about her old response: "We'll see! We'll see! Why don't you just say *no* and get it over with?"

"Because that means I'll think about it."

"No you won't!" She'd yell back and stomp off to wait downstairs on the porch.

I wouldn't bother to ask any more, just pick up my share of the stuff we needed for swimming and join my sister, knowing my mother would answer us with the standard lecture: "You know this is vacation and when it's over, it's over, and we go back to our regular lives in Brooklyn. You can't expect things to be the same back home as they are here. Daddy and I have to work and you have to go to school. It's nice here and it's different and we need our vacation, but it's not forever; nothing is."

As we got older, she would add in Italian, *"Tutto finisce, tutto passa,"* which means everything comes to an end and passes away. Whenever I heard the phrase as a young person, I hated the thinking behind it and rebelled against her easy acceptance of the reality that everything had to end. As an adult, however, I've often heard her repeat that phrase to me during difficult times and have found comfort in the concept of the finiteness of both good and bad times.

After our swimming time was over, the newly arrived families would be greeted at dinner with applause to welcome them. While I always joined in the clapping, especially if the evening meal had brought back a friend from another year, I'd always wish we were the ones being applauded because we'd just arrived. Knowing you had only one week left was like knowing you would die someday, except that on vacation you knew the exact number of days that were left for you to enjoy.

I always took comfort in the rituals at Twin Lakes, and found the fact that everybody had to leave and that no more guests came after Labor Day until the next summer reassuring to me as a child. Having grown up with the communal rituals of the Catholic Church (where everyone, even the Pope, went to confession, received Communion, and had to go to Mass) these group "hello's" and "goodbye's" made me feel this was a confirmation of the fact that arrivals and partings were a part of life for everyone. As the years passed and I matured and experienced different kinds of losses and endings and had my share of first time jitters, the significance of group rituals—like baptisms at the beginning of life and wakes and funeral masses at life's end—took on a deeper significance to me. However, I never felt more comforted than during the times I stood together with my sister and our parents and waved a last goodbye to friends from the faded first floor porch of the Cosgrove's farm house.

Chapter 6

Laughing in School

By the time we returned to Brooklyn from Twin Lakes, my yearly fantasy of an endless summer vacation had given way to the realization that the number of days before school resumed had grown much shorter. The nightly setting of the sun just a little earlier than a few short weeks ago highlighted my awareness that we would soon be back to the books. The reality of how quickly the once endless supply of June days had melted into one another in the heat of July, leaving only a small puddle of easily counted mid-August drops, filled me with the impossible desire to rewind the calendar like the spring of a music box whose tune I couldn't bear to have end. Like a resident of Catfish Row, I felt living was just easier and less complicated in the summertime.

Some of that feeling was due to the fact that since I had entered JHS 228 the past September and had found myself in the "SP-1" seventh grade class, my experience of school had changed dramatically. While the rest of the world in that summer of 1960 focused on the upcoming Olympics which would begin in Rome at the end of August, debating whether the fact that JFK was a Catholic would affect the outcome of the November Presidential election, and waiting to see how long of a sentence Lt. Gary Powers would receive from the Soviets who had captured him after shooting down his U2 plane and putting him on trial, my concern was how best to use the precious few weeks of freedom left before I returned to school for ninth grade. In short, I had come to dread school.

Although I would technically be a high school student in September, having successfully, if unhappily, completed a year and a half of the three years of the junior high school curriculum in my accelerated SP class, I was not yet thirteen years old and would still rather focus on summer dreams instead of fall realities. Having always been one of the youngest due to my November birthday, I did not look forward to competing with the real ninth grade girls who filled the other classes and referred to us "SP's" as "SR's" for "Smart Retards," because inside my deepest secret world I felt like what they called us. I knew I was book smart but life ignorant and I didn't like this feeling that was underlined every day for me in school.

Before the painful limbo that was junior high, I had always loved school. Although I had never gone to kindergarten, because my mother's boss at the Brooklyn Army Base where she worked then wouldn't allow her to take an extra half hour of her accumulated leave every morning so she could take me in herself and allow my Granma to be home with my baby sister. She told me this story when I had asked why I hadn't attended school before first grade and ended her explanation with the fact that her boss had died of cancer a year later, as though this was his karmic punishment for depriving me of kindergarten.

Despite this deprivation, I had done beautifully from the first time I'd sat in a classroom. I'd loved almost everything about elementary school, starting with the desks, which were bolted to the floor and stood unmoving like soldiers, silent and permanently on guard; they gave my almost six-year-old soul a feeling of permanence, order, and security, which no description of school by my parents was able to convey. The very immobility of those desks was consoling to me as I made my first real transition from home to the outside world, and their permanence silently promised me a smooth passage into that world. The grain of the wood on the desktop, which my father told me was oak, looked rich to me; even the little scars from other children's pencils made me feel I had become a part of the history that we studied just by using the same desk as those phantom students of the past who'd left those marks.

I knew when I left for the next grade, some of the scars from my pencils would be there, too and other younger students would add to them and continue right on into the future. A fat, long groove had been cut into the part of the desktop closest to the one in front of it. Pencils, crayons, and sometimes, a skinny ruler were kept in that groove; to the right of this was an unused round hole that my father told me was probably an old inkwell that once been used to hold a little bottle of ink for fountain pens from the days when he had been in school.

Years later, when I asked him why he could sign his name with both hands, he told me that when he had been learning to write, he'd been discouraged from using his left hand by a teacher who had hit that hand with a ruler and had encouraged him to only use the hand that was closest to the inkwell: his right one. This had only managed to make him write uncomfortably with the hand the school preferred and he had continued to use his more dominant hand (the left one) at home and in school whenever he wasn't being observed. Having never been the victim of corporal punishment at home or in school, I didn't get what had happened to him until I was older. My father's ambidextrous ability, which I found amazing despite its cause, and his presence itself was connected in my mind in a positive way with the space for the inkwell that faced me every day on my desk at school; every time I saw it at the beginning of the school day, I thought of him at home asleep after his night of work as a pipefitter and insulator at the Brooklyn Naval Shipyard.

Whenever I finished my test or assignment at school before the other students and sat waiting for the teacher to call time, I would sit quietly with my hands folded together to signal that I was done, but in my mind I imagined myself dipping a quill pen into the inkwell, which now had been filled by a fancy glass bottle of dark ink, and preparing to sign an important document, like Thomas Paine's *Common Sense*, or perhaps a letter to Benjamin Franklin. Sometimes the teacher would catch my eye and smile her approval that I had completed my assignment, nod, and thereby allow me to get out of my seat and drop off my work on her desk; I would do this, taking a book from the small library at the back of our classroom as I returned to my seat. The speed and efficiency with which I completed my elementary school assignments, both at PS 105, where I attended first grade through the middle of third grade, and later at PS 95, which I attended until my sixth grade graduation, allowed me to frequently indulge my hunger for a good read, and firmly established school as one of the brightest lights in my childhood sky.

Those extra few minutes while everyone else was still working added up. They were a part of my introduction to good literature disguised as castoff classroom library books, of which each classroom that I learned in had an abundant supply. In those spare minutes I read *Russian Fairy Tales* (all of which were written before Russia became the Soviet Union), where the stories were told to a young girl and boy by their grandmother, who sipped tea through a sugar cube that she placed in her mouth behind her bottom teeth when she needed to moisten her throat so she could tell them another story. A large illustrated book called *Norse Myths* introduced me to Thor, Freya, and Loki, the jokester, who I pictured as meaner than the illustrator had shown him, and who reminded me of Annemarie, always playing cruel pranks. I even tried to read *Evangeline*, but found it too sad. The dirty, worn covers on those books, which were opened to me with the key of my ability to work quickly and efficiently on my regular assignments, disguised a secret and limitless world that I had been allowed to visit throughout my elementary school years. They were as important a part of my early education as the assignments themselves.

My happiness with my abilities in school had culminated with my uncharacteristically doing something unethical and peeking at my grade on the group IQ exams that were routinely administered in the sixth grade to all the students in the city of New York. I remember being chosen by my sixth grade teacher, Mr. Samuel Reiss, as being trustworthy enough to carry the graded girls' exams down to the main office along with a boy in my class named Peter Di Sieppa, who was chosen to carry the boys' tests. I was delighted at being chosen for this honor, having great affection and respect for Mr. Reiss. He was a wonderful teacher and also had a great speaking voice, which was much in evidence when he read to us on Friday afternoons for the last fifteen minutes of the school day if we had completed all our assignments and tests for that week without excessive fuss or talking. Having him read stories aloud to us from many different books, including the Bible, was a treat that I looked forward to as the week came to an end.

Although I trusted Mr. Reiss, and he in turn trusted Peter enough to give him this plum assignment, I didn't—having seen too many times when Peter would smile his best Eddie Haskell smile at a teacher and then proceed to give that same teacher, including Mr. Reiss, the middle finger as soon as his or her back was turned, leaving his classmates shocked and amused in spite of themselves. Most of us fellow classmates were both in awe of and frightened by the smoothness and audacity with which he behaved. He didn't appear to be affected by a fear of being caught and he acted as though the rules that the rest of us followed didn't exist for him. At recess, he'd been heard to shout out at a younger kid from fourth or fifth grade in the schoolyard who'd asked to be included in a game with the sixth grade boys: "If you want me to say urine, go drink some!"

That word, substituted for "you're in," was shocking behavior in a time when people never even said the word "cancer" aloud in polite company and it both amazed and frightened us. Of course, we'd all laugh, simultaneously ashamed and relieved we hadn't been the one singled out by him. Like Anna, Peter was a master at wearing two faces and I didn't like his real one. So I cautiously went down to the office with him to deliver the tests.

He made a point of publicly holding the door of the classroom open for me to walk through first into the hallway, carrying my stack of IQ exams. As we walked down the three flights of metal stairs toward the office, he stopped on one of the landings in a place that was hard to see from the stairwell and casually started looking through the boys' tests, which were stacked in alphabetical order by last names. His was near the top of the pile and he expertly flipped to the back page where the total grade and the teacher's initials were and read his IQ He smiled, flipped the booklet closed, returned it to its proper place in the pile, looked at me, and gave an upward nod of his head, indicating it was my turn.

Seeing the conflict on my face he said, "You're smart, just like me. Don't you want to know *how* smart? Come on, if you look too, then we can tell each other and you'll always know the score...at least on the exam."

I didn't answer, just worked my way down the pile to the N's and pulled out my exam, peeking at the last page as though it were a doctor's diagnosis of my health. It said, "Total Score: 144." *Was that good?* I wondered, baffled by a mark on an exam over 100%. I didn't know, but I'd find out. I closed the booklet and put it back into the pile, nodding to Peter as we resumed our trip to the office, where we dutifully handed in the tests and began to walk back up to our classroom.

As soon as we were alone in the stairwell, Peter said, "What was your Intelligence Quotient? How smart are you?"

I swallowed and said it was my business.

He laughed and said, "I bet it wasn't as high as mine. I got 139. You know, 150 means that you're a genius and can probably do anything you want. I know because my uncle's studying psychology and he tells me stuff."

I tried to digest the fact that I was only six points below what Peter said was a genius, all the while wondering if he was truthful or trying to trick me. He did know a lot of stuff. What should I say?

I answered, "No, not that smart; just 134."

He smiled, satisfied with the answer, and we both ran up the rest of the stairs, stopping for drinks of water before returning to our classroom and our work.

I didn't tell anyone what I had done, but I did ask my mother if she knew how high of a mark you had to get on an IQ test to be considered a genius. She smiled at the question, but she looked into it and later told me that 150 was considered genius level; after that point I felt different about school, as if I knew it wouldn't be fun anymore.

Not knowing I had begun to cross the threshold from childhood into adolescence intellectually as well as physically, I blamed it on that exam and on the fact that I had peeked at my score. Even confessing it to the priest, who didn't give me a big, difficult penance to do, didn't make me feel any better, only like I had lost something in finding out the score I wasn't supposed to know. I thought about the story of Adam and Eve and the Tree of the Knowledge of Good and Evil and felt like I had taken a costly big bite that I could neither chew and digest nor spit out.

A few months later, my parents received a letter that said, due to my excellent academic record and those IQ test results, I had been invited to attend Hunter College High School for junior and senior high instead of having to attend my local schools to continue my education. It was an honor to be invited to join this invitation-only program for worthy public school students and, for a while, it was a topic of conversation in our house and even on the block.

My parents were enormously proud, but didn't think I should go for a lot of reasons—the main one being the ninety minute subway ride all the way to East 68th Street in Manhattan that involved changing trains and transferring to the IRT subway, that I would have to do alone every school day. They didn't feel an eleven-year-old girl should have to wake up extra early and come home much later for the next six years just to attend a good school, when we had perfectly good schools a short walk away in our neighborhood in Brooklyn.

"Save that daily grind for when you have to go to work and you don't have a choice about it," was their often repeated philosophy, which they also had followed by staying in Brooklyn after my father returned from World War II because they felt that it was better not to have a long commute for work.

Only Mr. Collaro, Marissa's father, who was as proud as if I had been his own daughter, and who took the subway every day to work in Manhattan, thought I should go. He was the only one of the fathers on our block to have what was called a "white collar" job, and he went to work every day in a white shirt, jacket, and tie. I'd heard my mother say he could afford to give me advice because he made the incredible sum of $10,000 a year and, therefore, looked at everything differently from the other parents. Since the school was free, I didn't know what his salary had to do with the matter, but wisely kept my opinion to myself.

My Uncle Dom thought it was a great opportunity for me, but agreed with my parents about the subway ride and told me that he thought I'd also miss all my friends from the neighborhood, especially Marissa. Of all the objections to my traveling into the city (as we called Manhattan) for school that were offered, the only one that made sense to me was Uncle Dom's. We had lived on the same block since I was in third grade and Marissa had been my best friend for practically all of that time. Although she was a year behind me in school and we would be in different schools until she graduated the sixth grade and came to JHS 228 the following year, I could still see her every day after school, unless, of course, I was busy traveling home on the subway from the city. So, in declining the invitation to attend that special Manhattan school, my parents had actually done me a favor—or so I thought, until they did accept the second academic honor that I was offered.

Along with some of my friends from PS 95 who had done well academically, I was to be enrolled in the 7 SP class in JHS 228. The New York City Board of Education had decided the best way to deal with bright youngsters entering the city junior high schools was to take these young adolescents and have them complete the three years of academic work (seventh, eighth, and ninth grades) required for a junior high school diploma in two years instead of three, thus accommodating their intellectual abilities while ignoring the needs of their emotional development. The emotional needs were often in conflict with the academic ones, and it was as if the flame under the simmering pot of early adolescence had been turned up just enough to cause the contents to threaten to boil over daily.

My friends and I from PS 95 all missed the extended family feel of our old elementary school, which was a place where teaching virtually ended for the day on Wednesdays at two o'clock, while ninety-five percent of the students left the public school for religious instruction, which was referred to as "released time." We walked on our own or were escorted the few blocks from Avenue U and Van Sicklen Street to Avenue T and Lake Street, guarded by a street patrol of moms holding up signs to stop the traffic on the corners, to be given religious instruction by the nuns of Sts. Simon and Jude Catholic school. We all felt as if we had been ripped away from our comfortable, homey elementary school and thrown poorly prepared into the lobster pot that was our new junior high school with its academic expectations of us that far exceeded our past experiences, and we all weren't ready to live up to these new expectations.

I later took it personally when my junior high math teacher, Mrs. Kane, informed us, as she gesticulated with a long piece of chalk to make a point to the less mathematically gifted of our SP class, which included me: "In my class, it's sink or swim. No floating!"

My first year of junior high had been a disaster academically, but I do remember a lot of raucous laughter in the awful, dark basement room that passed for a cafeteria, where we seventh graders were given the absurdly early lunchtime of 11:15 am to accommodate the large numbers of baby boomers being educated at the school. We girls from PS 95—myself, Mary Zinni, her cousin Annie-Pat Bari, Tina Carcioffo, and our new friend Rosie DeMarco— who had gone to PS 97, soon formed a strong bond of friendship. We had all been recently demoted from the position of "smartest" that we had held in elementary school to that of "not quite the dumbest, but close to it" as we found ourselves competing quite unsuccessfully in the academic snake pit that was the 7SP-1 class that we had been assigned.

Our class walked together to all its subjects after a fifteen minute homeroom when we arrived at school, and everyone knew how everyone else was doing in all the subjects we studied every day, since privacy of grades and consideration for the feelings of the students in a transition year were alien concepts in the public education system in Brooklyn (as well as the rest of New York City) as it existed then. Only the kindness of some individual teachers and the strict discipline that was maintained in the classrooms (at least when the teachers were around) allowed poorer students to maintain some dignity in the face of less than stellar academic achievement.

To counteract this awful new reality that we shared, our lunchtime—all thirty-five minutes of it—was filled with non-stop talk and frequent laughter. We PS 95 girls and Rosie from PS 97 almost always sat together and, among us, everything—teachers' names, guessing who wore a toupee, even the contents of a friend's lunch—was up for grabs in terms of laughter; the only rule was it couldn't be mean. Stupid, dirty, vulgar, absurd, and ridiculous were fine, but outside of the lunchroom we were forced to eat more than our share of mean from a lot of teachers and classmates, so the unwritten rule was: "No mean laughter at each other's expense at the lunch table."

We must have been a bunch of obnoxious pre-teenagers, talking and laughing non-stop, while scarfing down our sandwiches and trading desserts, but those observing us from the outside didn't realize that underneath our annoying behavior, we helped each other to grow accustomed to a scary new environment by one of the oldest human methods: group support.

The only day we ever attracted the attention of the lunchroom attendants was the time that we made Mary Zinni laugh so hard at a story about one of our teachers that the milk she was drinking actually spurted out through both her nostrils in a huge, disgusting double gush of white liquid while she dropped the rest of the small container onto the floor, convulsing with laughter. We were all so shocked by this, and by the fact that she just continued her laughing that we all nearly fell off our chairs with the strength of that contagious spasm of laughter, screaming and breathless, tears streaming down our faces and laughing innocently, completely, and thoroughly as only young adolescent girls can. We barely escaped detention by cleaning up the mess we had made before the lunch lady told us to do it, suffering only indignant looks from the teachers on duty instead of a more formal punishment, and giggling all the while as we did so.

Not only were my friends and I not making the grades we formerly had in general, but we were doubly chagrined to find ourselves in the lower half of the class in Italian, the foreign language of choice for all students in the 7SP −1 class, the SP-2 took either French or Spanish. None of us had ever spoken Italian before since most of our parents had been born in the US and we felt the double whammy of shame at doing poorly in an academic subject, as well as not succeeding in learning the language of our grandparents. For me personally, the second failure was the more shameful one.

Since none of the public schools taught Sicilian, I had especially wanted to succeed in Italian; it was one of the things I had looked forward to the most when I chose what foreign language to study in preparation for attending junior high school. By learning it, I would be able to feel at one with my ancestors from Sicily and southern Italy and also consider myself an educated person who knew a romance language—what my father had explained the languages derived from Latin (which he himself had studied in high school) were called. One of the things that I especially liked about Jacqueline Kennedy, the wife of the President, was that she was able to speak three of these languages: Spanish, Italian, and French and had given speeches in each one which had helped her husband get elected.

However, I found myself, at the beginning of seventh grade, frustrated in my attempt to achieve this goal of learning Italian because I had a problem that I was unable to articulate to myself to our teacher. In studying the language, the simple concept that a one-word verb could convey what would take two or three words to do in English had me completely confused. I simply didn't understand that the one word *parlo* meant, "I am speaking." I didn't comprehend this one-word verb was all I needed to convey both the tense (present) and the action (speaking), as well as the person (first person, singular) and also that (unlike English verbs) the one-word verb needed no other word to help it. So, I kept doing well in straight vocabulary quizzes, but failed tests where I had to use verbs, continually and erroneously inserting unnecessary helping words with them.

For the first few weeks of the term I struggled mightily with what felt like, in retrospect, a simple concept. During this time, I worked hard on my pronunciation and continued to memorize all the vocabulary I could in the vain hope that it might pull me through, and prayed for the ability to actually recognize what I had done wrong and what it was that I had failed to understand. I remember looking at several quizzes that I failed because I had inserted the word *sono* (am) after the word "Io"(I) and before the verb that could have stood alone, such as *guardo.* So the sentence that should read, *Io guardo* (I am looking) or at its most basic, *Guardo,* was incorrectly written by me as, *Io sono guardo.* This continual error earned me a series of almost failing marks in the subject I had thought would be my best one.

When I finally got the concept of the one-word verb acting efficiently all by itself in the present tense, and the light bulb went on, it was late in the game for a 7SP-1 student. The first marking period was upon me and I found myself having to explain to my parents how I had an average of sixty-five percent in Italian and expected to get that failing grade on my report card; the passing grade in an SP class was seventy-five percent. The fact that I had never failed any subject before and cried when I told them caused them to be kind to me. Once I explained I now understood the concept that had eluded me for the first few months of school and promised my marks would now improve dramatically, my father told me about his struggles with high school Latin, and encouraged me *never* to be afraid to ask for help when I didn't understand what was being taught. My mother asked me if I'd mind it if she explained what I had told her to the Italian teacher at Parent/Teacher Conference Night so she could emphasize the teacher should take more time explaining anything to me that I didn't understand; of course I agreed she should do this.

I was comforted by her also saying that even smart kids sometimes didn't always understand something the first few times and was truly grateful for their understanding as they both signed my report card. I vowed to do better in next marking period, so that the next report card, which was due around Christmas time, would once again be a source of pride for our family. I acted confident in my ability to do this and felt that way, having overcome alone the biggest academic problem of my young life, but

I knew deep inside we all thought maybe we had made a big mistake by putting me into that 7SP class.

It wasn't just our now second-rate academic performance that had demoralized me and my friends during the first few weeks of that school year, however, but the fact that, out of the four other girls in our class whom our friend Rosie DeMarco had known at PS 97, two had turned into watered-down versions of that evil Anna and her nasty sidekick Annemarie. While all four of the other PS 97 girls always got ninety-five percent or above on every test, two of them, Bonnie Levy and Mary Anton, were kind of nice and would even sometimes try to mouth the answer to a difficult question if they saw you struggling to give an oral answer in class when a teacher called on you unexpectedly. The other two, Berni Cravitz and Rhonda Linden, got even better marks (ninety-five percent was on the low side for them) had the best clothes, handbags, and hairstyles and loved to ask you what your mark was on the latest test when they knew you had done especially poorly.

They knew so much about our marks because the teachers never saw through them and even let them mark the test papers of our short answer quizzes, the kind of tests that had done me in that past fall in Italian, so I knew their viciousness and sense of superiority first-hand. They'd stand next to you in the hall or in the back of the classroom, one on each side, and look up and down at your outfit, never the equal of theirs, and then smirk and loudly say something like, "How'd you do on the Italian quiz? I bet you got a good mark because, after all, you're Italian!"

They'd belt out the last two words together like it was a big joke between them that they'd rehearsed in advance, which of course they had, savoring the humiliation of a classmate whom they'd deemed infinitely inferior to themselves both before and after their attack. Although I wanted to slap the nasty smiles right off their faces, all I was able to do was hold back my own tears. At the same time, I'd say something to them using the Italian words I did know, and Granma Mary had told me not to use, push past them and get away from them as fast as possible. They didn't only pick on me, but enjoyed doing this to every girl that they looked down on in the class, which included all of my friends. They left Bonnie and Mary alone because they'd gone to school with them since kindergarten.

Some of my friends, like fragile and petite Tina would actually cry in front of them when they did this to her. This often prompted Mary Zinni and her cousin Annie-Pat to run to her defense and tell them to leave her alone or they'd get them in Gym class, where we would sometimes manage to extract a small drop of revenge by "accidentally" hitting Berni and/or Rhonda with the dodge ball in the head or stomach. Even then, we were usually careful to control our natural desire to retaliate and keep it within the acceptable limits of the gym teacher's rules of engagement.

Once these two even made the mistake of picking on Francine Russo—the prettiest and most well developed girl in 7SP-1 from PS 95—who had gotten into the class on brains, but had then met a boy who was a third year high school student over the summer before junior high school. She had then decided to virtually ignore every subject except home economics because she said they would get engaged when he graduated and got a job. Even with this non-academic plan, however, Francine and her best friend, Ilana Terrazza, who went out with the best friend of Francine's boyfriend, did better than anyone in my little group in almost every subject, including Italian.

On one of the rare occasions when she had messed up on a science quiz, and Berni and Rhonda had tried their routine on her, Francine had simply told them to shut up and leave her alone or she'd slap their faces and then get her boyfriend and Ilana's to come by after school and fix them so they'd never bother anyone in the class again. Witnessing her reply, my friends and I felt that, regardless of what our mothers said about her, Francine had earned her place in our SP class. We even talked about nominating her for Class President and Ilana for VP for having delivered a real "voice of the people" speech by threatening to deliver some Brooklyn justice to two girls who richly deserved it.

Unfortunately, the only real effect was Francine and Ilana were prudently left alone while the rest of us, boyfriend-less and miserable, were continued to be tortured about any bad marks. Although it was awful to have them in our class, I think Berni and Rhonda caused the rest of our group to grow closer and, ironically, to do better academically so they wouldn't have as much ammunition to use against us.

We once did see a small measure of revenge; however, it was perpetrated by Fate, not by us. One day Berni came into school late, a highly unusual occurrence for her with her perfect record of attendance on top of everything else about her that appeared to be perfect. She arrived during our study hall period were we sat in the auditorium and everyone looked up at her when she came in and gave her late pass to the teacher on duty because of the way she looked. Her hair was messy and her clothes were disheveled. She also looked like she had been crying—yes, crying!

Although I usually tried to ignore her unless it was absolutely impossible to do so, my head snapped up from my notebook when Mary elbowed me and whispered sharply: "Rosemary, look at Berni! She looks upset!"

Upset? What was this all about? I thought to myself. *Was there a crack in the shell of perfection that surrounded her?* Would I live to see Berni *cry* in front of all of us?

Oh goody! My bad angel was thrilled. I really hoped so.

It would be nice after all the times she'd made us feel like crying; and it would be sweet revenge for the couple of times that Tina had broken down herself under Berni and Rhonda's relentless meanness and had cried in class. I decided to leave my homework for after school and only pretended to do it while I listened like my whole future depended on my hearing what was going on as Berni sat down next to Rhonda in the row in front of us and whispered to her in a harsh, gulping voice, trying not to cry. I strained my ears, as did every one of my friends sitting in the row on either side of me. This was too juicy to miss.

What had happened was Berni had lost her new leather handbag, which the rest of us had coveted as soon as we had seen it, on the city bus while coming to school a bit late after seeing the dentist. None of us were able to afford to have leather handbags and we all had make due with spongy vinyl ones that Berni had informed us were "cheap imitations of the real thing." She told Rhonda that she'd had an early morning appointment so she wouldn't be late for school, a typical kind of perfect behavior for her, but had left her handbag on the seat of the bus when she'd picked up her books because she'd been studying for a quiz we'd already had that day and had almost missed her stop. She hadn't realized this until she'd walked to the door of the school and looked for the note to hand in; only then did she realize she didn't have her handbag. She had been so upset that she'd turned around and walked home, but her mother had already left for work, so she couldn't get into her apartment because she didn't even have her key. It was in the bag with all her money and her school GO card. By the end of this tale, she was crying and kept saying: "They have my money, my address, and my keys! I lost the note, too! I have to call my mother and tell her!"

Rhonda patted Berni's shoulder and raised her hand to get the teacher's attention, explaining what had happened to her and the study hall teacher sympathized and immediately let them go to the main office to use the phone.

In terms of revenge, this was better than anything I could have imagined, and I hadn't even done anything to her myself. So I could sit back and watch her little drama, innocent of any complicity in it, and watch her dissolve into a puddle of tears while worrying what her mother would say and do for a change. Maybe it wouldn't have even happened if she hadn't been so horribly mean to us, and drawn bad luck to herself by always trying to be so perfect.

Imagine my surprise when, during lunch-time, Tina, who was probably Berni and

Rhonda's biggest victim, said she felt sorry for Berni.

I was so amazed that I blurted out, "Why? Don't you remember how many times she made you cry on purpose? Now she's crying because of her own stupid mistake. She left her own perfect leather bag (that she shoved in our faces all the time) on the seat because she was studying to be even more perfect! Now she finally knows how it feels to screw up! Good for her!"

My friends looked at me from over their sandwiches with a mixture of shock and admiration. I knew most of them felt the same way, but wouldn't say it out loud.

"You're right," Mary said.

"I could feel bad for that happening to anybody else, but not for her."

Annie-Pat silently but emphatically nodded her agreement.

Rosie DeMarco said, "I know them from PS 97 and that's the first time I ever saw either of them cry."

"Look," I said, "we didn't do anything to her, all we're doing now is enjoying what she did to herself, and we would feel sorry for her if she had ever been nice to us before this happened, but she was never nice. I'm not feeling sorry for her, because she did it to herself and I'm feeling okay today because she's too busy with her own troubles to torture me, and I'm not confessing this because I didn't do anything to her, even though I wanted to a lot of times."

And with that final remark, I bit into my sandwich.

Tina said, "I still hate her, too, but it was a beautiful bag. I'd love to have one like it and I'd die if I ever left it on the bus. My mother would probably kill me for that, too."

Rosie nodded her head in agreement as she chewed thoughtfully on her pepper and egg sandwich. Then she swallowed carefully and said, "Maybe we feel a little bit bad because the bag was so gorgeous and we know we'll never have one like it."

"Not until we get jobs and buy our own bags," said Mary. "I'm going to be an RN someday, and if Berni comes into my emergency room, I'll use the dullest needle on her that I can find. Watch now and you'll see that the teachers will be even more on her side than they were before because of this. It'll probably be sickening to see her telling them the story of why she's so upset."

Mary proved to be right. "Poor Berni" was a phrase that became overused in the week or two following the loss of her bag, but not by anyone in our group, even Tina, who studied harder like the rest of us, and tried to avoid "poor" Berni's influence by her own efforts.

By the end of the academic year, in June 1960, I'd studied so hard that my marks were once again back to my previous level of achievement, and I had gotten onto the honor roll. The reward was that, having suffered through the past year, I could now look forward to finishing junior high school in the 9SP-1 class and graduating in June of 1961, which I did.

Years later, on my first trip to Italy in 1989, I was easily able to ask our Roman guide in Italian for the directions to the church of *San Pietro in Vincoli* (St. Peter in Chains) so I could see the famous statue of Moses, sculpted by Michelangelo that we had learned about in our junior high school Italian class. While there, I actually thought about Berni and Rhonda for a minute, delighting in the feeling of how far I had come, not only on my trip to Italy, but in my own life.

I also thought about Mr. Peter Munisteri, who had continued to teach me the language of my ancestors for another few years at Lafayette High School. He had taught us lyrics to popular songs of the time like *"Volare"* and *"Arrividerci Roma,"* asking us to memorize their lyrics so that we could continue to do what he called "thinking in Italian," a process where the words flowed from us like music. Everything Italian was important to this wonderful teacher: culture, music, art, and history were all incorporated into our studies as he stood before us and gesticulated to make an important point, often rising onto his toes and stretching his five-and-a-half foot frame upward, mustache twitching and arms gesturing with the excitement he felt while trying to inspire in us the great love of the language he taught and so obviously adored.

He encouraged us never to be anything but proud of ourselves and of the language we studied, and told us that he, himself had never visited Italy until he had been teaching for a few years and had enough money for travel. After a year in his class, I finally began to feel the flow of the music of the language and I say, *"Tante grazie!"* to him for his inspiration.

When that guide in Italy answered my question and gave me the directions to the church housing the Michelangelo statue, he asked me if I had studied Italian in Florence, because as he also told me in a gently scolding way, my Italian accent was more Florentine than Roman, implying, of course, that the Florentine was inferior.

All over Rome there are remnants of the Roman Empire, and it is still possible to see the letters: SPQR on some of the remaining buildings. The letters stand for the phrase, *"Senatus Populus Que Romanus,"* which translates to mean: "the Senate and the People of Rome." In the ancient rivalry between the city-states of Italy, the Florentines used to joke that this actually stood for, *"Sono porchi questi Romani,"* meaning, "These Romans are pigs," to reinforce their own superiority.

Old rivalries die hard between cities and countries and, especially between people, but I felt more forgiving than I had been in junior high because the words still flowed for me and Italian verbs would never hold the same power to confuse me again.

So I didn't take offense at the guide's assessment of my accent at all, just told him (in Italian) that I had actually studied my Italian in Brooklyn, the part of New York City that shared the name with the chewing gum that was so popular all over Italy. I smiled at him and felt good about that.

Chapter 7

Shrimp, Dracula, and Uncle Dom

One of the best things about returning from vacation was the fact that we would soon be seeing our Uncle Dom again. My mother's brother, who lived nearby and had worked with my father at the Brooklyn Navy Yard, had come along on vacation with us once or twice before, but not this summer. Since my sister and I always looked forward to having him come over for dinner, as he did several times a week, we immediately thought about him when we got back, knowing he usually called to check in with us soon after we returned from vacation. On these occasions, when we heard the phone ring—even if its sound echoed through the kitchen window and out into the driveway as we unpacked our car—we knew it would be our uncle calling. My sister and I would race each other into the house to try to be the one to answer the phone, leaving our father to finish unloading our suitcases and bags.

That day our mother was way ahead of us and we found her already talking to her brother when we came into the kitchen through the side door that led from the narrow alleyway that we shared with the Angelini's, our neighbors across the way. We stood next to the kitchen table and openly eavesdropped on their conversation:

"You got them, Dom, that's great. We'll see you around 5:30 then," she said while waving her hand to warn us to be quiet while she was on the phone.

Then she hung up and told us to go outside, help our father with the rest of the bags, and tell him that our uncle would join us for dinner on the shrimp boat. Puzzled, we looked at each other and did as she told us; our father smiled when we told him and then he handed us our smaller suitcases to take inside.

Seeing our faces, she tried to reassure us by saying, "Don't worry. Everything's okay and you'll be happy when you see your uncle."

But we did worry and, as we walked back into the house with our bags, Alice and I said "Shrimp?" and made the kind of face at each other that expressed our confusion, surprise, disgust, and a mild sense of having been betrayed by our uncle. He was usually our ally, and held this special status because of his one-step-removed-from-a-parent role as well as because of his intrinsic kindness to us and his sense of humor, which perfectly meshed with ours.

Unlike many other Southern Italian-American families of the time, whose roots were in the seaside towns near Palermo or Naples, our family did not eat fish often. It was usually relegated to Fridays (especially during Lent, when we abstained from eating meat and couldn't convince our mother to let us have pizza or spaghetti with ricotta for dinner) and this was just fine with my sister and me. Even on those Fridays that saw fish on the menu, the dinner was likely to be Mrs. Paul's frozen fish sticks or, if we were especially unlucky, fishcakes, which we also hated but managed to eat as long as they were covered by huge gobs of tartar sauce.

As an adult who loves many kinds of fish, I realize this aversion was partially due to the fact that my mother didn't enjoy preparing fish, except for *baccala,* the salted cod that is a staple of Neapolitan cuisine, which she loved and we hated. We Brooklyn-born girls wouldn't eat it, just moved it around on our plates while she railed about how spoiled we were when it came to what we would and wouldn't eat.

Having been raised in poverty after the early death of her father a little while before the Great Depression, my mother just could not spend a lot of money on a food item or ingredient when another, cheaper substitute was available. Coupled with her tiredness after work and her desire to get dinner on the table quickly, this frugality virtually condemned us (unlike most of our friends) to a culinary life devoid of fresh, well-prepared fish.

After Granma Mary died when I was eight years old and my mother got a part-time job in the cafeteria of an elementary school in Coney Island, which qualified for government funds to provide lunch for lower income children, my sister and I often felt we were forced to relive our mother's own culinary childhood, with choices of sustenance rigidly limited by economic necessity. To our horror, she and the other "cafeteria ladies" secretly brought home the leftover food rather than throw it away at the end of each day as the regulations required. I realized later in life that only bureaucratic fools, light-years removed from real life by reams of paper and tomes of rules, would have expected working class women of my mother's generation to throw away perfectly good food just because those rules said to do that. This action would have been the moral equivalent of a grave sin to all those hardworking women who were the backbone of the school lunch program in the city, no matter what their ethnicity or religion.

My mother told us that they would often give extra milk, another half of a sandwich or an extra apple to a child on the lunch line who they knew was hungry, or who'd asked for seconds and had eaten the food. These housewives might have been out of their own kitchens and at work, but they were still moms themselves and were there first and foremost to feed the kids in their role as white-capped "lunch ladies."

Whenever we complained about any of the food she'd brought home, my mother would tell us, "I remember how it felt to be hungry and be grateful for the food you had. We never complained it was whole wheat bread instead of white; we were just glad to have it. You girls just can't understand that."

It was our family's version of "The children in Europe are starving, so don't complain, just eat it all" speech that was repeated in houses all over the country in the decade following World War II. So, we shut up about it (to her, at least) and drank our milk from tiny half-pint containers and took day-old peanut butter or American cheese sandwiches on whole wheat bread wrapped in waxed paper to school. My sister and I were some of the only children who stayed in school to eat lunch from brown paper bags, unhappily sitting on the hard wooden benches that ringed the walls of the school basement at PS 95 with the few other children whose mothers had to work and couldn't provide the lunch of hot soup or a fresh sandwich that most of our contemporaries enjoyed from 12:00-12:40 every school day. Although I didn't like this arrangement, I read my current book while eating, traveling far away from our unsatisfactory lunchtime situation in my mind; but my sister, three and a half years younger than me, hated it, feeling she was treated especially unfairly by our mother's abrupt return to work after Granma Mary died. We both missed Granma's nurturing presence in different, but equally important ways.

Finally, Alice rebelled at having no one to play with or talk to while eating her lunch and also about being teased by other kids, who called her "orphan" and insisted something be done to improve the situation. So our mother relented and said she would trust us with keys to the side door and tell the school that she was once again allowing her children to go home for lunch. From fifth grade until I went to junior high the next year, I was in charge of getting my sister back and forth to school in the middle of the day and making sure that she ate her lunch. I also had to be sure the door was locked behind us when we came into the house and again when we returned to school for the afternoon.

This worked out well until I got to the sixth grade, where a lot of the kids were given a little money to go out and buy their lunch and then stroll around on Avenue U in good weather before returning to the schoolyard for the afternoon lineup. Then it was my turn to rebel and my relationship with my sister suffered because I felt it wasn't fair for me to be expected to babysit her at lunchtime every day for no money when I wanted to be with my friends some of the time. I didn't take this issue up with my mother, however, because she would never have let me be with my friends at any time where it conflicted with what she saw as my duty to my family, and that duty required me to be with my sister every school day for lunch.

My sister was a little more reasonable, since she, too, wanted to have a little more freedom and had begun to see we could sometimes be allies as well as sisters. So we worked out an elaborate system where I would ask to go to the bathroom on those days that I wanted to go out to lunch with my friends and would then pass by her classroom, try to get her attention by tapping on the glass in the door, and wave to her in her front row seat. This would let her know she was on her own for lunch that day because I was going out to eat with my friends. Although this sounds like a simple way to do things, eliminating the need for us to find each other in the chaos of the yard at lunchtime dismissal, we often got our signals mixed up and she was angry at me for forcing her to eat alone as well as for the kind of lunches she was forced to eat.

As food became increasingly tied up in our minds with disappointment, we both became even more suspicious of what we were served to eat at home, especially if it wasn't a part of our mother's usual dinner repertoire. This was especially true of fish—all fish except for tuna that we saw come out of a can, and even that innocent fish wasn't much to our liking, because our mother insisted on buying the supermarket brand, which she said was more economical (translation: "cheaper," as my sister and I would say to each other as we rolled our eyes to heaven in frustration) than the Bumble Bee solid white tuna that Mrs. Collaro prepared for her kids.

Whenever we saw the successful "Sorry, Charlie" TV commercials that featured the below-par tuna fish who tried continually and unsuccessfully to get picked to be in a can of Star-Kist brand, we actually identified with him because we, too, weren't able to get near the good brand. After all, when it came to brand names and choice cuts of meat, or even just a regular school day lunch that wasn't sec-ondhand and served in your own kitchen by your mother, my sister and I always felt we had been assigned to the second-class dining room, where we had to serve ourselves.

Another reason to be wary of any kind of unknown food was that our mother had once prepared *tripe* (the lining of the stomach of a sheep that has a characteristic honeycomb pattern), which some considered a delicacy, covered in mozzarella and tomato sauce, and told us that it was eggplant *parmigiana,* which we loved. When my sister and I complained the eggplant tasted different and was abnormally chewy, she smiled and told us to eat it anyway. So we both immediately did the chew-and-run-to-the-bathroom routine that we had perfected after my sister had chewed and swallowed some mackerel under equally false pretenses and had thrown up after eating it.

I found out later that *tripe* is also slang for "rubbish" and was often used as a quick verbal comeback to someone making an obviously false statement. We could have adopted it as our culinary mantra, which was part of why we hated fish. Our mother wasn't even the sole culinary culprit in our lives, either. Once, having been invited by Grandpa Joseph to see something special that he had prepared to go with *"La Gloriosa"* that night, I went downstairs to his basement kitchen only to hear him say he had bought fresh *pulpo,* which turned out to be an octopus. He pulled it out of a brown bag that appeared to be almost moving from within and plunged it alive into a pot of boiling water that he had on the stove. Horrified, I turned and ran back upstairs and warned my sister about it before the table was even set for dinner.

As soon as we were old enough to realize we couldn't count on honesty to be served with dinner, my sister and I scrutinized our meals as they were cooked for anything that struck us as odd. If something exotic did make it to

191

the table, we would declare we had a stomach-ache or felt dizzy before dinner rather than try eating something that probably would make us sick anyway as we tried to chew it. Despite our mother's lectures, my sister and I mutually decided we would rather starve than eat something that might have been the star of our nightmares before it appeared on our dinner plate. Because of my experiences growing up, I am still not a fan of those food shows that take you around the world and show the "exotic" things that people consider food. My children know I won't even eat sushi and they have learned to live with that.

So, with the pleasures of our vacation still lingering in our minds, it made us feel especially sad that our beloved Uncle Dom, who had always stood up for us in the past, would be the food betrayer this time. He would be over soon with shrimp for dinner! How could he do something so un-uncle-like when he had always understood how we felt about strange foods?

He had even taken us out for pizza on a Friday night during Lent when we hadn't eaten the fish cakes that our mother had served for dinner; it had been a choice between that and the frozen perch filets that our parents ate and we had chosen to fast as well as abstain that night. Uncle Dom came over to babysit us so that our parents could then go out to the movies (a rare occurrence for them) and we had been only a little surprised when he said he was hungry so we should all go out to the avenue for some pizza.

So we all went out together to keep him company, and even ate with him so he wouldn't feel like he had to eat alone. He even said we didn't have to mention the pizza to our mother because it was his idea and he'd tell her. He winked at us and said he hated fish cakes, too. He had understood we hated the fish sticks and the perch, so why did he bring us the shrimp, we wondered?

While we had begun unpacking and putting our dirty clothes in piles for the laundry, the clock had continued to tick, and soon it was 5:30 and time for dinner. A few minutes later we saw our uncle pull up in front of the house and wave to us from his car. We ran to the side door to meet him and when he came up those stairs from the alleyway, he carried a big brown bag, only a little smaller than the ones that held groceries and it had little spots of grease on the bottom. My sister and I didn't run to kiss and hug him the way we usually did, remembering the bag with the octopus. Why were disgusting fish always in a brown bag? He put it down on the kitchen counter near the window and something strange happened. We smelled the shrimp aroma in the air and it smelled...well...good, actually. I looked at my sister and we went over to kiss him and he simply said, "Hello." His smile was mischievous and his eyes twinkled as they did when he had a good story to tell us.

Then he said, "You two look nice and brown from the sun. I bet you had a good time on vacation. Want a sample of dinner?"

When we shook our heads, saying we had eaten a big lunch on the road home, he kept smiling at us in the teasing way he sometimes did and said, "Come on, try it. Have I ever lied to you or steered you wrong about food before?"

My sister and I looked at each other and she nudged me with her elbow to go first, the usual procedure when it was something that didn't look promising. I tentatively nodded and moved forward closer to the bag, slowly extending my right hand as if whatever made that good smell might suddenly metamorphose into a lizard or some other disgusting thing and bite me, instead of the other way around. Uncle Dom took a small fork from the drawer, reached into the bag, stabbed something, and handed the fork to me with an unrecogniz- able plump, roundish shape impaled on its tines. The shrimp was golden brown with a coating of what looked like breadcrumbs, and a pretty pink and white color peeking through in between the crumbs. I put the end of the fork to my nose and sniffed it again; still good. I opened my mouth and took a big bite of it. Absolutely delicious! I smiled and shook my head up and down, still chewing on the firm, but not rubbery flesh of the shrimp. Alice held out her hand for the rest of what was on the fork; she liked it, too. We looked at each other and Uncle Dom looked pleased and laughed.

"Can we have another one?" We said almost simultaneously, laughing out loud.

"I knew I'd regret it if I introduced you two to shrimp. They're good, aren't they? Some people like them with a little lemon juice and tartar sauce or ketchup, but I like them just like this: plain and freshly fried."

"No tartar sauce for us, either," I said, remembering we'd used it to kill the taste of the fish cakes.

"They taste too good by themselves, right? Would I ever steer you girls wrong about food? Never!"

We felt ashamed about our lack of trust and offered to set the table for dinner while he sat down and relaxed. Our father walked in then, having completed his maintenance on the family car to ensure its readiness for work the next week, and the two of them sat and talked.

To our surprise, our mother, who had slipped out and gone to the grocery store while we were busy with the dirty clothes, returned with a bag of goodies to accompany the shrimp. She put her grocery bag down and unpacked fresh tomatoes, onions, and lettuce for a salad and as well as the macaroni salad from the local deli that we loved, and even a glass bottle of Coca Cola each for my sister and me, a rare treat on a non-holiday. Then she took three glass mugs out of the freezer and filled them with beer and the grownups clinked glasses and drank. Alice and I did the same with our cokes, feeling that even though we were back home, the vacation wasn't over yet.

* * *

Although he had frequently rescued us from bad food, the real reason my sister and I loved our Uncle Dom had nothing to do with eating. He was often around; having gone through a divorce (or "The D" as my mother referred to it when she spoke about it to my father) and often ate dinner at our house and spent time with us. Aside from cryptic references to my uncle's marital status, usually made when the adults thought we were out of earshot, all we were supposed to know was he had gone to Mexico (an unusual vacation destination for anyone from our family) a few years ago and had returned with a gift of lovely, delicate, little leather purses for my sister and me. Hers was green and mine was red and they were shaped like the fancy purses we saw women carrying to Mass on Sunday or when they were dressed up and went out to dinner, only they were smaller. The leather they were made from had designs etched into it, which brought to mind a phrase that we had heard about: "hand tooled." We had never seen anything that nicely made specifically for children.

We loved the bags and had used them to pretend we carried them to go out to lunch in the city with our lady friends who wore lipstick, hats, and gloves and went to lunch at fancy restaurants all the time. We knew our mother was upset by the real reason that he had gone to Mexico and we felt bad about showing her how much we loved the bags, which would only remind her about it. So, we usually played with the purses in our room, compounding the secretive nature of our behavior by practicing putting our hair in curlers and trying on lipstick, thinking, if she caught us doing those things that she disapproved of, at least it would distract her from the purses, and the awful fact of "the D."

Since he also worked in the Brooklyn Navy Yard, but as a welder not a pipefitter, Uncle Dom and our father also had a lot in common. They always talked about where they found a good parking space, close to whatever gate they had to use to enter "The Yard" as they called it. This was an ongoing quest for them, since a "good" space meant close to whatever gate they had to use to access the ship they were presently working on, since different ships were in different dry docks for repairs or construction, and "The Yard" had many different entrances and gates for admission to the particular ship they were assigned to work on. This proximity to the gate was especially important when they had to work overtime or had a night shift and went home after the surrounding neighborhood was quiet and dark and the streets were deserted, so their quest for the proverbial good parking space never ended. I can recall many evenings when their pre-dinner conversation revolved around their success, or lack of it, in what I came to think of as their parking game.

If one of them found a block that was newly empty, due to the completion of a project on another ship, they'd let each other know, sharing their own secrets with each other, much like my sister and me. We would listen to the two of them talking about gates and parking spaces and comparing notes on their respective apprentices—whether they wanted to learn the job and had initiative, or were lazy and hopeless—and we didn't understand everything they discussed, but felt good about the talk and their friendship anyway. We were proud of the fact that the two men closest to us in the world, who had both fought in World War II, had built and repaired our country's ships to help keep our Navy strong and capable of protecting us. We were also happy that they were friends as well as relatives; their talk about their work made us feel both safe and protected by both of the men in our family whom we loved, and that was great.

Because he wasn't our parent, Uncle Dom had a special and favored status that put him somewhere between a teacher and a friend. Because he was a good listener, we could sort of complain to him about our mother and he'd understand right away, since she was his sister. He was a safety valve for us and allowed us to let off steam without doing any real damage, as long as our criticism was fair and didn't go too far. During my adolescent years, when I needed to escape and my friends weren't around, he showed understanding of my intermittent but urgent need to get away from my mother. When this happened, he often volunteered to take me to the movies, just as Granma Mary had done when I was little. At that time I didn't think about the fact that both of them, mother and son, had helped me out when I needed it in much the same way. It is important for me now to remember and acknowledge how they both helped me so much when I needed it just by sharing their love of the movies with me, and taking me away and into another world with them. Just by being with me and doing something pleasurable they gave of themselves to me and I will never forget the gift of their presence that they gave to me.

Unlike Granma Mary, Uncle Dom favored westerns and horror films instead of movies filled with music and jokes, like The Court Jester with Danny Kaye, which she had enjoyed. Although I had enjoyed the musicals when I was younger, the horror films took first place in my adolescent heart. At first, my mother disapproved of my choice, but relented after I promised I wouldn't get anyone up but myself if they gave me nightmares. So, even in summer, I spent a lot of nights sleeping with my head under the sheets during the next few years, until the vivid images of the most recent horror film faded a bit with time, but it was worth it. It made me feel more like a grownup because I dealt with the fears by myself, and I had my Uncle Dom to thank for that, too.

In the late 1950's and 60's, Hammer Films, a British film studio, produced a succession of movies starring Christopher Lee as Dracula and featuring Peter Cushing as his nemesis, Dr. Van Helsing. These films, although definitely of the horror genre and therefore unqualified for the distinction of serious films, were a cut above the usual Saturday matinee schlock. They were usually period pieces with elegant-on-a-budget costumes, filmed in lush color and featuring British actors, whose diction and dignified bearing even in a horror film made a great impression on me.

I was immediately aware the movies released by Hammer Films had a distinctly British take on the horror stories they released, which were often based on famous classic tales of terror such as Bram Stoker's *Dracula*, which was the one book that my father had said frightened him when he had first read it himself as a teen-ager. Even if these movies had the same goal of attracting audiences who would pay for the privilege of being frightened as their American counterparts, they were light-years above

The Blob or The Crawling Eye, which were more the standard fare at the Saturday afternoon matinees that my friends and I usually attended. There was an elegance of language as well in many of these British horror films that reminded me of Sir. Arthur Conan Doyle's *Sherlock Holmes* stories, which I also loved.

After a good dose of the Hammer films, I was spoiled for the other trashy movies and even became a bit of a snob, often refusing to go with my friends to the usual Saturday movies. To me it felt like eating the "cardboard cake" that my father rejected as not worth the calories when my mother tried to pass it off as dessert. Like my father, I felt this junk was not worth my time anymore. The Hammer movies also gave me a desire to read the books on which some of these classic films had been based. Of course, I tried *Dracula* first and was immediately caught up in the fact that, although a novel, it had been written as a series of actual entries in various characters' diaries and letters. That gave it an authenticity that a straight third-person story might have lacked and the vivid images of the evil "brides" in the castle attacking helpless Jonathan Harker didn't leave my mind as easily as the movie images had. Whether it was the cumulative effect of the visual images of the movie as well as the images conjured up by the written words, it was a good lesson to me in the control I had to assert over my imagination for my own good, and also just to get a good night's sleep.

After Uncle Dom took me to see The Horror of Dracula at the Fortway Theater on Fort Hamilton Parkway (where Granma Mary had taken me when I was little and we had lived on 57th Street) I was thrilled to be sitting in the adult section of the theater and watching that scary film. I'd found out that this film was pretty faithful to Bram Stoker's novel, the way the version with Bela Lugosi had been, and wanted to see it. However, while sitting in the section reserved for grownups, not the smoking section, and a few minutes into the film, Uncle Dom asked me if I'd be okay alone for a few minutes while he went to the back of the theater, had a cigarette and then brought us back some popcorn. I lied and nodded my head and then watched the next few minutes through a gap in the fingers of the hand I held in front of my eyes, which I pretended to be using to scratch my head when he returned.

In the course of the next few years, we went to some of the great movie theaters in the borough of Brooklyn which, although on the decline even at that time, were still in good enough condition to allow me to appreciate the architecture and design that had made them true movie palaces, the antithesis of the multiplex shoeboxes we sit in today. I would happily trade the latest in surround sound and stadium seats for the elegance of those old theaters, constructed in the days when men wore jackets and ties and women wore hats and gloves to go to the movies.

I remember in particular the curved mosaic that was constructed in the niche that surrounded the drinking fountain in the Arabian nights-themed Fortway Theater. The reflective tiles appeared to be gilded and were so elegantly opulent, forming a peacock that reflected light from the water as it gushed out of the spigot of the fountain, that you could imagine drinking from a palace fountain in the movie Kismet. On the right side of the movie screen, at the curved perimeter surrounding the seats, was the area designated as a smoking section, which was separated from the farthest seats by columns and was dimly lit. There, if you let your imagination go, you might see dancing girls from the movie behind the people having a cigarette during the show, the glowing cigarette ends metamorphosing into lightning bugs in the warm summer air of those Arabian nights. I miss those elegant places, where going to the see the theater was often as exciting as the movie itself, but not as much as I miss Uncle Dom.

We went together to many movies during my difficult adolescence and I particularly remember going with him to the last double feature show at the Brooklyn Paramount theater where we saw The Last Train From Gun Hill with Kirk Douglas and Anthony Quinn and The Man Who Could Cheat Death with Anton Diffring and, of course, Christopher Lee in 1960 before the theater closed. Although it was sad to me that the theater was purchased by Long Island University as part of the expansion of the downtown Brooklyn campus of the school, it seemed at least fitting that it went out with both a western and a Hammer film on its marquee at the end. Today, the old theater is a part of the school's gymnasium and is in the geographic center of the downtown renaissance area of a Brooklyn that Uncle Dom would no longer recognize as his home borough.

The Fortway Theater lasted longer than the Brooklyn Paramount, although in a much sadder and shabbier state than it was in my youth, when the ghosts of the old movie palaces were more clearly visible and you still catch a glimpse of their former grandeur. The old secular temples of the Dream Factory that projected their vivid images onto larger than life screens and transported us to other places and times that we kids from Brooklyn could never hope to visit are now as much a memory as the old borough where we grew up. However, into my young adulthood, I could still see the place as it was then, when Granma Mary, and later Uncle Dom, and I used to frequent it, and I miss it, but not as much as I miss the people who used to take me there.

My Uncle Dom was one of the adults closest to me, not just because we were related by blood, but because he took the time to listen and to care about me when he didn't have to. My sister and I knew he had made his own mistakes, but his imperfections gave me hope that, despite all my own shortcomings and errors, I'd one day be able to function as an adult too.

During many of the small triumphs of my youth—when I was invited to attend Hunter College High School, and had achieved good enough grades to be able to attend Brooklyn College, and later became a teacher and then married my husband—his pride in my accomplishments was as great as if he had been a second father to me, which in many ways he was. I think he knew how much I loved him and some of his pride in me made him a little happier in his later life, after he had been beset by many troubles and sorrows. I know he made my life better just by being in it, and I will never forget him.

Chapter 8

Dancing With The Naked Baseball Player

I reconnected with Marissa and her family as soon as I finished the many chores my mother assigned me, which took the rest of the weekend and felt like punishment following the fun of our vacation. I was allowed to walk home with Marissa when we met after Mass the Sunday after we returned and we immediately planned how we'd get together and walk to the library the next day, talk on the way there, and catch up on everything that had happened to us in the past two weeks.

She had been away on vacation, too; her family had spent a week on Long Island with her cousins at their grandfather's summer-house, which I had been invited to visit many times. I had never been allowed to go because it would have meant an overnight stay, and my mother didn't allow us to sleep away from home unless we were with her. I was sure Marissa would have more exciting things to report to me than the bonfire and ringing the bell at the Twin Lakes house because she and her cousins were allowed to walk to the bay beach near her grandfather's house and could stay there alone for the afternoon, too. There were boys at that beach, mainly her cousins and their friends, who provided another reason for my mother to say "No" to all their invitations to visit with them there.

If Marissa hadn't had problems of her own with her mother, we wouldn't have remained close friends with the beginning of adolescence because I started to notice the looks she got from boys, many of them older boys. Although she was a year younger than me, in the last few months she had developed physically at such a rapid rate that she began to resemble Sofia Loren, in figure as well as face. Although I was jealous of her for being able to wear a bra size bigger than my mother's, while I still wore what was referred to as a "training bra" (as if my tiny breasts were preparing for the Underwear Olympics where they would suddenly jump out of my chest and take the lead in the Sexual Attractiveness Sprint), I still felt sorry for her in a way. It was easy for me to see she was more than a little overwhelmed by suddenly being looked at in a sexual way by those boys, which made her mother even more protective than usual.

"Don't talk to anybody you don't know!" and,

"Don't go with anybody even if you know them!"

These warnings, formerly played in the background at a low volume, had become the loudly blaring soundtrack of her life in those past few months—as her blossoming external maturity, with its concurrent sexual overtones, had triggered the warning bells in her mother's mind. So, she was constantly reminded by her mother that she wasn't as grown up as she looked, and that, young men couldn't look at her and know (or care about) her age and might mistake her for someone who was "available." We had both been constantly admonished on how to behave so that we didn't become one of "those" girls—the kind who were wild and got into trouble—and ruin the rest of our lives. One thing that had not changed since my grandfather's hasty emigration from *Porto Empedocle* was the high value put on a daughter's sexual innocence until she was married, and all of our grandparents and parents had proudly carried that value along with them all the way to Brooklyn.

When Marissa had gotten her period for the first time, her mother had slapped her gently across her left cheek "for good luck," something other friends of mine reported to me as well, although I was completely unfamiliar with this custom. They all said it was done by your mother or aunt or grandmother—sometimes all three—to wish you well and to hope you would one day be able to become a mother yourself, but sometime in the future after you were married, and definitely not any time soon.

I always thought that it was a strange way to wish someone good luck and welcome her to the club, but rather felt like a warning about what awaited you if you didn't do the right thing. However, this understanding of the hidden meaning of the ritual didn't prevent me from wishing that I could have any communication from my own mother about sex—the most forbidden of topics in my family—even a slap, if it meant she'd only talk to me like a real mother. How, I wondered, did this category of human experience, and my earnest desire to learn more about it, become equated with wanting to be a bad girl, a whore, a *putana,* or, as we called them in Brooklyn, a "hoo-wa"? Why did wanting to know anything about sex automatically make you a contestant in the Slut Olympics? My curiosity wasn't stifled in any other area to the degree that it was when my questions had something to do with sex or reproduction.

All I did know was if I wanted to avoid my mother's bad side, I had to get as much information as I could from "other sources," as my social studies teacher, Mr. Townes, had suggested to us the previous year, when he advised us that we had to get our term papers researched without quoting from the text-book. Gathering information about sex proved to be quite a little trickier than when I had to research the rise of the Mau-Mau in Kenya for my term paper, which brought me a grade of A-. I had the library and the encyclopedia at my disposal for that assignment; for this one I had found my sources narrowed down to three: other girls, magazines, and books.

Since it was too embarrassing to admit my ignorance of this topic when, as an almost thirteen year old, I knew so much about many other things, I had to be careful about how I got information from other girls. Whenever sex was discussed by my friends, I did a lot less talking and a lot more listening, absorbing as much as I could and filing it away for future reference, memorizing facts as though they were crucial to my final grade in school. Words like "menstrual cycle" and "ovaries" were secretly added to my internal vocabulary list, to be understood and integrated into my knowledge of myself and other people as sexual beings, but never to be spoken aloud, at least not at home.

Magazines and pamphlets that were given away by the manufacturers of what were referred to as "women's sanitary products" were added to my internal bibliography of sources, which provided many of these new words. Yet, Marissa and I thought the best of these sources were likely to be the forbidden novels that told about what people actually did together in bed. We found *Peyton Place* by Grace Metalious in her mother's headboard bookcase while babysitting her brother one Saturday night and, to us, it was like finding the Rosetta Stone of information about sex.

Even now, there's a scene from the novel that still puzzles me and many of my post-graduate educated friends who've speculated about what Betty really did to Rodney Harrington with that scarf. Although I can now imagine several interesting scenarios, I'm not absolutely sure and have finally accepted my lifelong puzzlement about certain sexual matters as a permanent part of me—an acknowledgment that my desire to know as much as possible about whatever interests me will never be satisfied, even if I do have a lot more personal experience as well as the Internet to smooth my pathway to knowledge.

Our ability to be honest with each other about our lack of knowledge concerning many sexual things served to help cement the bond of my friendship with Marissa. Mrs. Collaro's explanation to her daughter about getting her period didn't include much extraneous information about sex in general. We were both still in the dark concerning a lot of things that Marissa felt too ashamed to ask her mother about, so we were left with Grace Metalious' infamous book as one of our main sources of information.

Another source was Anna. Although we both hated and feared her, she knew things that we wanted to know, so we were both polite and acted a little friendly to her in the hope that she would take pity on us and not shame us publicly too often, but also to learn whatever we could from her about sex. Her attitude toward us was that of a cat playing with its food before devouring it. Sometimes she'd talk to us condescendingly and occasionally treated us as almost-equals, but mostly we were the audience at her show. If she deigned to drop a crumb or two of information that we found valuable, we paid for it by allowing her to constantly condescend to us and make fun of us, one at a time. Her philosophy, like a meaner version of my mother, was to divide and conquer. So, if Marissa was the butt of Anna's joke or pointed comment, I laughed, but not too hard, just enough to stroke Anna's ego and make her feel in charge, and Marissa did the same when I was the target.

Marissa and I had talked about this a lot and we had both agreed to allow this as long as it didn't go too far. We were determined to stay best friends and there was only so much we could hear about each other from Anna. Our loyalty to each other could be stretched, but never beyond the point of dignity. This was a lot easier when the three of us were together but, alone with Anna, we each found it difficult to maintain our balance and, if Anna was with

Annmarie, we avoided them at all costs, staying in the house and doing anything our mothers needed doing— even helping with housework— rather than subject ourselves to their combined sadistic stings like those of a spider/scorpion combo right out of a schlocky horror movie.

Soon after my father had fulfilled a long-delayed dream and actually bought a new car (his first and only one), a black 1960 Plymouth Valiant, with a push-button transmission, which I would inherit eight years later and drive until the brakes failed to catch until the last second before arriving at the Staten Island tollbooth of the Verrazano Bridge, I met Anna. She was standing near her father, who was short and rotund with a perpetual cigar, sometimes lit and sometimes not, in the corner of his mouth in front of her stoop. Anna watched him wipe the non-existent dust off the fender of his new turquoise and white Chevrolet Impala sedan that was parked in front of their house. She waved to me immediately and insisted I come closer to admire their new car.

"Isn't it great!" She bragged. "Much more eye-catching than black," she said with a condescending dip of her head in the direction of our new car.

Before I could defend my father's choice of color for his new car by reminding her that he had to park it at the Brooklyn Navy Yard, where it was better to be inconspicuous, she cackled and continued, "I'm glad you have a new car, too. Now Marissa's the only one of us who doesn't have a new one."

She spoke as if we were friends and Marissa was the outsider, but I was too smart and too suspicious of her to ever desire or believe in that fantasy. I knew she'd use the same trick on Marissa when I wasn't around, to keep her off balance, too. Marissa had told me and we'd talked about what to do when this happened and Anna tried to trick us into betraying each other. We'd decided to say as little as possible when this kind of thing happened.

I answered, "Your family's new car is beautiful. Congratulations! I have to go back in because I forgot the money my mother gave me to buy bread. See you!"

With those words, I waved and went off, laughing to myself because Marissa had told me that, in fact, her father was going to buy a new car too, a Thunderbird, with an unexpected but welcome bonus he had recently received from his boss. She was excited about it because he had taken her to the showroom when he ordered it, and I knew they would be getting it in about two weeks. That would fix Anna and, no matter how nice her car was, it wouldn't change her father from looking like a meaner version of Lou Costello into looking like Mr. Collaro, who could have passed for the young Sean Connery's Italian cousin. Dealing with Anna all the time made me grateful to have a best friend as nice as Marissa, and I liked her family, especially her little brother, as much as I liked her. Although it was a chore for her, babysitting her brother was a treat for me.

There was another family that I babysat for, but not as often. The Ragusa's lived across the street near the corner of Avenue U in one of three large apartments above the store on the corner. They had three daughters close in ages from four to seven and I loved to sit for them. Mr. Ragusa was a New York City Police Detective and he and Mrs. Ragusa only went out to the movies occasionally and never stayed out past eleven pm, so my mother thought it was okay for me to babysit for them. The girls were sweet and always cooperated when I sat for them, getting into their pj's and brushing their teeth and combing their hair with no fuss at all.

The key to my success was I didn't try to make them go to sleep, just sat in their room with them reading stories until the youngest one had dropped off to sleep. Then I would talk to the older two girls quietly and answer their questions about school and whatever they wanted to talk about until it was ten o'clock. I knew this was a half hour after their regular bedtime and told them that they had to go to sleep because, if their parents came home early and found them still up, I'd never be able to sit for them again. It usually worked, but I was always tired when I got home from watching them.

Sitting for Marissa's brother was much easier. Her sister, Maryanne, was always sent downstairs to her aunt, Mrs. Collaro's sister, for the evening because Mrs. Collaro didn't think it was fair to leave us to watch both Markie and his sister. Upstairs in her apartment, Mrs. Collaro usually left us a huge assortment of cold cuts and Italian bread to eat if she and her husband were going out for dinner. A feast of *soppresata, capicola,* and *mortadella* with pistachio nuts rested on a platter already overflowing with boiled ham, Genoa salami, and even Swiss cheese. When we were hungry we'd take the platter out of the refrigerator, uncover it and cut up the bread into sandwich-sized pieces. Then we'd scoop out the soft middle of the bread leaving only the crisp part of the crust hollowed out so we could pile our sandwiches high with each and every meat and the cheese as well as slices of a ripe tomato from Marissa's grandfather's garden in the backyard.

Sometimes we'd roll little pieces of the soft, white dough that had been discarded from the inside of the bread into tiny bread "meatballs" and throw them to Markie, who'd try to catch them in his mouth as we finished making all the sandwiches. Then we all stuffed ourselves the way only the young and still growing can and took turns playing with Markie while we packed up the remnants of dinner and put them into the refrigerator for Mrs. Collaro to use the next day.

After we'd eaten, when Marissa usually lost patience with Markie, I took over the responsibility for him, which consisted of playing, singing, reading, and telling stories and, his favorite: talking like Donald Duck. Later, I let him have his favorite snack before bed, cornflakes with milk, which he called "cornflakes for milk," on a tray in the living room while we watched The Honeymooners. He loved Jackie Gleason and liked to imitate the way his eyes got big in his head when he was angry. We'd sit together, with Markie in his little pajamas, and I would say "To the moon, Alice!" and he'd laugh in delight. He was aware of being the youngest child with two older sisters and when he was allowed to do more grownup things, like staying up and watching a TV show with us, it made him happy.

When it was time for bed, he rarely fought with me because he knew he'd already stayed up longer than his parents would have allowed; he also knew I would sit on the floor next to his youth bed and pat his back gently until he felt asleep, soothing him into his dreams. Mrs. Collaro had taken him out of his crib because she thought it was safer for him to sleep in a low bed rather than to keep trying to climb out of the crib all the time. Although I'd heard people talk about the "terrible two's," I found it much easier to deal with a child who could talk than to try to guess what was wrong with an infant and feel the frustration of knowing I wasn't able to understand what the baby needed.

Many of my Saturday nights in the past months had been spent at Marissa's house babysitting for Markie, with Marissa more anxious for him to go to sleep so that we could raid her parents' bookshelf and read up about things we weren't supposed to know about. Thanks to *Peyton Place* and the dictionary, we had learned about rape, unwanted pregnancy and abortion, and other forbidden things. But, aside from using it as an informal source of sex education, the book surprised me as I learned from reading it how similar a small New England town was to our own neighborhood in Brooklyn. Everyone there knew everything about their neighbors, just like in our part of Gravesend; except for the character of Mr. Rossi, the people certainly weren't Italian American, but were much like all the people we knew. I thought, except for the secret of the unmarried pregnancy and little details like owning a dress shop, Constance MacKenzie was a lot like my mother. She was determined not to let all those nosy people know her business and she was strict to the point of meanness with her daughter, Allison, who dreamed of being a writer. The wishful and dramatic part of me enjoyed that parallel with the novel, too, thinking that maybe someday writing would figure into my life as well.

Interspersed with our reading was the occasional attempt to smoke a cigarette that Marissa had managed to sneak out of her mother or father's packs of Kent or Newport as they lay unguarded around the house in the hectic minutes before they went out. We would make sure that Markie was asleep soundly before she took out the contraband cigarette and lit it up in the bathroom with the window open and the exhaust fan on at the same time.

We knew if he ever saw us smoking, there would be no way to keep him quiet about it. First, he would ask us a million questions and then mention it to Mrs. Collaro. He wouldn't tell her as soon as he saw her, like Marissa's sister would, but during a conversation about nothing, or when she bathed him or when he ate, or, for sure, when he saw someone else light up a cigarette—or whenever it came into his head. It would be like a sword in the air over our heads, floating around and ready to swoop down and destroy us at any minute, and that would be the end of my babysitting, on Saturday or any other night or afternoon.

My mother would see it as just another proof of the fact that she couldn't trust me when I wasn't with her and would be doubly annoyed at being told the news by another parent and have them knowing about it too. Mrs. Collaro would feel obliged to tell her, as one parent to another, because it had happened in her house and would probably feel a little guilty herself because she knew my parents didn't smoke, and that would be the end of it for me. So, the few times we did try a cigarette, we avoided having Markie catch us smoking at any cost.

Once, when Marissa had sneaked a cigarette out of her father's pack and put it up the sleeve of her blouse, Markie almost gave us away. He pointed to her arm and said: "What's that?"

I gulped and scooped him up before Mrs. Collaro came back into the kitchen with her laundry and took him to the bathroom where I pulled out the manicure kit that we used to do our nails when we were tired of reading. I pulled out the nail whitening pencil, which was supposed to give you the look of a professional manicure when you rubbed it under the white at the end of your nails. I showed it to him and held my finger up to my lips, saying: "Ssh! We're both going to get manicures tonight and we want to surprise your mother so your sister is hiding this pencil until they go out.

"Me, too?" He asked. He was a smart little kid and wouldn't keep his mouth shut unless he was in on the secret.

"Sure, if you want one!"

"Yes! I want a manypure, too."

"Okay, you've got it, but boys only get clear polish, okay?"

"Okay, but I want the pencil, too."

That was how Markie came to have clear polish on his toenails and wrote on the bathroom tiles with the nail white pencil; after we'd rubbed the tiles clean, we decided we had to be careful about everything we did in front of him, not only about the smoking.

* * *

Later, after the summer when we had returned to school, we would meet in Marissa's basement a few afternoons a week after school to watch American Bandstand with Dick Clark and practice the latest dance steps. We'd include Markie once in a while so that Mrs. Collaro could go to the chiropractor and have him take care of her back, which hurt her a lot since she picked up Markie, or just to give her a little time to do her housework in peace. When we heard the music for Bandstand go on, we'd take turns teaching Markie the steps, sometimes with our younger sisters if we felt particularly generous.

After school, we'd rush home and then out again after a quick snack and gather in front of the old basement TV, switch it on and, as soon as we heard, "Da-da-da dada, da-da-da dada da-dum, Da-da-da dada, da-da-da dada da-dum," the distinctive theme song of the show, it was our signal to be ready to see the kids come into the studio for the show, which was televised live from Philadelphia. Marissa and I especially like to see the "regulars," the kids who went to be on the show every day after school, the same way we watched at home.

They seemed like people we might know, except for the fact that they were older teenagers with boyfriends whose parents let them dance every afternoon and vote on songs and be on live TV.

The main attraction of the show for us, aside from the great live music it featured, was the fact that these were regular kids like us who lived in Philadelphia, a city that had a lot of Italian Americans and a Naval Shipyard, too, just like Brooklyn. We couldn't imagine our parents allowing us to do what they did every day after school—to go on television and dance with boys—so instead we watched faithfully every day that we could. These weren't actors or glamorous stars, just a lot of kids like us, and that was what drew us to the show along with our kind of music performed live and voted on by those same teenagers. Only something truly serious—an appointment with the dreaded dentist, or a high fever—could interfere with our watching and dancing.

This vicarious pleasure felt so real to us that we would talk about the "regulars" and the good-looking host of the show, Dick Clark (of whom even our skeptical parents approved) at school every day as though they were people we knew. It was a phenomenon that was shared with almost everyone in our age group, making the show our generation's American Idol.

We did all the new dances as soon as they appeared on the show—The Twist, The Pony, The Mashed Potato, The Locomotion—but

Markie's absolute favorite was The Twist, and, being cute and chubby himself, he liked Chubby Checker. It was also an easy dance for little ones to do, and Markie loved to swing his arms back and forth in time to the music as he danced. When he was upset, we could usually make him feel better by asking him which dance he wanted to do and then putting on the record and dancing with him.

One of the best things about American Bandstand was seeing the original musical artists perform their songs and then watching a panel of teenagers vote on them and say what they did or didn't like about the music. Watching them made us feel like we had a voice, at least about music, and some control over something, even if it was just expressing an opinion about a popular song. We liked to hear the kids who judged a new song talk about why they did or didn't like it. The beat, the words, the music, all contributed to whether or not it got a high score and would become a hit. It was far from "serious" music to our parents, it certainly wasn't Sinatra, and some of the songs were absolutely silly or just awful, but it did help us to develop the ability to break down music into its elements. We'd listen to our little AM transistor radios and hope to hear a song that we'd liked had become a hit. If we liked a song that had premiered on Bandstand, we'd save up our money and buy the single of the song on a 45-rpm record for ninety-nine cents and play it over and over and dance to it when we weren't watching TV.

In years to come we would see "Little" Stevie Wonder perform his song, "Fingertips" and we all became big fans of his music. Marissa remarked she thought it must take a great deal of both talent and self-confidence for a kid who was so young and also blind to appear on television and perform live. It was an era when we weren't often exposed to people with any kind of disability, except for the Down syndrome kids (who were referred to as Mongoloid in that pre-PC era) who we were used to seeing in many of the local *Pasticcerias*. For some inexplicable reason, a great number of families who owned those pastry shops had a Down syndrome child, and these children were the one standout exception that I recall to the practice of keeping people with mental and physical disabilities out of sight.

I even recall a classmate who had been sick and eventually died of leukemia and was mourned, but the cause of his death was not spoken about openly. The word "cancer" was not mentioned freely, as though the condition itself was contagious and avoiding the discussion of it would protect the rest of us. Maybe that's one reason we were all so impressed by Stevie Wonder, but I think it was the combination of his likeable personality and the overwhelming musical talent he obviously possessed that impressed us. Marissa said even then that she thought he would be successful and famous and she was right; Markie was immediately partial to any performer who had the word "little" in front of his name, especially a talented one.

We loved The Shirelles' music as well as the fact that they were also girls, like us only a little older, who were gutsy enough to use their talent at singing to make people happy and to make money; it was an intriguing idea that took you well beyond the wonderful music of their songs. While we went out and bought "Will You Still Love Me Tomorrow" (which was the first rock and roll record by a girl group to reach number one) and listened to it on our radios and sang along with it, they made music history and we had watched them on Bandstand.

We also got a chance to see what fashions and hairstyles the increasingly self-aware "regulars" wore onto the show. The magazines we read, like *Teen* had begun to feature stories about them and their lives, too. We tried to imitate their hairstyles, experimenting on each other, and tried also to piece together similar outfits to those they wore from our own clothes and a few, inexpensive accessories. Yet, most of all, we loved dancing together, not worrying about how we looked and just enjoying ourselves. It was our first taste of what would become reality TV in the basement of Marissa's grandfather's house on West 5th Street and we loved it.

Chapter 9

In My Head and Around the City

Although my mother wasn't friendly with the neighbors, and liked to keep her life private, she was familiar with all the resources that our great city had to offer. She often took my sister and me with her on her expeditions to make use of all that was free and available to us in the city; her attitude was it was absolutely foolish not to take advantage of all the free things available to any New Yorker who was smart enough to navigate the buses and subways. She was determined that we grow up knowing not just our little neighborhood, but what was around us and available for the fifteen cents it took to ride public transportation. She often told us that other people from all over the world had spent thousands of dollars and traveled to New York to see the things we were lucky to have so easily accessible if only we made the effort. We had mixed feelings about this. If the destination was a trip to Manhattan Beach any sunny day, or to the Coney Island Boardwalk on Tuesday evenings in the summer to see fireworks, we were more than willing to accompany her.

In the summer, we often met our father at Coney Island after he got out of work, if he had the day shift, to have dinner there and see the free fireworks show that followed after sunset. On those nights, instead of sneaking bites of our dinner into our napkins for secret disposal and sweating in our hot kitchen at home, we gorged ourselves on food from Nathan's Famous, which we enjoyed in the cool ocean breezes that blew across the boardwalk. We took the Sea Beach subway from the Avenue U Station to the end of the line at Coney Island, where it was elevated high above the ground, giving a panoramic view of the rides, the beach, and the boardwalk. Then we walked out of the train car and down the stairs and continued a little farther to the corner of Surf Avenue where the original Nathan's stood and still remains today.

It wasn't a fancy dinner out. You walked up to a counter where men in white paper hats that resembled the ones we made out of newspaper pages stood behind the counter ready to serve you, and just yelled out your order to one of them when it was your turn. It was an unspoken rule that everybody knew what they wanted before they got up to the counter. If you took too long to read the menu signs and the line moved you to the counter before you were ready, you weren't from Brooklyn and would be jostled to the side to read on your own time while others ordered:

"Gimme two with mustard and sauerkraut, two French fries, and an orange soda. No, make it a coke!"

"I'll have a BBQ'd pork on a roll with extra relish!"

"Gimme a lean corned beef on rye, heavy mustard and a cuppa coffee, black!"

My sister and I loved to listen to the people ordering, our ears soaking up the speed and surety of their voices, all the while imagining we were old enough to bark out our requests and be served any number of delicious treats for dinner—no worries about sodium or cholesterol at Nathan's, just big appetites to be satisfied. You got your order on a little grey cardboard tray and then went over to pick up napkins, straws, and more ketchup or mustard if you needed it.

All around on the walls were large posters with black and white photos telling how Nathan Handwerker had started with a small hot dog stand right there on the corner of Surf and Stillwell Avenues and relating the story of how he became incredibly successful because of the delicious quality of the food and the quick service. We also knew there was a hot dog eating contest there on July 4th every year, where each of the contestants tried to eat the most hot dogs and buns in a twelve-minute period. The contest was a kid's dream: winning fame (and maybe fortune) by eating free hot dogs!

We would wait for my father and meet him out on the sidewalk in front of Nathan's, kiss him hello, and then give our orders to him and our mother. Then we'd walk into the place with them and my sister and I would continue out to the Boardwalk in the back to wait while they got the food and we all looked for a place to sit and eat our meal together.

Sometimes, when they made plans to go to the fireworks, my father would tell my mother to stop and get knishes instead of French fries to go with our hot dogs and sandwiches and we'd make a little detour on the way from the elevated subway station to stop at Shatzkin's for the knishes. They were the best ones our family had ever tasted; their flavor has never been duplicated and I'm sure it never will be in our era of "healthy" eating, when having a bagel makes you feel that you should go to confession.

The front of the store where the knishes were made as well as sold was open and you could stand right outside the glass of the window and watch the elderly ladies prepare them. First, they took a round piece of dough and rolled it out, then patted it thin, like the dough for a tiny pizza crust. An ice cream scooper was then filled with that special mixture of mashed potato, kasha, diced sautéed onions and spices from a large container on the table and was dropped onto the dough. Finally, they would slap another circle of flattened dough on for the top and pinch the sides together so it looked like a large, overgrown ravioli. Finally the knishes were fried or baked. If we were lucky, the knishes were still warm when we bought them and were infinitely better than French fries with our dinners. It was heavy and satisfying food that stayed with you and took hours to digest.

My parents both had a great deal of affection for Coney Island. My sister and I got the feeling that they had often gone there together when they were younger in the time before they were married. They had told us many times about a wonderful amusement park that they had gone to called Luna Park that had many rides for adults to enjoy. My father had described it to us and from his words it sounded like it had been a fantastic place, with a grand entrance that had two large curved slivers resembling the crescent phases of the moon; one had the word "Luna" and the other the word "Park" written across them. There were also high towers and three circles that looked like wheels suspended above the moon-like slivers. Everything was lit up at night and had a magical quality to it. When a person entered the park, all of this made you feel small as you passed underneath it to go in. My sister and I had never seen it, though, since it burned down during World War II.

The way my father spoke about it, I thought it must have been terrible for him to return from the war and find out Luna Park was gone. I wondered if he ever passed by the place where it had been and looked at that spot with longing for what had once been there. However, an Italian company has recently rebuilt it and the new Luna Park is now a favorite destination of our grandsons—a fact my father would have been pleased to know.

At that time, my sister and I regretted we had been born too late to see it ourselves, but we did have Steeplechase Park to enjoy. The one remaining amusement park in Coney Island was a wonder itself. Our parents had taken us there and we both loved and feared the place. We loved to see the huge face that sat above the main entrance gate with the words: **Steeplechase, the Funny Place** on it.

We always tried our skill with the ride that we called "the barrel." It was just that: a huge barrel constantly turning at a fairly quick speed; it was big and dark and a tall adult would have a hard time trying to stand up straight in it. Although it was more of a walk than a real ride, we loved trying to get through it without falling down. The trick was to walk as though trying to climb up the wall and to keep away from other people who had stumbled while maintaining your own balance and still moving ahead. This trick of walking up the wall to compensate for the turning of the barrel was my first experience in something that demanded my extreme concentration and I felt good when I was finally able to do it after many failed attempts.

Although they usually weren't daredevils, my parents had once taken my sister and me on the famous ride that gave the park its name, The Steeplechase, and I will always remember how scared all four of us were as soon as the ride began. My sister and I were split up, each riding on a mechanical horse in front of a parent who sat on the rear of the two person saddle. Since I was the older one, I rode with my mother. The parent was supposed to sit behind the child and put their hands around the girl or boy to protect the child and keep them from falling off as the ride picked up speed, but that was only how it happened in theory. The ride had originally been built in the early twentieth century and was merchandised as a place where it was acceptable for the gentleman to put his arms around a lady in front of him, protecting her.

What had appeared socially daring in 1900 was physically terrifying to us fifty years later. The tracks that the horses were attached to had been rebuilt in 1907 after a fire and were routed around the outside of the building, traveling at a quick speed and picking up more speed as the horse traveled on them around the curves. There were two different tracks with four horses to a track, and one set of horses was set higher than the other. You had no choice as to whether you were on the higher or the lower track; it was the luck of the draw. All the tracks wound around the building, both inside and outside of it for the duration of the ride, which was advertised as: "Half a mile in half a minute and fun all the way!" Talk about truth in advertising!

On The Steeplechase, you were essentially on a fast roller coaster ride with no car around you to protect you, only a carousel horse that you had to hold onto to avoid becoming the next attraction at the park as you sailed through the air and hit the ground below. The ride was so fast moving that people lost hair bows and even eyeglasses in the wind once the ride started and the horses were off. It was a present day tort lawyer's dream. Although I never heard of anyone dying on the ride, I truly believed my mother and I would be hurled right off the end of the building every time that we rounded a curve. I had never heard my mother scream in fear until we got on that ride and I was truly surprised my underpants were still dry when the ride ended and we all staggered off, grateful to be alive.

When we did get back onto the ground again my parents both looked as if they had been in one of those wind tunnels that they used to advertise on TV, disheveled and, I'm sure, upset with themselves for having taken us along on the ride. After that I remember having nightmares where I was being tossed into the air and would wake up gripping my bed with a pounding heart and the sensation that I had jumped from a moving car. My sister had bad dreams from what we came to call "The Horses," too, and I let her come into my bed when she woke up frightened because I knew exactly how she felt.

Neither of us told our parents about the nightmares. I remember how my mother had clutched both her own purse and me with a desperate, steely grip while we were on the ride. I could only imagine how my father, who always sought to protect us, felt. After our experience on that ride, any time we walked on the Boardwalk past the entrance to Steeplechase Park, we'd hear screams being carried in the air from the people on the same ride as they flew along on the outside tracks. Then the sound would disappear as they were whisked inside the building again and my sister and I would look at each other and shiver, remembering it all. The fireworks sounded calm and beautiful compared to "The Horses" and I would watch them with a sense of peaceful awe, always being reminded of the beginning of The Honeymooners, the TV show that Markie loved, and wondering if they had filmed the fireworks at Coney Island on a summer night.

* * *

Another place that both my parents had taught me to love and visit often was the Brooklyn Public Library. When we lived on West 5th Street, the branch I went to was on the eastern side of West 6th Street just north of Kings Highway. It wasn't far from the Highway Theater, where I used to go on Saturdays with my sister and my friends to see a lot of matinee double features. Most of my friends probably preferred to go to the movies rather than to the library but, as much as I loved movies, I was a library lover first. You had to have money to go to the movies, your mother had to allow you to go, and then she had to approve of what you saw and the people who went with you.

All I had to say to my mother was that I had to go to the library for school, and I was usually out the door with her approval, but that was only one of the reasons I loved the library. The more important reason for me was my father had explained to me that, unlike many of my friends' families, we had never bought a set of encyclopedias because of the library. He said one of the best things about living in our country, and especially our city, was we had the finest books available for us to read for *free*. All you had to do was get a library card and you could borrow books and even records without paying a cent for them. He told me that the libraries usually had more than one set of encyclopedias available for use and they updated them pretty regularly. If you needed to check on facts for a report for school, instead of looking them up in an older, outdated encyclopedia, you could get the best and most recent information at the library. If you needed to find out information about something complicated, you could go to the main branch of the library.

The Main Branch of the Brooklyn Public Library was, and still is, located at the corner of Flatbush Avenue and Eastern Parkway, overlooking Grand Army Plaza, Brooklyn's answer to Rome's Arch of Constantine and Paris' *Arc de Triomphe*. That building has always looked to me like a stylized flattened benevolent giant whose arms are outstretched, welcoming and waiting to embrace those lucky mortals who walk through its grand front entrance. The building is an art deco splendor that has been lovingly restored and still bears on its stone front the inscription that set my mind on overdrive as a child when I first read it:

HERE ARE ENSHRINED
THE LONGING OF GREAT HEARTS
AND NOBLE THINGS THAT TOWER
ABOVE THE TIDE
THE MAGIC WORD THAT WINGED
WONDER STARTS
THE GARNERED WISDOM THAT HAS
NEVER DIED

From the first time I visited the building with my mother and read the words, I felt the library had spoken to me, telling me how important it was to understand what the written word was capable of, to treasure it, revere it, and never abuse it—in short, to have respect for the countless souls who had taken the time they were given and attempted to leave something of themselves to other people because they wrote down in words what they knew or felt, or had imagined. It was an awe-inspiring thing for me to think about, and left me feeling much as I did in church when I was moved by a Gospel reading.

As a Catholic I had been taught (and truly believed) God had spoken through the prophets in human language. What was the Bible, after all, but words that had been inspired by God and were written down for the edification of future generations? The first human stories had been passed down orally, but were only preserved for those who followed after they had been written down. The Italian language of my ancestors had been spoken in many forms for years, but was polished, formalized, and written down by Dante Alighieri in his *Divine Comedy*. Words were, and always had been, the currency of my life, flowing through my mind and heart and spilling off my lips as I tried to communicate, as essential to me as the blood that flowed inside me and nourished my body.

Visiting the library was, in some ways, like going to church for me. You had to be quiet and respectful in your demeanor in both places because of what was alive there. Every Catholic church, no matter how grand or small, was a holy and sacred place because it housed the Eucharist, and every library, no matter how humble or grand, was a secular shrine to the written words it housed. I knew I wasn't the only one who felt this way.

After I finished reading *A Tree Grows in Brooklyn* and felt sad because I was done with the book, my mother suggested I try another, lesser known novel by Betty Smith, *Tomorrow Will Be Better*. I read it with delight, realizing for the first time that a writer could sound more like a friend if you read more than one book by the same author and became aware of the writer's cares and concerns that they dealt with in their books, as well as the characters that they created. These fictional people always appeared to be formed from different little parts of the writer, even if they were based on other real or imagined human beings.

At one point the heroine of *Tomorrow Will Be Better*, Margie Shannon, describes how much she looks forward to going to the library in the evening with her husband. Even though she is in an unhappy marriage, she manages to draw comfort from being there with him and choosing books to read while he looks through back issues of Popular Mechanics magazine. I imagined she looked like me, only born a few decades earlier and with the hairstyles of her era: fishhook curls and shingled hair, which were vividly described in the book. Although I didn't think of myself as genuinely unhappy, as Margie was, I often escaped from my real life into books as she did.

I remember being embarrassed in my own classroom because I was so engrossed in reading *The Song of Hiawatha* by Longfellow after finishing my work in the fifth grade, that I screamed out loud when a classmate knocked on my desk to get my attention because the teacher wanted me. I had been so engrossed in my reading of the passage where Hiawatha is fighting against the almost invulnerable Megissogwon, who is trying to throw a large stone down on him, and the knock felt like the stone hitting my desk. It was like waking up from a dream because of an event in the real world, like a phone ringing, and being so startled that you scream yourself awake from the other state, and I did just that and then had to explain myself to the teacher and the rest of the class. I didn't reveal to them, however, that I often became more engrossed in whatever I read that I was annoyed at having to go on with the next lesson, preferring my book to whatever was being taught, especially if the lesson was math.

I devoured many books from the class library, indulging my indiscriminate passion for reading with great pleasure long before my powers of discernment about the content of the book I held had developed. I had learned from the *Russian Fairy Tales* book in our classroom that the grandmother who told the stories to the children sipped hot tea from a glass, not a teacup, with a cube of sugar held behind her front teeth to sweeten the brew, thinking neither my dentist nor my mother would have approved of that.

I'd even tried some of the *Sherlock Holmes* stories by Sir Arthur Conan Doyle, and had been especially frightened by the *Adventure of the Copper Beeches*, where the innocence of the countryside was depicted differently from my own experiences in the country at the Twin Lakes house. It made me think living in the city, even with all the nosy neighbors whom my mother couldn't stand, was far preferable to the isolation of the country, where neither you nor your neighbors could see anything that occurred in another house because everyone lived so far apart. That story made me realize that although I loved the country in the summer, I probably would have hated it in the winter. It was bad enough to be inconvenienced by a big snowstorm in Brooklyn, where it was hard to get around only a few days every winter because of ice and snow. In the country you might be really isolated many times during storms and I couldn't stand the idea of being stuck inside for a long period of time. Although nobody I knew was like the villain of the story, it still made me decide never to move to the country for good.

All of this love of reading and my reverence for the written word eventually led to my desire to become a writer, but I couldn't admit this to myself. I viewed writers with as much reverence as I viewed the Sisters of St. Dominic, who had devoted their lives to God and who were the teachers at Sts. Simon and Jude School, where I went for religious instruction every Wednesday afternoon through eighth grade. I saw their decision to live a religious life as a nun as all-encompassing, affecting every one of their actions and decisions every day. This was how I saw being a writer as well, but I wasn't sure I had that kind of devotion in me, at least not yet.

I had enjoyed reading *Little Women* and its sequel, *Little Men,* so much that I decided to read *Invincible Louisa*, a biography of Louisa May Alcott, when we were assigned to read a biography for a book report at school. She was my favorite author at the time and the depiction of her life in the book only convinced me more that a writer had to be devoted above all else. Louisa was devoted not only to her writing, which made her famous, but also to her family, especially her father, Bronson. Due to the failure of her father's experimental "Temple School" in Boston in 1839, his family lived in modest circumstances. Another unsuccessful attempt at Utopian farming that also ended in failure in 1844 even denied his wife and four daughters the luxury of living there in poverty and it was Louisa's writing that actually supported her family although she was always loyal and remained devoted to her father until his death.

I was particularly impressed by a scene from the book where Louisa gets off a train at a railway station and sees a large crowd assembled and waiting for someone famous to disembark from the train. Louisa asked a porter who the famous personage on the train is and he responded: "You!" She couldn't believe all those people were there to see her, but I could. From the first time my mother began to read *Little Women* to my sister and me as a bedtime treat when we were old enough to read for ourselves, but had been home sick for a few days, I had been captured by the naturalness of her writing. Although the book was full of references to unfamiliar things like *blanc mange*, and dresses that were scorched in the back from the wearer being too close to the fireplace, the day-to-day story of a mother and four daughters struggling to live a good life with the father away during the Civil War was written in a timeless human style that resonated with me.

The chance to meet the author of such a popular and beloved book was as exciting during Louisa's lifetime as it is now, when endless popular author meet-and-greets are big business at both the mega bookstore chains and independent stores. I liked Louisa even better because she was so unaware of the extent of her own popularity. It appeared she hadn't stepped out of the role of devoted daughter and into the part of successful popular author. This made her an example to me of how to remain human even after achieving great success, and encouraged me to think that perhaps I, too, could put words onto paper and dream of having others *want* to read them some day. After I read her biography, but before I had ever heard the word, she became my secret mentor. Even while my mother read aloud to us from *Little Women*, I imagined being a writer like Louisa and, of course, Jo—not now, of course, but... maybe someday.

* *

For me, it was the library, but I think my mother's favorite place to visit for the cost of a subway token was The Museum of Natural History in Manhattan, or, as we referred to it in Brooklyn: the City.

"I have to go into the city today."

"My brother got a good job, but he has to go into the city every day."

"She's sick. She has to go to a doctor in the city."

"She didn't get into Brooklyn College, so she has to go all the way into the city to Hunter College."

All these common expressions of how removed we felt from that borough across the river that had swallowed up the once-independent city of Brooklyn, were what we expected to hear from fellow-Brooklynites. We of "The Borough of Homes and Churches" (which was how my elementary school city history book referred to Brooklyn) didn't feel as much estranged from Manhattan as we felt that we had everything we needed in our own borough without having to cross the river, so why do it unnecessarily?

A fellow student of mine from Brooklyn College once said to me that people from Brooklyn didn't know Manhattan, but people from Queens, like him, did. I told him that he was right; we felt we didn't need to know Manhattan as well as people from Queens did, but I don't think he got it, even after I reminded him that he had chosen to come to Brooklyn for his higher education for a reason: it was the best education he could get at a branch of the City University. I forgave him his ignorance because he was, after all, from Queens.

My mother, who had worked in the Empire State Building during World War II, both terrified and thrilled us with the story of how she had been there working when someone jumped out of a window to commit suicide as she was typing away at her desk, usually agreed with these sentiments about Manhattan. However, she would have answered that question about why leave Brooklyn with the words "to become more educated." This was another reason to take advantage of the great public transportation system–as long as you did it under your parent's watchful eye. Thus, from a young age, I have memories of riding on the buses and subway cars.

I even recall a subway car that had straw seat cushions whose fibers cracked and split with age and would pinch your skin if you wore a little cotton pinafore or sundress. If the seat looked questionable, my parents would put a handkerchief down on it to protect my skin before I sat down on it. This was all before my sister was born in the early 1950's and we started going around more often in the car when my father was home on weekends. I also remember many times after my sister was born and I had learned to read when I would try to read everything I could see, especially the signs on the street, the buses and in the subway cars and even on the platforms. I thought the people who wrote the subway signs must be from Brooklyn, too, because they said:

"To City"———————> with an arrow directing you if you were going into Manhattan, and

<——————— **"From City"** with another arrow directing you back to Brooklyn on the opposite platform. This made a lot of sense to me because, if you could read the signs, you'd never go in the wrong direction and get lost: the

thing that many kids and their parents feared most on the subway.

Not everything on the subways made sense to me, however. Whenever it wasn't too crowded and I was allowed to stand up and hold onto the pole, I'd especially enjoy seeing the ads and trying to read all of them. One of my favorite ones to look at was the "Miss Subways" sign that told about a pretty young woman who worked or went to school and whose name and photo were put up with the other ads for people to look at while they traveled on the subway. I thought it was an honor to be chosen for this but my mother told me how foolish she thought it was for a young woman to have her name and photo up in the subway car where anyone (meaning strangers—specifically men) could see it.

She said no one would become famous by being a Miss Subways, but that a lot of people could find out your telephone number and call you up and annoy you, and who knows what kind of crazy guys looked at the photos. I looked at it differently after she said that, wondering what kind of mothers those women had who didn't explain to them that they lost their privacy, especially if they weren't getting anything to make up for the loss.

Another thing that confused me was the sign about keeping your hands away from the doors. The signs that I remember all looked like they said: "PLEASE KEEP HANDS OFF THE OOOR," not "DOOR."

The first letter looked like an "O" to me and not a "D", and I wondered if they spelled the word door differently in the subway than they did above the ground. When I finally asked my father about it, he looked closely at the sign and told me that if I looked carefully at it I would see that there was a straight line on the first letter of the word, and that it was a "D," but he admitted it wasn't clear enough for someone who had just learned to read or had bad eyesight. Since he wore glasses himself, that made me feel better and we used to joke about it afterward, reminding each other to close the "ooor," or not to leave the "ooor" open when we got home.

Although it was a long ride to West 81st Street and we had to change trains a few times, our whole family loved the Museum of Natural History and the Planetarium that was attached to it. We, like Holden Caulfield of *The Catcher In the Rye*, loved to see the canoe with the Native American Indians in it that was right inside one of the entrances to the museum. It appeared huge to us and we loved walking all around it in a circle so that we could see the people in the canoe from different angles. We studied their expressions and their clothes, or more specifically their lack of clothes.

We usually took the stairs and not the elevator to the different floors of the museum and

I loved those marble stairs—they were so wide and long and high that they made me feel at once smaller and more grownup as I climbed them. We would stop on a floor and my mother would look at the floor plan and we'd decide if we wanted to see what was there, or go up another level to the next floor. We had visited several times and my sister and I always argued about what our favorite exhibit was, as if the one we liked in particular was in some way superior to the other choice. As we returned time and again, the favorite one was always subject to change as we saw new exhibits—at least, they were new to us.

One stop we always made was the room where there were real animals, stuffed and posed as they once were in life and presented in their natural habitats from all over the world. A lion family (called a "pride") might be killing and eating a wildebeest in a glass cage next to a scene of a polar bear coming across the ice toward an Eskimo who was ice fishing. My father told us that a lot of the animals had been donated by people who had hunted them a long time ago and that some of them would never be allowed to be killed anymore because they were in danger of becoming extinct, like the elephants that used to be hunted for their ivory tusks, which were then used to make piano keys and kept as trophies, but that it wasn't legal to hunt them anymore. While we were happy to be able to see the animals, we always felt sad they had been killed—except for the monkey, which was donated to the museum after it had been someone's pet for many years and had died of natural causes.

We almost always went to the top floor to see the dinosaurs, but on the way, had to pass the room where there was a giant squid hanging from the ceiling, which always gave me the creeps because I felt like it was ready to pounce down on us from above. I hadn't read Jules Verne's *Twenty Thousand Leagues Under the Sea*, but I owned the Classics Illustrated comic book about it and I had seen the movie where the squid wraps itself around the sub and almost destroys it. I didn't even like calamari, so I hated the squid and never went willingly through that room.

My sister loved the dinosaurs, especially the Tyrannosaurus Rex, so we went there every time we visited. I acted as though they bored me, but found the little descriptions of their habitats and the drawings of what they had probably looked like fascinating and sobering. The idea that such huge creatures could just have been wiped out made me feel we were particularly vulnerable as human beings and I didn't like to think about that a lot. I consoled myself with the idea that we were still here looking at their skeletons a long time after whatever had happened to them, which scientists still aren't sure about, had turned them into museum exhibits. To my almost adolescent mind, it was another example of intelligence triumphing over brawn: we feeble but ingenious creatures now looked at the huge and impressive remains of those gigantic creatures who would have instinctively eaten us as a snack, had they not been reduced to their bones. Scientists, who devoted their lives to study and teaching, had found those creatures' bones and dug them out and reconstructed them into the skeletons that we studied and looked at in the museum.

When the dinosaurs were done, we'd often head to the planetarium, which you could access through the inside of the museum in those days. If we had time, we'd watch the Sky Show, which changed throughout the year. The lights dimmed in a huge circular auditorium and a specially designed projection machine magically transformed the darkened dome above the audience into the night sky, or the Milky Way, or took us hurtling back through time to see the birth of the solar system. If we didn't have enough time for the show, we'd go to the scales where you could find out how much you would weigh on another planet, and decide which one you might like to visit in the future.

* * *

As different from the Museum of Natural History as a building could be, Radio City Music Hall was another Manhattan place that became a much-loved part of the city to me as

I grew up. Although my friends talked about being taken to see the Rockettes and Santa at the Christmas Spectacular, my family often attended the Glory of Easter show. It featured a segment where all of the Rockettes, dressed in white robes and carrying bouquets of lilies in their arms, filed in and mounted the stage as only the Rockettes could. As the music they walked to reached a crescendo, they simultaneously lifted their arms and their Easter lilies formed a huge, but delicate cross. The other stuff on the program, usually involving bunnies, colored eggs, and flowers was forgettable at best, but that cross held me; it was at once corny and moving. No other place was like the Music Hall, where a movie was usually paired with the stage show, and you spent the better part of the afternoon there if you were lucky enough to go to this spectacular art deco entertainment palace, which, thankfully has survived, and even thrived to this day.

The combination of the impressively large marquee outside that lead to the huge, carpeted entrance to the lobby where your ticket was taken served to prepare you for something bigger than you had ever seen at another mere movie theatre. When you finally entered the lobby itself, you saw the truly grand scope of its scale, as well as the graceful sweep of the main staircase, which in my mind even dwarfed that of the Titanic. If you visit the Music Hall today, you'll still see tourists snapping photos inside the entrance to the lobby, as enthralled as its first visitors were. I didn't know about the period of the architecture when I first visited, but I did know there was something just right about the way the movies and stage shows were presented there, which couldn't help but diminish the other movie theatres I frequented by comparison; they just weren't Radio City. They couldn't be because, even if they had been built at the right time, they hadn't been preserved the way that the Music Hall had.

I often thought if they went by the inherent beauty of the structure, then the Academy Awards should have been presented at Radio City Music Hall. I was extremely relieved when, having endured hard times, and even having been in danger of being demolished for a short time, the building was given a much-deserved reprieve. It made me especially happy when, in 1997, the venue was chosen to be home for the annual Tony Awards broadcast, honoring the best plays, musicals, performers, and writers of the New York Theater. Except for the year 1999, when it underwent renovations, it has housed the awards ceremony ever since and is now thriving, although the weekly stage show had been reduced to the Christmas season only, with that season extending from mid-November to early January.

When we emerged from the Music Hall after spending the better part of the day there, my imagination was always on overdrive from the experience, as often happened when I went to Manhattan. On the subway ride home to Brooklyn, I'd smile knowingly at Miss Subways and dream my dreams, keeping both feet on the floor and my hands off the "ooor."

Chapter 10

Teach Me

$\mathcal{E}$ ach year, with the end of summer and the beginning of school, all of my friends prepared in different ways for the return to routine and the loss of freedom that we experienced like an annual, ritualized group punishment. Since I had skipped the eighth grade and was going directly into the ninth and Marissa was just beginning seventh grade, we knew we would have more schoolwork and that our babysitting would probably be limited to a few weekend nights a month. Depending on the homework load, we probably wouldn't be able to get together to watch American Bandstand every afternoon either, but might be reduced to only a few times a week. We were forced back into the schedule of regimented waking, sleeping, and eating that our parents all lived by. In short, we found we were growing up and without liking it at all.

Our summer clothes, consisting of mostly shorts and sleeveless cotton blouses, would soon be replaced by school clothes, and mine never quite managed to resemble those of my peers enough to keep me from standing out in JHS 228, where clothes were much more important than they had been in PS 95. As much as I tried, I was never able to escape the familiar and awful feeling of dread that sprouted in my stomach and circulated out to all my limbs, weighing me down, whenever we went shopping for school clothes. Going shopping for clothes with my mother (who usually insisted my sister and I shop together with her) made me feel like I had on one of those old undersea diving suits that only permitted the wearer to walk slowly and awkwardly forward, attached to an air hose that controlled every movement and kept you alive in an environment where you weren't supposed to be able to breathe, but only if you didn't try to stray too far from it, and never attempted to cut yourself loose.

The problem was that all the clothes and shoes my mother took us to buy were being purchased with my younger sister, not me, in mind, and I knew what this would mean to me on the first day back to school. I *hated* clothes shopping. It was horrible to be made to see all the new styles at our shopping Mecca on Fulton

Street in Brooklyn, and know, whatever cute styles Abraham & Straus or the other department stores might be showing, they weren't for me to wear. I had resigned myself to my nasty nickname of "Rosemary Longcoat" several years before when my mother had decided the best way to economize on clothing costs was to buy my winter coat two sizes too big and let me "grow into it." Like the homemade haircuts of my earlier childhood, where my bangs were perpetually uneven because they were cut at home, it felt like fashion would not be an area in which I dazzled anyone. During this command performance shopping, which demanded my presence while silencing my opinions, my main goal was to skulk quietly around the sidelines until my mother had bought whatever she wanted to buy for us in the way of clothes, and save all of my fight for the shoes, where I sometimes had some clout in the choices made for me if I lied about what they allowed and didn't allow at school in the area of footwear.

This year, all my hopes were pinned on being allowed to buy a pair of Hush Puppies in grey suede with laces and their famous soft soles, *the* shoe that all the other girls had already been wearing for a while. Saying laces weren't allowed wouldn't do the trick in this case, so I started to talk about the fact that my friends said our junior high school required soft-soled shoes. This would rule out the horrible and dreaded saddle shoes that I had been assigned for as long as I could remember, and rule in the soft and sweetly named shoes of my dreams. Just like "Cuban heeled" pumps was a more acceptable way of saying "more grown up shoes," the "soft-soled shoes" line might smooth the way for me with my mother. Wearing the Hush Puppies would allow me to fit in easier than the hated brown and white saddle shoes, which often had people asking me if I went to Catholic school when I had my still-long winter coat on and they couldn't tell if I had a uniform on underneath it. While it might be wonderful to read about Nancy Drew wearing saddle shoes on one of her adventures, I was aware those stories had been written in the 1930's. It wasn't far enough along into the century to make them stylish again and I hoped they never would be. My mother didn't believe in style for schoolgirls, just practicality, so I absolutely hated to do my pre-school shopping with her, except for school supplies, that is.

Nothing made me feel as excited about the possibilities of the new school year like buying a new loose leaf and some marble covered note-books. The fresh, sharpened but unused, pencils were lovingly put into my pencil case, as they had been every year since I had begun the first grade, with all my hopes and dreams for the new school year still as intact and undamaged as my writing instruments. Since this would be the first year of high school for me (the city at that time divided many of the junior high schools into seventh through ninth grades), we had to wait for the individual teacher's instructions before setting up an individual notebook or section of a loose leaf binder, but I liked to have some notebooks purchased ahead of time so I wasn't scrambling with all the other kids at Taverna's 5 & 10 on Avenue U for all of my school supplies on the first afternoon as soon as school got out.

My mother agreed my sister and I could buy some of our supplies that we would need anyway, regardless of the requirements of individual teachers, so we loaded up at John's Bargain Stores on pens, pencils, sharpeners, pencil cases, crayons for my sister and colored pencils for me, and we were also each allowed to buy one or two marble composition books and a loose leaf binder with some dividers and loose leaf paper. I liked to buy reinforcements for the loose leaf paper, too, having learned the hard way in seventh grade that the papers that usually tear out of the binder and get lost are the ones with the information for the homework or test. I would sit dutifully for a while each day in the week before school and lick the reinforcements and attach them to the holes in the paper that surrounded the metal binders of the loose leaf binder, listening to the radio and trying to convince myself that the boring work would pay off after I was back to my classes and had the notes I needed.

The actual return to school on the first day back after the long Labor Day weekend was always a little anticlimactic for me, because I had already spent so much of the week before thinking about what awaited me back in school. In previous years, when I had just been returning to PS 95 for the next grade, I had mostly been concerned with what teacher I would have and whether or not some of my friends had been assigned to the same class-room. Having already experienced the cultural and intellectual shock of being assigned to one of the two Special Placement seventh grade classes (known as SP-1 and SP-2), I was already a little more cynical about what was coming in this new school year. My worries about whether my friends were in my classes were exchanged for worries about the subjects we would study. Since the classes were organized to be basically stable, with most of the same students together for two years, I knew my friends would be there, but the teachers were another matter.

I had learned the hard way the previous year that my success or failure in subjects that I found challenging, like math and science, was directly related to the instructors' abilities to convey the material to us, as well as their desire to do so. I had only left the warm cocoon of PS 95 one single year ago, but had already come to truly appreciate the devotion of the teachers I had learned from there, especially Mr. Samuel

Reiss, who had been my sixth grade teacher. Although it was unusual for a male to teach in an elementary school, we never thought much about that since he was one of the kindest and most devoted teachers I had ever had, and I missed both his gravelly voice and his practice of reading to us from a book of a student's choosing every Friday afternoon for fifteen minutes before we were dismissed if we had completed our assignments for the week. Nothing like that happened in school any more. The best we could hope for was a few minutes of free time in our home classroom before the day started and after the Pledge of Allegiance and the broadcasting or reading of the daily information that the Principal of our junior high school deemed important for us to know.

Although there was no Mr. Reiss, I had found a few teachers who were more special to me than the others and I had done better in their classes than expected. The surprising exception to this was in my study of Italian, where Mrs. Gertrude Grande, who stood out among the staff as more elegant, mature, and aristocratic than most of the other teachers, attempted to instruct us about the music and culture of Italy in addition to the grammar and pronunciation of the language. Although I admired her ability to convey a great deal of the information to us, while marveling at her beautiful silk dresses and perfectly coiffed hair and manicured nails, I still had a hard time in the beginning. As the girls in the class who weren't Italian American (but who did well in their study of the language) loved to point out, it should have been easier for me because I'd supposedly been exposed to some version of the language at home—wrong!

Both of my parents spoke English as their first language, having been encouraged to do so by all of the grandparents. Also, the dialect of Italian that they spoke was neither a grammatical match, nor did it share the same pronunciation as the Italian I learned in school. My Grandpa Neri, who spoke Sicilian, not Italian, as he frequently reminded us, was not even in favor of my learning what he thought of as the language of the North of Italy, so I didn't dare discuss my foreign language studies problems with him at all or risk hearing a lecture about how I should be studying Sicilian.

So, I disgraced both my concept of myself as a good student as well as my Italian roots by failing the first quarter of Italian with a shameful mark of sixty-five percent because I simply couldn't grasp the concept that both the subject, for example: "I" and the verb "am" could be expressed in Italian with one word: *sono,* which automatically conveyed the person, the action, or state of being and the tense in one simple word. It had taken me all of the first two months of the fall during the previous school year as I struggled along trying unsuccessfully to grasp this concept. I was continually afraid to receive my returned homework, quizzes, and tests because I knew I didn't get it, but didn't know how to express exactly what it was that I didn't understand to either my parents or my teacher, who might have been able to solve my confusion with a simple explanation.

However, when it came to the language of my ancestors, I was too ashamed to voice my shortcoming to anyone, even my friends, and so I struggled along until one day, I finally got it by myself while reading the assignment for the next day: a dialogue that we would read aloud in class. The triumph I felt at making that discovery myself after weeks of confusion remains in my mind and heart to this day, as an example of how I refused both to give up or to ask for help, a characteristic that I'm sure had much more to do with my proud and determined heritage than I understood at that age. From that point on, I immediately saw my marks in Italian improve to an eighty-five per-cent the next quarter, since this problem was the only one I had with the language. I also felt so much better about my ability to overcome an intellectual problem unlike any I had ever faced, that I actually looked forward to Italian as one of my favorite subjects, one in which my teacher eventually complimented me on my pronunciation, to my delight and the chagrin of the other girls who had mocked me when I had initially struggled. They had only taken Italian because it was thought to be an "easy" foreign language to learn, which they felt would help assure their admission to a good college since they were sure to do well in the subject. It wasn't their hearts, just their report cards, that were involved, so they could never understand what my struggle meant to me, and I never talked about it to anyone, even Marissa, at that time.

However, I never forgot what it felt like to be completely lost when everyone else was able to understand what happened and in the future, was a lot less timid about asking for help. I also would never make fun of someone who genuinely couldn't understand something, knowing well how badly that hurt. Studying Italian taught me not only about the language, but also about respect for those who struggled to learn—something I had never faced before—and it eventually made me a better teacher myself. The importance of a teacher's abilities to break down what sounded simple to them into bite-sized pieces for their students would remain one of the things that I admired the most in all of the teachers I would have in the future. I think it became one of my strong points when I eventually entered the classroom on the other side of the desk. It was good preparation for my work as a teacher to have to struggle so that I could understand how difficult the process of learning could be, having experienced that struggle personally and not only intellectually.

Another subject that I looked forward to was social studies, mostly because of the teacher, Mr. Townes. So many changes had taken place in the world during the last few years that we constantly had to have updated maps to help us with our current events studies. The school curriculum particularly emphasized the study of Africa, which was in the process of constant, and sometimes violent change as more and more countries moved from colony to independent self-rule. I decided to do an extra credit book report on Robert Ruark's *Something of Value,* which dealt with the Mau-Mau uprisings in Kenya. Mr. Townes had suggested a book report was always a good idea to build up credit so that you had a buffer of good marks to offset any unexpected bad test scores in the course of the term, and I took his suggestion. He was not only a good teacher, but also genuinely interested in world events himself; I had noticed him carrying a copy of Boris Pasternak's *Dr. Zhivago* along with his textbooks. I was impressed by the size of the book as well as by the fact that it wasn't a non-fiction work directly related to our social studies class, but rather a Nobel Prize winning novel about the Russian Revolution.

He was a handsome and distinguished looking man, tall and dark, with a neatly trimmed mustache that he sometimes touched when emphasizing an important point to us. Although he didn't teach English, he was responsible for guiding us through the process of writing our first term paper with varied sources needing to be consulted and cited. I decided, as long as one of our allowed topics was the structure of corporations, I would do a paper on the history of MGM, and learn about the motion picture industry in the process. He approved my topic and I set to work. It was the first time I did actual research and read a number of different non-fiction books on the history and the development of that motion picture studio, and I enjoyed using the indexes and doing the critical reading that was required to have a reasonable number of sources for my bibliography; what I hated was the typing.

As the daughter of a woman who had made her living for many years as a statistical typist, flawlessly typing unending columns of tiny numbers that she manually added up without error at her jobs at the Brooklyn Army Base and as a civilian employee within other branches of the Federal Government, I felt from the first day I tried to use our little portable typewriter that I would never master the skill of typing as well as my mother. I just sat at the keyboard and pecked my way along slowly and ineffectually. Seeing me struggling with the mechanics of doing my first real term paper, my mother finally agreed to help me by typing the bibliography page of the final draft after noticing the amount of erasable bond typewriter paper I had wasted, which was more than I had used on the body of the paper itself. She also proofread the final draft of the paper and, when it was done, told me she was proud of the work that I had done—no easy compliment to elicit from her. I felt doubly proud, both of the paper and of her unexpected compliment, which I felt was genuine. Although I received an A- on the paper, a mark I would normally have been proud of, it was the vote of confidence from my mother about my work that resonated with me.

I had frequently discussed my weekly Current Events homework with my father. Mr. Townes required us to choose an article from the newspaper, cut it out, and paste it into our notebooks along with a description of why we had chosen it and what influence we felt it would have on national or world events. It was the first time any of us had been required to do more than summarize the news article and our teacher's goal was to make us think about the effects of events on the country and the world we lived in. It was the beginning of my awareness of the significance of events that I had no control over on my life. Even though it was one step (or even 100 steps) removed from our day-to-day existence in Brooklyn, this weekly assignment had the effect of forcibly focusing the minds of a group of bright but as yet provincial young people—myself and my fellow classmates—on the external, and the attempt of a good teacher to refocus the intellect outward is part of what comprises good teaching. The fact that the notebooks weren't collected regularly, but might be called in at the end of any given teaching period for evaluation (which was a quarter of our grade) kept most of us honest as well as informed on current events.

Not all of the teachers we encountered in school had a profound effect on us. A number of them phoned it in and those were forgotten almost as soon as we passed out of their classrooms, but the whole ethos of the school as a workplace that was to prepare us for the future did permeate into the consciousness of most of us as we went through our daily routines. We saw ourselves as members of the same workplace and had that as a basic shared experience, much in the same way as our parents saw themselves at their jobs. We might not be enthralled by everything we were expected to do or have or imaginations captivated every day, but we were still expected to keep working every day. School was our job, and our parents mostly expected us to do that job the same way they did theirs, with consistency and diligence, even if we didn't like some or even all of it.

Some of our teachers, not responsible for subject areas, taught us by example; our homeroom teacher in 9-SP1, Miss Karnes, was one of those. She was one of the older teachers on the staff, and also one of the most energetic, which was obvious on the first day of school. We were informed we were responsible for showing up on time for her homeroom, which was an Art Studio, and to listen attentively to the daily announcements that preceded the Pledge of Allegiance. During the Pledge, she allowed no fooling around or slouching. She was not only older, but also old school, and proudly told some of the feistier boys that she had begun her career as a teacher in "neighborhoods where you would be afraid to walk," thus dispensing with the idea that, because she taught Art, she was a pushover when it came to discipline.

She tolerated no misbehavior of any type from the girls, either, and I vividly remember her walking over to Francine Russo and her best friend, Ilana Terrazza, and ordering them to take out the aluminum hair clips that they were fond of wearing in their hair, calling them "bedroom clips" and saying they had no place in her classroom and would be confiscated and thrown out if they appeared again. When the rest of us snickered at her phraseology, she let all of us know at the beginning of the term that the rules in her homeroom were The Law. She was tough, but she was also fair, and you knew where you stood with her and exactly how far you could go, which was reassuring to me because I had seen other homerooms explode into spitballs and thrown papers and books with other more tolerant teachers, thus setting a bad tone for the day.

I found her imposition of order, which guaranteed a calmer classroom atmosphere at the beginning of the day, reassuring. It was safe to be in her classroom; her rules protected the kids like me, who didn't have the fancy clothes, shoes, or hairstyles necessary to present a *bella figura* In the ninth grade SP-1 class. We were often the butt of the boys' jokes and the sneering comments of the popular girls. I specifically recall a day when Miss Karnes was absent and I realized how important her presence was to my sense of safety in school. It was a Monday and I had brought my clean white gym uniform, freshly washed and ironed (by me) to school because every Monday was supposed to be gym uniform check and, in theory, you could fail gym for having too many demerits for a dirty uniform. Although the check was haphazardly done, it had been weeks since I'd taken the uniform home and washed it and I felt I'd better not press my luck, so I folded it neatly and left it in the middle of the double desk I shared with the most obnoxious boy in my class, Sam Zazzi.

When I saw Miss Karnes wasn't there, I waited until after Attendance and the Pledge and then asked for the bathroom pass and got out of there for a few minutes while chaos reigned. When I returned to my seat, I couldn't find my gym uniform. Frantic, I looked all over and found it being kicked around the boys' side of the room like a football; it was filthy and covered with dust and even paint from the easels on the floor in the back of the room. I was furious, but couldn't do anything except pick it up and try to dust it off before the next period, which was gym class. I went to my seat with it and gathered my books, while Zazzi laughed like a hyena at what he had started and most of the boys joined in.

When the bell rang, I ran to a water fountain in the hall and tried to wash off some of the paint spots but only succeeded in smearing them. Of course that was the day for uniform check and I got the demerit and immediately vowed to get revenge, and all my friends agreed to help me. I stayed out of my seat after Attendance and took all my important stuff with me until Miss Karnes returned a few days later and I thought and thought about what to do to Zazzi. I didn't have to wait too long. She returned to class a day or two later and was not in a happy mood when she saw the state of the classroom.

A lot of her art supplies, including her poster paints and pastels for drawing, were in disarray and the bulletin board along the entire rear wall of the room was covered with hand-prints that had obviously been made by dipping a hand into a pool of poster paint. The handprints were reminiscent of what you did in kindergarten class, and Miss Karnes was unhappy about this unwanted "art" project that had managed to cover the display of her students' legitimate work. It wasn't easy to get your work on the rear bulletin board, and this act was an insult not only to her, but also to the students whose work had been destroyed.

It was the equivalent of flipping her and her students the bird, and you just didn't do that to Miss Karnes and get away with it. She was so outraged that she sent a letter home with us that night informing our parents that we all had to stay with her after school the following day, and for the next week, unless the guilty one(s) admitted what they had done and apologized personally to the students whose work had been ruined.

I saw my opportunity.

Although I didn't want to become involved in ratting out another student, we all knew this was all Zazzi's (we never called him Sam) work; his fingerprints were literally all over the back of our classroom. Coward and bully that he was, he never missed an opportunity to do something annoying or vulgar as long as he could sneak around and not get caught. My friends and I, as well as all the popular girls, had all put up with his crappy behavior—whispering filthy words to us during an exam while he simultaneously looked innocent and tried to copy from your paper—since the seventh grade. He cheated not because he had to, but because he liked to intimidate people into doing things that put them in danger of getting in trouble or just humiliated them. He had no respect for girls and women, in particular, but a lot of the boys didn't like him, either. They all stuck together because they were boys, but I'd seen some of them look upset at his antics like kicking my gym uniform around, and knew they wouldn't put themselves at risk to defend him.

So, on the first afternoon that we were kept in detention with Miss Karnes, my friends and I put our plan into action. The first thing we did after Miss Karnes reminded us all that we would be with her every afternoon until the guilty party confessed was to look at Zazzi, all five of us: myself, Annie-Pat, Tina, Mary, and especially Rosie, who had a special grudge against him from the time he had grabbed her behind in the back of the room when we rushed to get outside during a fire drill. She, too had vowed to get him, even if it meant taking her dog, a big, beautiful Irish setter named Red Flame, back to school (she lived right around the corner) right after dismissal to go after him. We had discouraged her from doing this, but she still wanted to get him, too. So we all sat in our seats, but turned our heads and bodies around in his direction, and pretty soon what we were doing became apparent to everyone and a lot of the other students, male and female, joined us in staring him down, even Francine and Ilana.

We didn't say a word out loud, just looked at him, saying nothing with our mouths and everything with our eyes. The five of us had agreed that if he didn't admit it after a week of detention we would all write anonymous notes naming him as the one responsible, but we hadn't counted on so many other kids backing us up and joining in the Great Staredown, and neither had he. My guess was he had no clue how much he was disliked by almost everyone in our class. Also, even the students who didn't like Miss Karnes because of her strict rules respected her because she was fair and, unlike Zazzi, she didn't pick on people arbitrarily out of meanness. If she didn't like you, but you did nothing wrong, you could get along fine in her classroom, and her basic sense of fairness had a great influence on us as students and commanded our respect.

After two days of detention, and two days of being deliberately ignored and frozen out of almost all the general conversation among the other students in our class, Zazzi finally confessed. We didn't know how or when he did it, but when we showed up for our regular homeroom on the morning of the third day, Miss Karnes told us all that we no longer had to stay after school and we were not to discuss it any more. So, we immediately started passing notes back and forth and speculating about the exact circumstances that had brought about this reprieve. I told my friends at lunch that I'd bet it was because we had all stuck together against him that he had given up and told the truth. Francine and Ilana, eating lunch nearby, overheard us and laughed, so I asked them what they knew about it.

"A lot," said Francine. Ilana laughed and slowly nodded.

We waited, knowing she'd tell us in her own good time. She looked at Ilana and winked, then motioned to all of us to move to their table. We did without bothering to take the rest of our lunches with us, hungrier for the story than for food. Dramatically, but delicately, Francine took the last bite of her sandwich, folded up the wrappings and put them neatly into their paper bag.

Then she looked directly at me and said, "If you had to guess, Rosemary, would you say I had something to do with Zazzi's confessing?"

I slowly nodded.

I hesitated, feeling this was some kind of a test that I didn't want to fail. Despite how different we were, I liked Francine and felt she was honest and could be counted on in a pinch—and Zazzi had certainly pinched us all in many ways.

"Okay," she said, "how would you think I could do something like that?"

I looked her right in the eye and said, "I'm not sure but I have a feeling it has something to do with your boyfriend, Frankie."

She smiled again and I knew it would all be okay and we'd get both the real story and her respect. She said, "You're right. He hates Zazzi, too. You remember when he grabbed Rosie's rear end during the Fire Drill and she wanted to bring her dog to get him after school?"

"Of course!" I answered for all of us.

"Well, Frankie heard that story from me and he said if I wanted him to, he'd have a little *talk* with Zazzi after school any day I wanted."

We stared at her in amazement.

"You told Frankie about that?" Rosie asked in surprise. "Why?"

"Because, in spite of what you think about his going to Grady and smoking and all, Frankie is a gentleman," she said proudly. "And no gentleman likes to hear about that kind of stuff being done to a nice girl by a jerk, so I told him because I didn't want her to maybe get herself into trouble along with her dog, and I didn't want him to get away with that kind of stuff. Listening to his disgusting talk is bad enough, but when he starts touching, then somebody has to do something about it."

"And Frankie was the one to take care of Zazzi, wasn't he?" said Rosie with a look of both admiration and surprise.

"Now, you've got the idea!" said Ilana, smiling at all of us in a way we hadn't ever seen before; we had all been admitted into their confidence and now we were all at least allies, if not close friends. "He told him he could tell the truth and save the whole class the trouble that he made for them, or he could take him on, man-to-man."

"Zazzi is a coward," I said. "He'd be afraid to take on a real man, especially someone like Frankie. I think he's got both manners and muscles, and he *is* a gentleman."

That made Francine and Ilana happy because I didn't just say it, for the first time, I *felt* it, too.

Before this, we had looked down on Frankie, for all the reasons that Francine had stated: He was definitely not going to college and was happy just to work on cars with his hands for the rest of his life. Also, he dressed like a James Dean tough guy, with his jeans and leather jacket, and usually had a pack of cigarettes tucked into his rolled up shirt cuff to draw attention to his muscular biceps. I had thought, aside from his car, one of the reasons that Francine was going steady with him was she was just another smart girl that had a weakness for a sexy-looking guy who was much cooler than the "intellectual" guys she would meet in college, if she ever went.

Now I felt ashamed, especially when Francine had used the word "gentleman" and had explained Frankie was as morally offended as we had been by what Zazzi had done, which would later have a name: sexual harassment. This put everything about Frankie, and of course Francine and Ilana, into a different light and made me and my friends realize we had been taught a lesson by all of them. It was a lesson about looks being deceptive and about judging the person by his or her character, that greater hearts and minds have always tried to impart to the young, and we learned it from two of our classmates that day.

* * *

Yet, it would take me another two years and I would be at a different school, Lafayette High School, before I met the teacher who had the greatest lifelong impact on me, and many other of his students, Mr. Irwin Maiman, a teacher of Creative Writing in the English department. You could only have him for a teacher if you were accepted into his elective course because of your good grades in previous English classes, and I had made the cut. In his class, we were expected to learn the vocabulary necessary to prepare us for the PSAT and SAT exams through daily drills and read American and British literature extensively, but that was not the core of what Mr. Maiman taught us.

We were also required to submit a weekly or biweekly creative writing assignment that he would read thoroughly and return to us with the most helpful comments about the content and, most important of all, with two grades: one for content and one for grammar. This was a revelation to me because he was the first teacher who actually acknowledged, by this system of grading, that there is a great difference between the intellectual and/or creative content of the writing submitted and the same writer's competence in grammar. Although a certain minimum baseline command of the rules of grammar (and spelling) was (and is) necessary in order for a writer to be able to communicate, Mr. Maiman never let misspellings and/or sentence fragments damn an otherwise good piece of writing.

Your grammar mark might, therefore, be lower than your mark in creativity; when that happened, you were allowed to rewrite the piece and resubmit it. Once, when I received pithy comments from him about a story I had submitted, I sheepishly approached him after class and asked him if it were ever permissible to rewrite a piece based on his comments about the creative part. His answer has stayed with me all these years: "Rosemary, a famous writer once said, 'I am not a writer. I am a rewriter.'"

This generosity and support for my efforts to improve my writing from a teacher I greatly admired, who was still a human being and could be easily approached, filled me with a happiness that I hadn't known existed before I had entered his classroom. Maybe I could also be a rewriter and thus become a writer, too. I hurried off to work on my story and was so encouraged by Mr. Maiman's kindness to all his students that I eventually submitted that story and others, and even some poetry to the school's prestigious literary journal of fiction, *The Marquis*, which had won first place in the statewide competition among all high schools for many years running. I eventually became a member of the regular staff of the journal and found myself going to the English office and reading and commenting on other people's work that was left in a folder on the desk in there for members of the literary magazine staff to pick, read, and return with comments and suggestions about the work. I had a few of my short stories and poems published in the winter and spring issues of my junior and senior years at Lafayette. This meant so much to me that nearly fifty years later, I still have the original copies of *The Marquis* where my poetry and stories were published.

Unlike other students of his, I lost touch with Mr. Maiman after I graduated and went to Brooklyn College. A little while ago, I looked him up on the Internet and found an alumni site from Lafayette High School, which listed his name on its "In Memory" page, and sadly, learned he had passed away on August 15, 2000. Good teachers never know how much they have influenced the students whose lives have been touched by them in the classroom. I think the presence of a teacher like Mr. Maiman transcends time and remains alive in the souls of the students who have been influenced by him for good, in both meanings of that word, forever and for better. The commentator who had written the information on his passing summed up his students' feelings about him simply and succinctly by writing: "To know him was to love him." His encouragement, work ethic, and high standards remained with me from the time I studied in his class, as did his essential goodness. All I can add to the sentiment expressed by the writer on the Internet is the word, "Amen."

Chapter 11

Birthstone Rings and Charm Bracelets

Although I felt right at home traveling around Manhattan to see the sights and experience the wider life of the city, as I grew older, I often felt less at home in my own neighborhood. While I loved the comfort of its familiarity and sense of psychological embrace, with streets, stores, and homes I knew like my own living room, Gravesend, like my mother, could often cross the line from embracing to smothering. I struggled with and against that smothering, and felt a strong and frequent desire to get away from both the neighborhood and her. Unable to do either as often as I wished, my struggle with her expressed itself in my angry silences whenever my mother sought to impose her notion of what I should be doing, wearing, or eating.

Outside of our home, but within the little world of Gravesend, my struggle to be myself often expressed itself through what I read or what I wore. My clothing was always a tender issue to me, since, although I read widely and looked through all the current magazines for stylish clothing and hairdos, I was rarely allowed to choose any of them for myself. So, what I invariably did to stand out was to cut my hair short.

I remember distinctly a time when I was in sixth grade and had uncharacteristically allowed my hair to grow into a "page boy" hairstyle, faithfully setting it on rollers at night and using hairspray so it would stay put. I had often watched the "Ozon Fluid Net" commercial where the dressed up mother picked up her baby from her crib before going out with her husband for an elegant evening. She cuddled the child and got her hair messed up as the baby joyfully played with it; then she put the baby back in her crib, used a comb provided by her unseen husband and ran it through her hair to fix the style, put on the coat that he held for her, and went out with him for a wonderful evening. The narrator told you that if your hair got messed up after using their product, all it took to fix it was a comb and a touch. I wanted that hair, but most of all, I wanted that life, so I used it.

My friends used other hairsprays that were cheaper, but I wanted the one that showed me my imagined future: happily married with a family, dressed up, sophisticated and well groomed, but still touchable. I knew what I wanted; I just didn't know how to get there, and if the hairspray helped me feel I was at least on the road, I'd use it. I instinctively sensed that road would have a lot of curves in it and I was right.

One day, I left my house through the front stoop when I saw Anna's mother on her next-door stoop and said hello. Although I couldn't stand her daughter, I was always polite to her, and on that day, she actually paid me a compliment, telling me that my hair looked nice the way I was wearing it. That did it for me; it ruined all the efforts I took with my hair to have the mother of someone I abhorred say it looked nice and I found myself in the haircutter's chair the next day having it all cut off. I thought then that the perverse pleasure I felt at wearing my hair in a short, pixie cut like Jean Seberg, even without her great beauty, could only be attributed to the fact that, if Mrs. Russo, who had produced a daughter like Anna, liked my hairstyle, there must be something wrong with it.

I was certain she had left out the word "finally" when she had first told me my hair looked nice in that style. I discovered she was a lot like her daughter the next time I saw her when she commented sadly to me that she was sorry to see I had cut my hair "just when it started to look nice." She confirmed for me that Anna had, of course, learned the art of giving backhanded compliments, and perhaps some of her sneakiness, from her own mother. However, the larger implication of getting my hair cut was that the part of me that still desired the comfort of the neighborhood was at war with the part that wanted a life that Gravesend couldn't offer. This was true not only of hairstyles, but also of jewelry.

When all the other girls I knew wanted birthstone rings and charm bracelets, I had wanted them too—at first. My First Communion had been celebrated with the gift from my parents of a birthstone ring in real gold, set with a topaz stone for my birth month. It was a delicate little ring which had a small, clear yellowish square stone embedded in gold filigree with a tiny ruby mounted on either side of it. It hadn't been sized properly, however, and was too big for my ring finger so I wore it on the middle finger of my left hand until it could be taken to a jeweler for proper sizing.

This worked well until we went on our annual summer outing to Jones Beach in Nassau County on Long Island, where the waves were always bigger and the ocean surf rougher than at Manhattan Beach. Although my mother had reminded me that the beach wasn't the right place for good jewelry and encouraged me to leave it home, I kept the ring on my finger anyway. I loved that ring, my first piece of real jewelry, so much that I risked losing it in the surf—which is exactly what happened—rather than leave it at home.

I had left it on the middle finger of my hand since I couldn't wait for that sizing, insisting to myself that it was fine there and I wouldn't let it get lost. Unfortunately, even my stubborn will had to bend to the force of the ocean, and I remember the moment when standing up after jumping into a wave and letting it pull me out and then back to the shore, I saw the ring pulled off my finger and sucked down by the force of the water. It disappeared into the knee-deep surf bubbling at the edge of the sand and was sucked down, disappearing into the shallow water. Standing in the ocean in disbelief, and then frantically digging at the muddy sand where I'd last seen it, I sadly learned the lesson that I probably wasn't the jewelry type after all. If I couldn't be counted on to avoid having my ring sucked down into the shallows—even after repeated warnings—I must not be careful enough to deserve fine jewelry.

Although I was not yet eight years old, I felt I'd never love another piece of jewelry so much that I wouldn't be prepared to lose it. This, I felt, was a good thing because what hurt almost as much as losing the ring was the fact that I had to admit my stubborn carelessness to my parents. They were okay about it, not scolding me too harshly, but letting me feel the loss by not replacing it, ever.

The surface result was I never again wore any jewelry I cared about to the beach; the deeper reaction was not to care about or desire to possess any jewelry other than a few pieces that had emotional significance to me. In the future, this would amount to not more than three pieces of gold jewelry, including my thin plain wedding band purchased from EJ Korvette on Fulton Street in Brooklyn for $18 in 1969, which is the only piece of jewelry that I've requested to be on my finger when I'm buried. I felt I had learned the useful lesson that you can't be careless with things that are emotionally important to you, and this loss was a small price to pay for the knowledge, while reluctantly admitting to myself that my own carelessness and stubbornness had caused me to learn the lesson.

While a lot of my almost-teenage friends were obsessed with receiving a charm bracelet for whatever the next big event was in their lives—birthday, Confirmation, Christmas—I disdained the idea of collecting little gold objects when what I wanted to collect were experiences. The little world of Gravesend, with its familiar streets, friends, schools and churches, which had felt idyllic to me when I was eight had begun to feel claustrophobic as I looked ahead to my thirteenth birthday that would come in the fall. The door that had been

partially opened with the offer of the scholar-
ship to Hunter College High School, and had
quickly been closed, left me with a longing for
something I couldn't have and was unable to
name. More often than not, in the past year, a
vague feeling of unease began to leak out from
some unknown place beneath my "just one of
the neighborhood girls" facade when I accompanied my friends on shopping or movie out-
ings on the weekends. I always longed for more
than they did, but I couldn't figure out or even
name what that "more" was.

I thought at least part of it was to visit
other places like the ones I saw portrayed in
the movies. If I could never be as elegant as
Audrey Hepburn or hope for a figure like Sofia
Loren's, at least I could plan to someday travel
to the places their movies had brought to life for
me. While I hadn't ever been out of Brooklyn,
except for our family's two-week vacation to
Pennsylvania in the summer, my mind transported me to all the places I read about or saw
in the movies. To assist me in my vicarious
travels, I could always make the shorter trip to
one of my favorite movie theatres: the Highway
on Kings Highway between West 6th and 7th
Streets. I had started going there with my sister
and some of our friends a few years before,
when our parents had allowed us to travel in
groups to see the Saturday matinees and get
out of their way for a few hours on the weekend
without getting into too much mischief.

The Highway was unique because, along with the usual Saturday fare aimed at kids they often had a second feature like Carry on Nurse, which featured Shirley Eaton before her Goldfinger fame, or Terry Thomas in Make Mine Mink. For me, these comedies served as an introduction to modern British comedy and, although they didn't show a lot of the country, made me want to visit Britain. I felt the British approach to humor was much more in tune with my own, and I secretly felt snobbish about its superiority to the ridiculous comedies starring Doris Day and Rock Hudson that most of my friends liked. I had sat through the movie Pillow Talk with Marissa and a group of my friends, but had found it a sort of slick, dirty movie of a minor kind, and not a funny comedy. Although I had laughed at it with my friends, it made me feel vaguely uneasy, and I knew my mother wouldn't have approved of it, and would have put it in the same category as inquiring about sex. I thought (and still think) a lot of my friends went to these movies to increase their knowledge of sex and to look at the clothes and sets to see how adults with a lot of money lived. The film was interesting to me only to the point that it gave me a peek into the fictional but possible life of a successful career woman who lived in Manhattan.

The part of the movie that annoyed me most was the way the plot drew the two main characters together through the use of a party line telephone connection. I had only remembered having a party line telephone for a short period of time when I was little (around 1950) and thought that it was a stupid plot device to have the sophisticated and successful Doris Day character forced to share a phone line with the Rock Hudson character, when we had moved way past that inconvenience in Brooklyn almost a decade before the time when the movie was set. I was probably the only one of my friends who felt this way and didn't confide, even to Marissa, how dumb I thought it was. She was willing to come with me to see my British comedies and I didn't feel right telling her that I thought they were superior to Doris and Rock's work and thereby risk losing my favorite movie buddy.

Only after his terrible and public death from AIDS did I realize how ironic my feelings about the Day/Hudson team had been: Pillow Talk in 1959, Lover Come Back in 1961, and Send Me No Flowers which followed in 1964, were all double entendre laden comedies that still manage to seem a little smutty even in our anything-goes era. The irony of featuring Rock as the womanizer and Tony Randall as the man with the less-than-macho personality was later exposed, when the front pages of the newspapers screamed Hudson's AIDS diagnosis. In a discussion we had after Hudson's death, a good friend pointed out that these movies, in retrospect, were classic Hollywood deception, since it was Tony Randall (assumed to be gay by a lot of my friends) who was the straight man, in both senses of the word, to the jokes, which were often at his expense. Randall later perfected his finicky, nervous persona on television as the neat nick Felix Unger in the early 70's version of The Odd Couple, in which he co-starred with Jack Klugman as Oscar Madison, the slob.

I had always liked Randall for his nervous temperament and felt that he, like the unappreciated, stalwart Scottie dog in Lady and the Tramp, should have gotten a second look from Doris if she were truly as smart as all that. None of these opinions about jewelry or the cinema were freely expressed to my friends, however, except to say to Marissa that I liked Tony Randall because he was so funny. She knew me well enough to understand I was always going to be a little different, and she accepted my pre-adolescent skepticism with a lot of good grace. In fact, I often felt I was responsible for giving a voice to her feelings of dismay and cynicism at the world also, not just for my own.

We had both been raised by mothers who were born into a time when the rules were The Rules, and you didn't question or ignore them. As we moved ahead to the beginning of our teenage years, we both felt increasingly estranged from that world, but Marissa was more willing than I was to maintain the fiction that life for us would be much the same as it had been for both our mothers. Maybe it was because her mother was a little bit younger than mine, or perhaps it was the general comfortable feeling of her family environment, despite the fact of her resentment of her role as the dutiful oldest daughter, that kept her from being as secretly rebellious as I was. Whatever the reason, she was the only one of my friends who was able to tolerate my honest feelings about a lot of the things we discussed seriously and I valued her friendship a great deal.

She wasn't available all of the time, however, and I found I had to settle for the company of the more girly girls who were more school acquaintances than friends if I wanted to get out of the house, as I more and more longed to do. So I had found myself a little more in the company of some of my chums from the SP class at JHS 228 and a little less in Marissa's company as my first year of Seventh Grade ended. Right after school ended for the summer, I was once even invited by my friend, Tina Carcioffo, who usually sat with me at our table in the basement cafeteria, to go with her and a group of friends to Manhattan to see a movie. Although Tina, who was the youngest of the three children by eight years—her older sister Lorraine was in college and already engaged—her mother allowed her to travel a little more freely than a lot of the other girls' parents because her father was a motorman on the subway. He would know his schedule and we would go to the Avenue U stop of the Sea Beach train and travel to the city in "his" train so he could be sure we got there safely.

While I much enjoyed the thrill of going into Manhattan without an adult to chaperone us, except for her father driving the subway train, I still had to sit through the movie that she chose, and that was the catch. As a result, I remembered the thrill of being on the subway without my mother better than I did any of the movies I saw. Before our trips on the subway began, I had gone along to see Imitation of Life with Tina and a few of the other girls from school at a local movie theatre and had found the story of one of the minor characters much more compelling than that of Lana Turner's character, who always looked out for herself before everyone else, including her own daughter.

Susan Kohner, the gifted actress who gave up her career to be a mother to her two sons, played Sarah Jane, the ungrateful daughter of Annie, an African American maid played by Juanita Hall, who gave up her whole life to care for her daughter and was also more of a parent to Sandra Dee, who played Lana Turner's daughter, than her own self-centered actress mom. Since Sarah's father had been "almost white" she found she could "pass for white," a concept I found fascinating. I'd never thought much about racial problems in such a personal way before, but understanding how Kohner's character had chosen a way of life that she thought would give her more choices, but forced her to reject her own mother resonated with me. Her rebellion sounded like a sensible thing to do at first, but she later lived to regret the choice she'd made and only returned to her Mother in time for her funeral. I identified more with her character than with Turner and Dee's, who both appeared so one-dimensional.

Of all the characters, Sarah Jane was the one who had gone with her desire to make her own life and had paid the price for that. I felt her troubles had a lot more to do with the racial problems in our country and her not feeling like she fit in anywhere than they did with her deciding to reject her mother the way Lana Turner had rejected her own daughter time after time in the story. Sarah Jane was more complicated and, therefore, much more interesting to me. Of course, since these were my school friends and not Marissa, I didn't admit to all these feelings and just agreed when they talked about what a great movie it was and how beautiful the dresses were. Of course, we had all cried at the end of the movie together, so I just nodded my head, agreeing with their comments as we walked home.

A more unusual trip to the Highway Theatre with my sister for a Saturday matinee double feature a year or two before had turned out to be an adventure of another kind. Although I usually rebelled at having to take her any place, none of my friends were around this time and I agreed with little prodding by my parents to go, as long as it was just the two of us. Since she was going to see a horror movie that she normally wouldn't have been allowed to watch, she even agreed to the "no friends along" deal and we proceeded to the movies fairly happily together. I remember when we got there, I met a boy I knew from PS 95 named Dom with his younger sister and we sort of commiserated together wordlessly as we stood on line to buy our tickets to get in.

Once inside, it was the usual Saturday afternoon craziness, as a dark theater full of kids loaded with popcorn, soda, and candy reacted loudly and sometimes physically to the schlocky sci-fi movie on the screen. The combination of a theatre full of kids who knew there was only one usher or matron to police them while they watched The Attack of the 50 Foot Woman and all the sugar that they had consumed made it noisy and more fun than if we had seen a good film. At one point, someone in our row threw his soda, and not just his popcorn at the screen, provoking an immediate response from the male usher in charge that day. We had seen him at that theatre before and knew, perhaps because of his thick eyeglasses, he was usually more ineffectual than the female usher, often reduced to waving his light and hissing warnings at the troublemakers, never being able to see who it was causing the trouble, but that day, he didn't let his poor eyesight stop him.

Without warning, he ran to our row, which was a few rows behind the kid who had thrown the soda, shining his flashlight on our faces and pouncing on my sister, pulling her out of her seat by one of her braids that I had painstakingly done for her before we had left home. My friend Dom and his sister and I jumped up immediately and started yelling at him to let her go, chasing after him as he pulled her along the aisle toward the rear, while simultaneously barking at us over his shoulder, yelling we were all getting thrown out. My sister cried with hurt and humiliation and all the kids in our row, including the culprit, yelled at him to stop, joined by almost all the other kids in the theatre who hated that usher almost as much as we did. But thrown out we were—a shock to all of us who were basically good kids—and we didn't know what to do for a minute, but stood on the sidewalk in front of the theatre blinking at the sunlight as our eyes adjusted from the darkness inside.

After I had tried to comfort my sister, who now snuffled more quietly, I turned to my friend and said, "This isn't right! What did we do?"

He looked more shocked than I was and shrugged his shoulders. Then he got angry, too, and said, "We should go back in there and get our money back, or go get a cop!"

"No, wait," I said, an idea forming in my head.

"I'll do better than that; I'll get my father. You two wait here."

With that, I took my sister's hand and pulled her along with me the few blocks to our house and did just that. Alice had stopped crying along the way, but one of her braids was all messed up where the stupid usher had pulled it almost out of the elastic that held it and you could see from looking at her that she was upset, disheveled and crying. When we got home, my father was working on his car and surprised to see us back so soon. As soon as I told him all the details of what had happened and he looked my sister over to be sure that she wasn't physically hurt, he hugged her, put the hood down, and told us to get into the car. Then he got into the driver's seat and returned to the Highway Theatre, parking right in front of the "No Parking" sign—something I had never seen him do before. I knew better than to question his actions and thought maybe he wanted a cop to come along at that time.

My friend and his sister were still there waiting for us and they followed joining the small parade as my father, sister, and me marched into the lobby right past the ticket seller's booth.

"Point him out."

That was all my father said.

We all saw the usher, still carrying his flashlight, near the booth where you bought candy and popcorn. We all pointed and said simultaneously, "There!"

By this time, the usher had seen us and was headed toward us with an angry and yet frightened look on his mean face.

My father stepped forward, simultaneously pushing me and my friends behind him and put his arm around my sister. He stepped right up to the usher, bringing his face within a few inches of the man's nose and said, "You remember this little girl?"

The usher sneered at Alice and said, "She's the one who was making trouble, so I threw her out."

"You put your hands on this kid and pulled her by her hair?" My father asked quietly, being sure he verified what the man had said.

"Yeah. Somebody's got to keep these brats in line. That's my job."

"So you pick on a little eight year old girl? Who told you that you could touch her, or any kid?"

Before he could reply, my father pulled his fist back and clocked the usher right in the face and he fell backward. We were all shocked and then delighted. Then we cheered out loud. It was as if the hero had climbed down off the movie screen and punched the real life villain, and my father was that hero to us. We caught our collective breath and cheered. It felt like the whole theater erupted as the news of what my father had done spread.

At this, the manager ran over, alerted by the ticket taker that we had walked in without paying. Not missing a beat, my father turned to him and said, "This is my daughter and that jerk pulled her hair and threw her and her sister and these two kids out because he was too much of a coward to go after the ones who caused trouble here. What kind of an operation are you running here? What kind of people do you hire to be around kids?"

"You hit him!" The manager said, shocked at what had happened.

"Damn right," my father said. "And if you're worried I hit a guy with glasses, well I'm wearing them, too, and he's welcome to try to hit me back if he has the guts. I'm a little bigger than my daughter."

"Please sir, calm down. We can straighten this out without that."

By this time the screen had gone dark, the house lights were on and every kid in the place watched the show in the lobby, some even standing on their seats to see better—a much more exciting one than the movie, anyway.

"You've got two choices," my father said. "Call a cop and we'll let him decide, or fire this creep and you can go about your business and my kids can feel safe when they go to the movies. I'll come back in an hour and we'll talk. I've got to move my car now."

He turned and ushered my sister and me and our friends out to the sound of cheers from all the kids in the theatre, who were now all out of their seats and cheering for him. The word had spread, Brooklyn style, about what had happened and my father was the hero of that day. We left and he drove my friends home before we went back to our house.

That afternoon, my emotions veered between exhilaration and fear. I thought about what could have happened if my father had blamed us instead of defending us. I also thought about how he hadn't hesitated once he saw my sister was okay and knew we told the truth. He had fought in World War II and had been on one of those tiny Pacific islands where the twin scourges of rampant malaria (and no quinine to fight it) and the Japanese were the constant companions of the GI's, so I guess the usher held no terror for him. Yet, he was still my hero for what he had done (which might have gotten him jail time and/or a ruinous lawsuit in today's society) and he always would be.

I never found out what happened to the usher, but he was never there again when we returned to the Highway a few months later after everything had quieted down and the excitement of that day had been forgotten. Of course, I told Marissa the first chance that I got and she was delighted that someone—a parent no less—had stood up to that bully of an usher.

She teased, "Now if we could only get him to do something about that woman matron at the Benson who they call 'The Truckhorse,' we'd be in heaven!"

Nevertheless, I avoided the Saturday matinees as much as I could from that time on and spent more time going to Manhattan on Tina's father's train after that. Marissa even got permission to join us a few times, too.

The movie I will always remember seeing at the Highway was Psycho, during that same summer of 1960. Psycho had been released in June, and I have no idea how I got permission from my mother to see it. Maybe I convinced her that it was an Alfred Hitchcock movie that was more along the lines of Rear Window or even The Man Who Knew Too Much, which she had taken me to see. That movie had been another film starring Doris Day; one in which she sang a lovely song that my mother liked a lot, "Que Sera', Sera,'" and even sang to us at home. Maybe my mother hadn't yet read about Psycho, and the warning that you had to come to the movie theatre and see it "from the beginning or not at all," an unusual requirement in an era when you went to the movies and saw the film from the point at which you arrived. I recall no other film of that time requiring you to be there for the beginning and not seating you if you tried to get in late. The theatres even featured music in the lobby while you waited and had an announcement that told the number of minutes until "Psycho time." Whatever the reason, I had a chance to see it and took it, even though Marissa and all my other friends backed out at the last minute, leaving me the choice of seeing it alone, or not at all. So I went solo.

As I was in line outside to get in on a hot day in July, a woman in front of me who had seen it before told her friend all about the twist in the plot, which was a big deal with that movie, so much so that the public was urged not to reveal the ending as part of the publicity surrounding the movie. This woman just blabbed happily along to her friend and revealed the ending, which is still a shocker for those who have never seen the movie. As I listened to her, I knew I could move back in line if I didn't want to hear about it, but being alone, I thought it might not be a bad idea to see it knowing the ending, so I wouldn't be as frightened and I could see if it all hung together in view of my knowledge. I would often see movies that had a plot trick a second time to see if they held up under my knowledge of the plot device, and Psycho definitely did.

Even knowing the ending couldn't ruin that movie because it was so well written and acted. I still remember being a little shocked in a different way than I had expected while watching the first scene, where Janet Leigh appears wearing only a bra and slip, attire that pushed the visual envelope in 1960 regardless of all the sexual innuendo in other films I'd seen. Her dress, or lack of it, as well as the fact that the movie was in black and white, gave me the feeling it was different from any other film I'd seen before. There was a sense of menace and a building tension permeating everything that occurred, even at the beginning, all of it accentuated by the brilliant musical score. Even knowing the "big secret," I was drawn into the story of a basically good woman who makes a big mistake when she does something wrong that is totally against her nature and steals from her boss.

Since deciding whether or not to play by the rules was such a big theme in my own life, I identified in one way with Marion Crane, the character she played, who had always done the right thing and had therefore postponed her own pleasure all of her life. I got drawn into her story, as did the rest of the audience, when she decided to steal the money that she thought would bring her the life she wanted. From that point on, I knew she was doomed and going to be punished in some grisly way. Although the particulars about her death hadn't been revealed by the chatty woman in line, I had seen all the ads with her screaming and so I watched a lot of the film with my hands over my eyes, peeking through so I could still see, but ready to close my fingers if it got to be too much for me. I thoroughly enjoyed being terrorized by the rest of the movie, even after the shock of the shower scene, and felt Mr. Hitchcock was a master at manipulating the audience from the first scene right through the twisty ending.

Despite her crime, the audience was on Marion's side—that of a basically decent person who goes a little crazy one day when faced with an overwhelming temptation. In a few minutes, a foolish action sends her life spinning into an uncontrollable downward arc and we felt everything she felt as she was pulled into the whirlpool caused by her actions. Having been so concerned about her, we felt the loss of her character as an almost personal thing when she is killed—just what the director wanted to heighten the tension and up the ante. If he could do that, what else did he have in store for us, we wondered with delicious dread. The answer was: a lot. And I resolved, even while watching it for the first time, to see the movie again.

When I told my friends about what I had done, they told me that I was crazy: first, for going to see it alone and second, for letting the ending be revealed to me before I even saw it. Given my recent history at that particular movie theatre, and my un-girly nature, I knew they wouldn't understand why I had gone alone after they had all disappointed me. When they asked me to tell them the ending, I wouldn't do it unless they promised not to get angry with me for ruining it for them, so most of my friends remained in the dark about the big secret plot twist. Mr. H. would definitely have approved.

As we talked about the movie, I learned some of my friends had not gone with me because their mothers wouldn't let them see Psycho and I found myself in the unusual position of having a bit of knowledge and an experience that even Anna didn't have at that point. So, having seen the movie all by myself served a purpose within my own little circle of acquaintances, cementing my reputation as being a little bit different, while giving it a slight boost because of my ability to go alone.

I reveled in my ever-so-slightly inflated rogue status, most especially around Anna, who was now the acknowledged authority on the block about what was cool. While I still loathed and distrusted her, I did rather enjoy her sort of seeking me out after she found out about my solo movie adventure.

One afternoon she found me sitting on my front stoop alone, reading, and quickly interrupted me to ask: "How did you get your mother to let you go all alone to see Psycho?"

"I don't know; she said it was okay, and nobody else was around, so I just went by myself." I answered, putting my book down and shrugging my shoulders, telling her the basic truth of the situation.

"I'm surprised you had the guts to go by yourself. After all, your sister wasn't even with you," She commented in her usual snotty way, accenting the words "your sister," as if they had quotes around them.

"I don't always do everything that people expect me to do," I responded, looking her right in the eye in what I hoped was a meaningful and enigmatic way.

Anna never failed to make me angry at her ever-present superiority, even while supposedly asking me about something I'd done that I felt was more independent than anything she'd ever do. I'd never seen evidence that she had the sort of quiet interior existence that was so much a part of me and my real friends, like Marissa. She always needed her entourage of frightened and sycophantic followers to prove to herself and everyone else how great she was.

Yet, more than that, I had begun to see her need to hurt and humiliate others had become almost a symptom of something inside her that was either wrong or missing. Years before I learned the terms, I instinctively knew her narcissism and her sadism demanded constant feeding. She was like a virus that needed a host, or even better, hosts, to feed on for its continued existence.

Despite how pretty she was, she reminded me of one of the Brides of Dracula, who are only able to maintain their facade of humanity if they continue to draw blood from the living. At that moment I felt sure if she were totally ignored by everyone for a week, her influence over us all would wither and die, leaving us all much happier. I felt like telling her that, but wisely (and self-protectively) held my tongue, because organizing that kind of boycott was far beyond my powers.

"Well, as my cousin likes to say: 'There's more to you than meets the eye, and that's a good thing for you.'"

When I looked puzzled, she continued, "You're smart enough to know you don't have that much going for you in the looks department, but I think you probably make up for it in guts."

I wanted to kill her for that remark, but instead found myself recalling the scene in the movie that had started this discussion in the first place, where the private eye, Arbogast, is killed quickly and without warning at the top of the stairs and then tumbles all the way down to die at the bottom in a heap. Of course, he was innocent and didn't deserve it, but picturing her in his place helped me to catch my breath, count to ten, and reply, "I'd rather be smart than a lot of other things I can think of."

She smirked, pretty sure she had hurt me, and then went on, putting her hand on my arm, "Oh, come on; let's not fight. Why don't you tell me how the movie ends and then I won't have to spend my money on it. Did I tell you that I'm saving up for something special?"

"No," was all I quietly said in response to both questions.

We stood in silence for a few awkward minutes and then I broke the silence before it became hostile and asked, "What are you saving up for?"

She positively beamed, instantly forgetting all about the movie and said, "Didn't I tell you?"

"No, or I wouldn't be asking you."

"Well, it's a new charm for the charm bracelet that my parents are getting me for my fourteenth birthday in two weeks. It's all fourteen-karat gold with a beautiful Florentine finish and they're giving it to me with a charm that has my birthstone in it. It's a real ruby and the charm's in the shape of a calendar and the stone is in the spot where the date of the thirty-first would be, the actual day I was born, so it's being custom made just for me."

I almost laughed in her face, but she continued to blabber on about it, so she didn't notice my reaction.

Then I stopped her with a question of my own. "If your parents are giving you a bracelet with a charm already on it, why do you need to save up money?"

"Well, I can't wear a bracelet with only one charm. It'll look like I just got it and I want a lot of charms on it so I'm buying another charm that I'm paying for myself."

Before I could ask, she continued: "It's a little Eiffel Tower and it's adorable. I just saw it in the window of Grimaldi Jewelers and I knew I *had* to have it! You know I study French and it's so cute! But my parents are making me pay for it myself."

For a brief moment I almost felt sorry for her because she sounded so excited about the bracelet, a piece of jewelry. Then I realized once she got it, she'd be showing it off to everyone and demanding we bow down or curtsy to it or something equally as annoying.

So I said, "Cheer up. You're going to high school in September. Maybe you can sign up to tutor someone else in French. I know Mr. Grimaldi will hold it on layaway. He did it for Marissa's birthstone ring; they had that specially made for her with a modern setting so it was expensive."

She didn't like that much. And that was why I said it: to steal her thunder.

"What about you? I'll have a charm bracelet and Marissa has a birthstone ring. What do you have?"

"I don't like jewelry that much," I answered. "I like to go into the city. As a matter of fact, I have to go in now. I'm going to leave early in the morning and my mother wants me to stay in tonight to get ready."

So I turned around and, before she could say anything else, I was gone.

Chapter 12

Tell Her Anything She Wants To Hear

Discerning who my friends were and deciding how to treat the enemies disguised as friends wasn't the really difficult part of my early adolescence. That distinction would be reserved for my constant reevaluation of how I felt about my mother, and my attitude toward her was as subject to change as the words uttered by a politician. Some days she would be my biggest supporter, immediately coming up to school to complain to my guidance counselor in person about Anna's friend, Annemarie, who had tried to kick me and push me down the stairs after a gym class one day, suspiciously soon after my conversation with Anna about the charm for her bracelet. When I had sheepishly told my mother about that incident, which had occurred when I hadn't even known Annemarie had transferred into my school, she became immediately angry and got the look on her face that meant immediate action would be taken to deal with the incident.

What she said was, "She must finally have been thrown out of St. Simon's (our local parish Catholic School). Too bad she didn't learn any manners there. Don't worry. I'll take care of it; and her."

While I felt happy that the matter was now in the hands of a higher authority, I also worried my mother would get me in even more trouble with this obviously vicious girl and was almost sorry that I had said anything to her. Nevertheless, my mother proved to be correct in her handling of the problem.

I went to school feeling a strange mixture of apprehension at what my mother would do, and relief because I didn't have to face this scary little dragon alone. I soon learned my mother had followed the appropriate chain of command in this kind of a situation, but would soon take a unique little detour of her own. At the end of the day, Miss Karnes called me up to her desk and told me that I was to report to the guidance counselor's office instead of going right home. Seeing my distress, she whispered to me not to worry, and that my mother was already there, waiting for me. I hurriedly gathered up my books and jacket, waved good-bye to my friends, and headed out into the hallway.

Neither terribly reassured nor surprised, I made my way quickly to the guidance office, hoping to get there before the real crush of students emptying into the halls at the end of the school day. My mother was already there. The inner door to the guidance counselors' offices was open and I was waved inside by my counselor, Miss Cara, who appeared to be speaking amicably to my mother as I arrived. I had never been called into this office before—a fact that I hoped would help bolster my side of the discussion of the Annemarie problem. Miss Cara smiled at me pleasantly enough and waved me into the second of three chairs she had set up opposite her desk.

Turning back to my mother as if continuing a conversation with her, she said, "I definitely understand your concerns for your daughter's safety in school, and I can see from her records that she's a good student in one of our SP classes. Just as you said, she hasn't had any kind of trouble before this."

This was said with a smile and a nod of her head toward me.

"She didn't have any *trouble*," my mother said firmly. "She was *attacked* by this other girl while walking down the stairs after gym class on her way to the locker room to change back into her clothes. Annemarie kicked the back of her sneaker and made her trip and then pushed her so she would fall the rest of the way down the stairs, but my daughter held onto the bannister and pulled herself up and got away from her."

They both looked at me and I nodded.

Miss Cara looked directly at me and asked, "You didn't report any of this to a teacher. Why not?"

I swallowed and answered, "I just wanted to get away from her. She scared me. I wanted to find my friends in the locker room so I wouldn't be alone with her down there after what she tried to do to me."

Miss Cara nodded her head at this, acknowledging I had acted reasonably, and asked, "Did you find them?"

"I did," I answered. "They know all about it; you can ask them if you want to."

I remembered then how nice they had all been to me, especially Francine and Ilana, who had actually offered to go with me to find Annemarie and straighten her out. I had declined their offer and asked them not to leave me alone, so we had all walked to our next class together. I hadn't been concerned once we were together; there was no way I would run into Annemarie in any SP classes since she wasn't much of a student.

"I don't think that will be necessary, but thank you for the information," she said in a softer but still teacher-ish voice. Then she said, "I'm going to bring Annemarie in now and I want you and your mother to stay here while I talk to her, okay?"

I nodded and my mother said, "Good. I want to talk to her myself."

Miss Cara said, "Mrs. Neri, I understand how you feel, but I will do all the talking at first."

My mother nodded her assent but her eyes didn't soften a bit. When Miss Cara left, she squeezed my hand and told me not to worry, but I didn't feel reassured.

The guidance counselor returned a few minutes later with Annemarie following her into the room. I could see she had her usual smirk on her face and looked sneeringly at me, but her expression changed when she saw my mother sitting with me.

Miss Cara got a third chair for her and moved it to the short edge of the rectangular desk at the side near the wall and turned it so that Annemarie could look at her by turning her head left and at us by turning it right. She looked a bit uncomfortable squeezed into the meager space between the desk and the wall, and I began to breathe a little easier. My mother said nothing, just glared at her with that stare of hers that I thought could melt the arrogance and reserve of a seasoned criminal—the look that I felt was the facial equivalent of a slap delivered with unexpected force. If there were a scale for scary looks, this one would have been a 9.5 out of 10.

Miss Cara told her that although she hadn't been at our school for even a week she had already come to her attention, and that was not a good thing. She flipped through her files from the Catholic School she had attended and looked up at Annemarie as she read bits of it to herself and frowned.

Finally she said, "You are being accused of something serious here. You kicked and tried to push this girl (pointing at me like a prosecuting attorney) down the stairs. We don't take the safety of our students lightly and if you think you can bully anyone here, you are wrong. If you don't stay away from Rosemary, you are once again going to find yourself in another new school, where you will not be the toughest one in the class by a long shot. Do you understand me?"

Annemarie opened her mouth to say something, but looked up, turned her head right and, feeling my mother's stare, wisely decided to keep quiet. Instead, she nodded and looked at Miss Cara. From that point on, she kept her eyes averted from my mother's gaze as if the glare that was being emitted actually hurt her. I began to feel better.

"I also want to warn you that none of your 'friends' are to bother Rosemary in any way, either," Miss Cara continued. "If she has any problems at all with anyone touching her or even teasing her, I am going to call *you* in and hold *you* responsible. This is the situation you have made for yourself here and these are your new rules of behavior. Do you understand?"

For the first time since I had known her, Annemarie didn't smirk. She said, "I understand."

"Good. Now I think we can all go about our business," Miss Cara said. She looked at my mother and said, "Thank you for coming in to let me know about this and for letting the school handle this problem."

My mother nodded, shook Miss Cara's hand, and said, "Thank you for helping my daughter."

Miss Cara said to me, "Just go on about your business and keep studying and getting good marks."

I nodded in reply, sure under other circumstances, this would have been the cue for Annemarie to silently mimic the words that were said behind the adult's back while managing to threaten or belittle me at the same time. However, not this time. Not on my mother's watch.

We all stood up. Annemarie was the first out the door. My mother took my hand and almost pulled me behind her as I waved a small goodbye to Miss Cara. We were quickly out the front door and down the steps of the now nearly empty school, but my mother would not stop for anything as I paused to rearrange my books for the walk home. Instead, she raced ahead with me close behind her for half a block until she caught up with Annemarie at the traffic light on Avenue T and walked right up to her. She put her face right up close to hers and performed the amazing feat of speaking while it appeared her teeth were clenched shut in rage. She spoke in a voice similar to what I would later hear used by Mercedes McCambridge as the voice of the demon in the movie The Exorcist and hissed, "Stay away from my daughter and tell your friends to leave her alone too or you won't have to worry about any guidance counselor because *I'll* come after you *myself.* Now go home—and study for a change!"

All the kids I knew used to say a joke was a "pisser" because it made you laugh so hard that you felt you would wet your pants, and I had always found it to be a vulgar but apt description of the feeling of loosening of bladder control because of deep laughter. Now the term had a new application: my mother's warning to Annemarie was also a *pisser.* There was something so starkly vicious and personally malevolent about the tone she used and the intent behind it that I thought that tough little Annemarie would cry or pee herself in fear. I felt sorry for her for a moment, and then remembered what she had been like when she had tried to push me down the stairs and how much she had frightened me; I pushed my sympathy away, knowing that from this moment on, she would never scare me or make me feel bad about myself again. She had met her match and better in my mother, who constantly tried (and usually succeeded) in frightening me into obeying her about most regular day-to-day things. The irony was she had never, ever spoken to me with the voice she had used a few moments ago. What must Annemarie, who had provoked her anger beyond anything I had ever seen before, be feeling?

Our generation had been taught to respect and obey most adults and authority figures and, although Annemarie had never shown much inclination to do either in the past, I felt things would change for her at least a little in the future. Having met one adult who could match and even surpass her capacity for viciousness when provoked might mean there were others out there who could do the same. This knowledge would serve to sober even a cruel bully like her, whose only real talent was her ability to inflict scorn on others and make them feel afraid. Now that she had felt great anger inflicted on herself, she might be a little less inclined to think she would win every bullying contest she might engage in. Go Mom!

However, after witnessing this brief incident, I also felt like someone who had been given a brief but potent glimpse into another hellish universe and was happy to be returning to my own relatively unscathed. I also knew my mother had been on my side and this made me feel at once protected, confused, and frightened. I was delighted not to have to go to school every day worrying about what Annemarie would do to me, and happy my mother's rage had been directed toward a worthy subject, but the depth of that rage itself still frightened me as much as it had protected me. Hopefully, I would *never* do anything to have it directed toward me. This was the quintessential lesson I learned from the incident: never do anything that would make me the focal point of the anger that had been unleashed in my mother against Annemarie.

Yes, the problem had been solved for me, but the solution had also frightened me and I vowed to be increasingly cautious in my dealings with my mother from that point forward. This incident had been a lot more than a Mama Bear protecting her cub; I wasn't sure exactly what it was, but I was sure I wanted no part of it as a regular occurrence. In the weeks that followed, I found myself thinking about every interaction with my mother in terms of what I had witnessed with Annemarie. Aside from the usual day-to-day stuff (take out the garbage, do the dishes, pick up your clothes), I tried even harder than usual to discern what kind of behavior it was that would possibly set her off and came to some interesting conclusions about that.

First, I realized my mother had raced in to school to defend me from someone whom she viewed as a potentially serious physical threat to me—a threat that would normally unleash that primal, Mother Bear reaction in almost any woman. I knew there had been cases of women who had done incredible physical things, like lifting great weight to free a trapped child, when faced with a life-threatening scenario, but this hadn't been an immediate threat; I had managed to get away. This had been a case of my mother not wanting to worry about my safety every minute of the day when school was supposed to be a safe place—and it usually was in 1960 in Brooklyn—so part of it was the physical threat to me.

My mother had told me that, when she was growing up on the Lower East Side of Manhattan and went to school, all the children of Italian immigrants were at once warned and frightened by their mothers' stories of *La Cosa Nostra* and the *Mano Nero* (Italian for the Mafia and The Black Hand). The boys loved to frighten each other, and most especially the girls, by painting their palms with ink and leaving the imprint on the doors of the school bathrooms. My mother and the other girls had been warned by their parents *never* to accept a drink or food from anyone they didn't know, for fear of being drugged and taken into what they called "White Slavery" by the Black Hand. I knew slavery of any kind was wrong, but felt there was something else to this old story and only learned later how great a part of the puzzle of my mother's anger was the piece that dealt with physical safety.

I knew in my gut that the second part of her reaction to the incident had to do with sex and, more specifically, with Anna, not Annemarie.

My mother's eyes had been opened at the beach that past summer when she saw the interplay between Annemarie and Anna and I think she knew on some level, even though I hadn't said anything to her, that Anna was the one behind this incident. My mother disapproved of Anna, not just because she was "spoiled rotten" and got anything she wanted from her parents—from clothes to jewelry to participating in activities that were more appropriate for a grown-up, but more because she was voluptuous and sexually precocious.

When she was dressed up and wearing heels and makeup, Anna resembled a chubbier version of Bridget Bardot much more than she did a Catholic schoolgirl. The high heels and makeup alone were magnets for my mother's disapproval when worn by girls younger than seventeen, but combined with Anna's sneering and wise-beyond-her-years attitude toward life, she became actually repugnant to my mother, who liked to see my sister and I with more innocent and well-scrubbed friends like Marissa and her sister.

She told us often that fourteen year old high school freshmen (like Anna) had no business dressing like grown women, and would only attract the wrong kind of attention by looking like she did. And all those sex jokes that Anna loved to torture us with were exactly the kind of thing that would have sent my mother through the roof if she had heard them being told to her daughters.

Although I hadn't told my mother about my conversation with her about her birthday charm bracelet, she was smart and knew Annemarie merely played Igor to Anna's Dr. Frankenstein and would do anything she asked. She also knew they were bad individually and worse together, and that something must have happened between me and Anna that had made her my enemy in the exact meaning of that word as I saw it defined in *Webster's New World Dictionary*. I thought that it was even fitting that the etymology of the word showed that it was derived from the Latin–*in,* meaning "not", and *amicus,* meaning "friend." Anna was a non-friend and Annemarie had been her soldier. Part of me could imagine us all as ancient Romans dressed in togas, plotting against each other, mixing poisons and wearing a dagger under the fold of our clothes. However, Anna's side had not counted on my General Mom being able to take on both of them barehanded or even weaponless—more fools they!

My mother never asked me what had happened between Anna and me, but I felt she was happy to have an excuse to put some more distance between us, and this incident had served that purpose for her. She had never wanted me to be friends with her at all and had always been annoyed by the fact that we drew her as a next-door neighbor when we moved to West

5th Street. Now the goal of our enmity by proxy had been achieved, to her great relief, and we were estranged.

Not long after the incident at school, while doing some housework together, she said to me, "So I guess you won't be seeing much of Anna anymore, right?"

Although I had no desire at all to ever see or speak to Anna again, I felt immediately that this was exactly what she wanted and it annoyed me that she was subtly demanding my acquiescence to her will as the belated price for her intervention on my behalf.

I discerned immediately what she wanted my answer to the question to be and replied, "Why would I ever want to speak to her again? That creepy Annemarie did her dirty work when she tried to hurt me. Anna is the head creep and I can't stand her. She was never a friend of mine and I'm sorry she lives next door to us."

My mother looked at me, wanting me to continue and I obliged by telling her the story of my charm bracelet conversation with Anna that I thought had provoked Annemarie's actions. She nodded her head and appeared pleased to have had her suspicions about the real reason behind the incident confirmed. For her, this revelation could only add the last layer of cement to the wall between me and Anna, thus ensuring her wish to separate us, and thereby protect me, was fulfilled.

Relieved as I was about the resolution of the incident, it had caused me to upgrade the sensitivity of my emotional radar to prevent me from ever being the recipient of what I had seen Annemarie experience. Soon afterward, I had several dreams involving a big, hissing monster and couldn't tell whether it was Annemarie, Anna, or my mother hissing at me, so I resolved to avoid all three as much as possible. It was easier to do with the first two: Anna had gone to St. Brendan's for high school and Annemarie was in the regular track in school and not at all anxious to cross my path again. My mother was a different matter altogether, so I tried to fend off any potential attack by being, on the surface at least, who she wanted me to be. This entailed a lot of living inside my head, but I had become adept at that and sometimes preferred it.

I studied hard and got good marks that fall, even in math and science. I auditioned and got the part of the announcer when our class put on a production of the "rude mechanicals" scene from *A Midsummer Night's Dream* as a special evening assembly program before the Christmas holiday vacation break. I was proud to have been chosen by our English teacher, Miss Engel, for the part, since I had to introduce the scene, which had been written as a play within a play by William Shakespeare, as well as read the last lines of the play, originally written for the character of Puck, (who is also called Robin Goodfellow in the play) to wrap it all up for the audience:

If we shadows have offended,
Think but this and all is mended
That you have but slumber'd here
While these visions did appear.
And this weak and idle theme,
No more yielding but a dream,
Gentles, do not reprehend:
If you pardon we will mend.
And, as I am an honest Puck,
If we have unearned luck
Now to 'scape the serpent's tongue,

We will make amends ere long;
Else the Puck a liar call.
So good night unto you all.
Give me your hands if we be friends,
And Robin shall restore amends.

Our class had been assigned this important final assembly program of 1960 and our little production was chosen because it was one of the Bard's light comedic plays, and would be a positive introduction to Shakespeare for many of the other students who would be reading the play in the spring term.

As part of the larger plot, six comic Shakespearean characters: Peter Quince, Nick Bottom, Francis Flute, Tom Snout, Robin Starveling and Snug, the Joiner, had practiced to participate in the four days of festivities celebrating the wedding of their ruler, the Duke of Athens to Hippolyta, Queen of the Amazons, by presenting a short playlet. However, their farcical attempt to retell the sad story of Pyramus and Thisbe is so bad that it becomes one of the funniest scenes—in keeping with the lightness of the rest of the play. An important character, Puck, is a mischievous sprite and a trickster who magically replaces Bottom's head with that of a donkey's for the amusement of his master, Oberon, the King of the Fairies, but undoes the damage once everyone has had a good laugh. The whole feel of the play delighted me with its magical characters, whimsy and refusal to live in the serious part of life—a lively contrast to many of the Bard's more serious works.

The whole production was a lot of fun for me since I had wanted the part and I got along fine with the guys in my class who played Bottom, Quince, Flute, and the rest of the Rude Mechanics who put on the scene. Some of them had gone to PS 95 with me or were friends of the guys whom I knew, and Zazzi was not involved in any of it. Also, I didn't have to worry about a costume since my role as the announcer was done in my usual assembly day uniform of white blouse and blue skirt. Since I had to stay after school for rehearsals, and even went back in the evening for the run through before the performance, I had also found an acceptable way to spend more time at school.

My friends and I had a great time with all of the work involved in producing the show and everyone participated by helping sew costumes and decorating the scenery that would bring it all to life. We talked about little else, and as the day for the show drew closer, I realized my participating in the show had achieved my secondary goal of getting me away from home and my mother, for a legitimate reason. I felt freer at school, now that I had nothing to fear physically and was in my last year of junior high. Knowing I would graduate in June and go on with a lot of my friends to Lafayette High School for three years made the problems that I had initially encountered in my transition to the junior high school seem to have happened a long time ago.

Our assembly production went over well with both the audience, who were moved to laughter at the sight of the guys from my class playing the parts they were so well suited for, and the faculty who were pleased to see that we had "brushed up on our Shakespeare" so well. The biggest laughs were drawn by my old buddy Dom, who had been at the Highway Theatre with me and our sisters the day my father had clocked the usher. He had played the part of Thisby, the doomed female lead of the playlet, in a dress donated by someone's mother and a wig made out of a new white cotton woven mop head—the kind that most of us usually saw at home soaking in a toilet filled with Clorox bleach and water. His appearance alone was enough to make the kids in the audience laugh, but, when combined with the twinkle in his eyes, his appealing chubbiness and his falsetto voice and his clumsy movements, he stole the scene from everyone else and got a huge hand at the curtain call.

If everyone in our class and all our teachers were delighted by the quality of our production, I was also delighted to have learned by my participation that school could offer me a refuge from my home. I had previously enjoyed school, even with the challenges that I had faced at the beginning of the seventh grade, but now I saw it could have an even greater place in my life. From that point on, I looked for things to get involved in and for clubs to join. I eventually expanded my school experience well into the afternoon hours when I reached Lafayette High School the next fall and was eventually admitted to the staff of *The Marquis*, the school literary magazine as a contributor, a great honor for me.

I also discovered babysitting for pay. My experience with Markie-boy came in handy when I was asked to sit on a regular basis for our neighbors who lived in a large apartment above a store with its entrance almost directly across the street from us. The father of the family was a New York City Police Officer and I remember helping his wife when the youngest of their three little daughters ran into the street as she tried to get her groceries up the two flights to their apartment one day. I saw the little girl drift over toward the street as I was coming back from the store for my mother and instinctively went across to her and told her to wait for her mommy to come back before she tried to cross. Her mother hadn't even realized she wasn't walking up the stairs behind her until she turned around and she raced out the front door of the building to look for her.

She was so relieved to see her with me that she asked me if I liked to babysit and I was hired immediately. Thus began my experiences as the official sitter for the three Di Palma sisters, whom I grew to love almost as much as Markie. They all had huge brown eyes with dark lashes that Marissa and I would have paid a lot of money to get, and were only two years apart in age. Although the apartment they lived in was above a store, it was decorated much more lavishly than my parents', with thick rugs and pictures on the walls. You could see from looking at their furniture that it was expensive because the wood was so shiny and well cared for. I was a little intimidated at first, but Mrs. D. quickly put me at my ease and said she would like me to help her out while she was home for the first few times, so I could get to know where everything was in the apartment. Later, she could trust me alone, knowing that I was familiar with my surroundings. Also, she said she felt good about leaving me with three girls to care for because she knew my mother was right across the street in case of a problem that I couldn't handle alone.

Although this struck the wrong note with me, since I wanted so desperately to get away from her, it proved to be a good thing. About six months after I began sitting for the Di Palma's, Mrs. D. told me that they were going to have another baby; "hopefully, a boy this time." This news made me think about a lot of things.

I was comfortable with the girls; talking to them, feeding them dinner and even getting them to go to sleep was a pleasure and didn't feel like work. I never forced their assigned bed time on them, but just asked if they wanted to hear a story; then I'd read to them from *Little Women* or *Tom Sawyer*, two of my own favorites that I'd bring over to share with them. They'd say their prayers and I'd tuck them into their three twin beds in a row (like a real-life version of the three bears) and read aloud, stopping to answer all their questions about the story until they nodded off. Then I'd mark the place in the book for the next time and tiptoe out of the room.

Even after they were asleep, sitting in the apartment reading alone, in the glow of the fancy living room lamp made me feel grown up in a way that my own home never did. It made me think about a time when I would have my own apartment and pay my own way with nobody to tell me when I had to go to bed on the weekend. When Mr. and Mrs. D. returned, asked me how things had gone, and paid me and set the date for the next time I'd return, I'd always feel a little sad. As Mr. D. walked me across the street and waited for my father to open the door to my own house, I knew I didn't want to return to the reality of being the child when I had just gotten comfortable in the role of competent semi-adult. Sometimes I thought I should be paying the Di Palma's just for the way that sitting for them made me feel about myself, but I did take my pay.

As Mrs. D's belly got larger and the reality of the new baby drew closer, I also worried I'd be able to care for the infant and still be good to the girls, not realizing a lot of women pregnant with their second child have the same misgivings. When Markie-boy was tiny, Marissa and I had only served as mother's helpers and we hadn't been left alone with him unless he was asleep. I knew about bottles and burping and even changing diapers, but it wasn't hands-on, not my hands anyway. I decided to ask about what my responsibilities with the baby would be, but all of a sudden, he arrived. My mother got a call letting us all know the girls now had the baby brother everyone had hoped for. She looked at me seriously and told me that she thought it might be too much responsibility for me to care for him alone, just as I had feared. Perversely, her acknowledgment of my secret fears had the effect of making me want to care for him, and

I nodded my head in agreement while trying to figure out a way to get around her. I shouldn't have worried.

Mrs. D. talked to my mother and told her that for the first few months they would take the baby out with them when I sat for the girls, or else I'd go over and help while she was home, much as it had been with Markie-boy. My mother agreed this was a good idea, but added after a bit of time had passed, she would always be home to back me up with the baby if they wanted me to watch all four children. The world of mixed feelings swirled around me at this announcement: relief that I wouldn't be pushed beyond my comfort zone in caring for him alone, mixed with annoyance that my mother and Mrs. D. both agreed I wasn't ready for the solo care of a newborn. Then I started to help with the baby after school and the seesaw tilted into gratitude that my skills wouldn't be tested for a while.

While I got used to holding a newborn—support the head and neck in the crook of your arm, watch out for the soft spot on the skull, rock gently to soothe him—the girls were both delighted and disgusted with their new brother and let me know about all of their feelings. The youngest (my secret favorite of the three) eventually asked me if I thought her parents wanted her to be a boy and were disappointed in her. I didn't know what to say, so I told her that she was probably special to her parents because she was the closest to remembering what it had been like to be a baby. This answer delighted her and she decided to "help" them by playing baby and asking to be cuddled and given a pretend bottle. I told her that, at age five, that was all she could have, since she didn't want her friends to call her a "baby" and she accepted my rules, playing that she was learning to walk and talk. She got past that stage pretty quickly and went on to tell me that she loved to see her brother get his diaper changed and could help me any time I needed her to do so. Thanking her, I wondered what her motives were, but knew I would take any help I could get.

The first time I sat for all of them alone at night, when the baby was about four months old, I realized I needed a lot more help than the girls could give me. The Di Palma's had me over a half hour before they were due to leave so I could go over everything: how long to heat the bottle and how to test the temperature of the formula on my wrist, where the Desitin and pins for the diapers were, emergency phone numbers, etc. I became more nervous as she went along, but feigned calm. I was comfortable holding the baby when she was there, but still had my doubts about being alone. My mother had agreed to be by the phone at home if she was needed, but I didn't want to involve her in one of the activities that I felt prepared me for independence from her. I said good-bye to the parents with a smile on my face and a flutter in my stomach. Unfortunately, I wasn't alone in the stomach trouble department.

Everything went well until I had to give the baby his bottle. The girls had eaten a pizza dinner and helped me clean up the kitchen afterward. They even got into their pajamas and brushed their teeth with no problems as I heated up the bottle for the last feeding before the baby's bed-time. I picked him up and settled myself with him in the rocking chair in Mr. and Mrs. D's bedroom next to the crib. The girls came in and I told them that they could stay, but they had to be more quiet than usual and not ask me a lot of questions because I wanted the baby to be calm when I fed him. They did as I asked and he fed happily and finished the bottle in what felt like one big gulp. When I lifted him up over my shoulder to burp him, the problems began. He began to cry real screams and go rigid against me, as if something hurt him. I put him down into the crib and checked his diaper for open pins, but found nothing wrong so I picked him up and tried again with the same results. He screamed and arched his back away from me. I tried walking him and patting him gently and then a little more firmly, but nothing worked.

This continued for what must have been a few minutes, but felt like hours. Finally, as I tried unsuccessfully to comfort him, I asked the girls to get the phone number where their par-ents were. As they ran to the kitchen to find it, he exploded in a huge burp and then vomited up what looked like the whole bottle of formula onto my shoulder and immediately stopped crying.

I called his sisters back in with relief and told them to forget about the phone number, saying their brother just needed to burp and spit up a little, but all of them had all noticed what I had been too preoccupied to see.

"A little!"

"A burp!"

"That looks like throw up on the furniture!"

Behind me, on the front of the beautiful piece of furniture that stood taller than me was a line of thick, curdled white vomit. It slowly dripped down the front of the highboy like the residue of a volcanic eruption, slowly proceeding at its own pace and taking the finish off as it dripped down like slowly moving lava. I didn't know what to do first: change him, wipe off the vomit, or cry, but I gathered myself and asked the girls to get some paper towels and wipe the mess off carefully and try not to take off any more of the finish with the towel.

They immediately helped, but we saw from the first swipe of the paper towel that we were only making it worse, so I asked them to stop and we would show it to their parents when they got home. Then I put their brother onto his changing table and took off his vomit-soaked clothes and began to change his diaper. That was when the smell hit me. I had been too pre-occupied with my vomit-induced terror to notice the awful odor coming from the diaper but it hit all of us now. They all cried out in descending order of age:

"Yucch! A mustard poop!"

"Disgusting!"

"I don't want to help you with *this* diaper!"

I told them that they didn't have to stay in the room if they didn't want to and they all took me up on my offer, deserting me like people fleeing the sound of an oncoming missile. Now it was just me and the baby and the poop. I tried the best I could to clean him up, asking the oldest girl if she would stay with him while I got a warm, soapy washcloth ready to clean his bottom and she helped, since most of it was cleaned up by the time I called on her for assistance and because she was the most curious about how I would handle this situation.

The others drifted back in too, gingerly sniffing the air at the doorway to the bedroom before deciding to re-enter. When I got back with the washcloth, they all cooed at their brother and made him smile. I put some Desitin on his bottom and we changed him into a fresh, clean pair of footed pajamas, and all was right with our little world again—except for the highboy. I decided to worry about that later when their parents got home. In the meantime, I thanked the girls and told them that I would let them tell a favorite story when they were in their beds instead of reading to them that night. They were happy to get away from the scene of the vomit and climbed right into their beds and each told a fairy tale aloud. I sat holding the baby, who was now wide-awake and happy. We said goodnight after the last story and I wanted nothing more than to crawl into bed myself, but tossed them a kiss and went out with the baby in my arms.

I was still holding him an hour later when the Di Palma's returned. He was calm but cried whenever I'd tried to put him into his crib. Mrs. D. took him from me gently and thanked me for taking such good care of him, making me even more reluctant to tell them about the furniture and the vomit, but I did. They looked at their once-beautiful chest and sighed but didn't fire me, saying the baby's stomach had been full of acid. They said they would have to have the front refinished, but the baby was fine and that was what was important. I felt awful and told them I didn't want any money, but they insisted on paying me. As I walked home with Mr. D, I knew they wouldn't call me again to sit for the baby and I proved to be right. They didn't. In fact, they all moved to Staten Island to a one family house the following spring and I never saw them again.

And when my mother asked how everything had gone I told her what she wanted to hear:

"Fine, but I don't think I'll sit for the baby again."

She looked hard at my face, but couldn't discern any lies there, because, for once, what she wanted to hear was the essential truth.

Chapter 13

My Favorite Sin

I had been given the great gift of being born intelligent instead of beautiful. Although I didn't appreciate it until many years later, my intellect has proven a lifelong friend for which I am unfailingly grateful to the Lord. When I was almost thirteen, this fact was a truth I reluctantly came to see as inescapable, and I willed myself to think maybe having brains instead of beauty was a positive thing. I reasoned if I used my intellect, I would be able to improve my looks—after I made enough money—but trying to fix dumb was almost impossible. That was a truth I was strong enough to face and accept even if I still secretly longed to be good looking.

My birth family had a hard time with the truth, probably for generations before I was born. This problem was inevitably revealed whenever my sister and I wanted to know the true facts or circumstances surrounding the many family mysteries and tiny bits of secrets we always sensed and heard discussed in whispers around us. We were never privy to the real truth behind all the cryptic adult references to things we knew had an effect on us, but were never openly discussed in front of us, unless they were discussed *sotto voce* (in whispers) in Italian, which neither of us understood until we studied that beautiful language years later.

As a direct result of my aversion to any deliberate and unnecessary deceit, I've spent more than forty years of my adult life trying to rectify this familial failing for my own sake as well as that of my husband, children, and grandchildren who are now the future of my family. I've also become good at telling when someone is being deceptive with me, and always make it my business—especially in monetary matters—to demand clarity and honesty from anyone who is close to me or important in my life. I'm also good at spotting a big political lie, especially the ones that are repeated so often that many people come to accept them as the truth. I wouldn't have survived in Nazi Germany or the Soviet Union and would have been one of the first to flee.

* * *

When he questioned Jesus before reluctantly sentencing Him to crucifixion in order to avoid any civil unrest (which would reflect badly on his ability to rule his province as the representative of Caesar), Pontius Pilate asked, "What is Truth?"

We don't know with absolute certainty if he asked that big question sincerely or as a frustrated, cynical, and ambitious Roman official stuck in an inhospitable backwater, trying to govern an ungovernable populace. I suspect it was the latter reason; his famous hand washing is a huge tell. Even governors can have uncomfortable moments when conscience attempts to assert itself. Our family problem wasn't that dramatic, but incredibly persistent.

My family's issues concerning truth was an especially strong problem of my mother's and started to bother me when I was young. Her untruths were often mixed with my anger at her in a sticky and unpalatable concoction that I could hardly bear and would never swallow. I often felt like her lies could suffocate me and that made me want to scream, but instead of fighting for my right to breathe in the truth, I too learned to lie.

Although I don't remember my Granma Mary ever lying to me in the time she was with me, my memory has an indelible imprint of the big important falsities I heard my mother frequently try to pass off to us as truth. Foremost among these was the phrase: "But Rosemary, you know you're my shining star."

This infrequent but powerful refrain rang false in my head from the first time I heard it and she said it to me often enough for the words "shining star" to grate against my eardrums in an almost physical way–like the clanging of a loud alarm clock bell that rips you unwillingly from a calm, sweet sleep in the early morning hours. Maybe it was the use of those two "s" words following each other like twin snakes which sent my blood pressure soaring up as high as my potent but hidden anger. Whatever the reason, that particular phrase—which no one else ever used with me— always sent my personal lie detector needle off the chart. The reasons for my visceral reaction weren't at all complicated.

First, the phrase was often used after I complained about a privilege or a material thing that my sister or my friends had which was being specifically denied to me by my mother. Second, it was usually accompanied by a casual and trivializing brush of her hand against my head of short-cropped hair, which I'd had no say in styling.

Most important, the tone in which it was said always matched what my sister and I called her phony-mommy voice; a cloyingly sweet and soft tone we seldom heard in her genuine everyday conversations. This tone was reserved for two purposes only: either to convince someone of her sincerity when she was actually being deceitful, or else when she was simply indulging herself by speaking theatrically.

Whenever we heard this tone in her voice my sister and I would secretly make eye contact and mimic sticking our fingers down our throats as if we wanted to induce vomiting, in a pantomime of our Ancient Roman ancestors' practice of using the *vomitorium* so they could return to the banquet and eat more.

Our purpose, however, was to show how repellant her tone was, not to make room for more of her tainted food. Even if we were in another room we could both visualize her unsuccessful imitation of Doris Day at her most optimistic and sunny with that vocalization (a tone we knew to be as different from her real voice as was possible) as if she were acting as her own ventriloquist. We both found it at once creepy and ridiculous, a perverse combination that summed up its effect on us. We knew her real self too well to be fooled and we hated her phony-mommy voice whenever we heard her use it with others or us. It was like listening to a bad actress who has taken on a role that was way beyond her range, seeking to substitute blatant theatricality for missing talent. My sister and I found her substitution of inflection for veracity unpalatable and we were never fooled by it.

Lies are untruths, or things said, which are the *opposite* of truth, and are they are usually told for a reason, large or small. They are often employed to bring yourself out of an embarrassing situation: such as hurting a chubby friend who asks, "Do you think I look heavier in this dress? Like I gained weight?"

But more often, my sister and I had found our mother lied just to keep things easy for herself. For example, she would have a stock answer for a neighbor who might unexpectedly invite us to go along with their family on an excursion: "Oh, we'd love to, but we have something that weekend."

It could be anything from visiting a non-existent relative in upstate New York to an appointment with a doctor, whatever came to her mind to get out of it would do, and she always had an answer ready. Sometimes my sister and I would try to guess what she'd say if we even thought a conversation with a casual acquaintance would lead to another fruitless invitation to "get together."

Her frequent lies led me to understand why there are laws in many civilized countries that prohibit lying under oath in trials and have severe penalties for people who do this and thereby commit perjury. In our childhood, we had no such law in our family and my sister and I both suffered emotionally in its absence. In numerous instances, when we tried to express to our mother how not being listened to in a conversation about a grievance, or to tell her the reason for not being allowed to do something had upset and angered us, her default response was almost always to deny our feelings right to our faces. She would say we had "misunderstood" her or we couldn't understand her words. No matter what, she always tried to make us believe the reason why we had these feelings was due to *our* poor perception and inability to understand *her*. The actual problem was we *did* understand and none of our feelings were false, especially in reaction to how unjustly we were often treated.

As I was to learn much later in therapy, her obvious and annoying use of the mechanism of *denial*—or telling yourself that what is occurring or has happened is not going on or never even happened—is an emotionally primitive one. It's easier for the young child to think that a negative experience such as a physical or verbal slap never occurred, rather than face the fact that a beloved adult is capable of cruelty or impulsiveness or other human failings. Although often a negative trait in later life, *denial* often starts when we are little and trying to maintain our mental balance when faced with two irreconcilable facts: Mommy or Daddy loves me, but Mommy or Daddy hurt me. While my sister and I never knew until later in our lives what caused her to be so deceitful, we did know, especially as we progressed into adolescence, that our mother was a champ at lying herself out of anything and then shoving the fault for any problems right back onto us.

Denial defended our mother from having to admit to herself or to others that life is often difficult, ugly, and inconvenient. Her way of coping was to push away that reality and lie to herself for her own comfort or self-protection. This continued throughout her life, rarely recognized by herself, but evident in her behavior toward us.

As a teenager however, my immediate concern was not to find out why my mother's favorite response was "no" or even to discover why she denied my feelings. My goal was to get out of the house and enjoy my own life like my friends were, so when necessary, I learned to lie even better than my mother did. Going out with my friends to do some shopping was usually allowed, so I did a lot of that. My babysitting money soon became a key to unlock the front door of my house. Movies were good too, sometimes accompanied by my sister, but often with my friends and usually in the afternoon when it was cheaper. Once, when I went to see a cheesy vampire movie (*not* released by Hammer Films) whose previews had featured the brides of Dracula wearing low-cut, sexy shrouds, I told my mother that I was going with my friends Marissa and Tina to see Please Don't Eat The Daisies starring: Doris Day! I actually did and do like Doris Day and feel she wasn't properly recognized for her singing, dancing, and acting abilities as well as for being the survivor of a hard life of her own. She brought a lot of joy to many people and, as she got older, also chose not to give into bitterness, but to do good instead. The goal of my deliberate lies, which often contained a perverse kind of private joke like the Doris Day reference, was to give myself the freedom, which I increasingly had to fight to achieve.

Lying came easily to me and made me feel I had finally found a way to break free physically just as my friends had done. My simple goal was to get outside and away into the world for a little breathing time without my mother hovering over me—emotionally or physically—and trying to micromanage and alter my life so it matched hers perfectly, like a crazed dressmaker who only produced garments from the same pattern while disregarding her clients' actual needs and wishes. I was sick of being told how to save my babysitting money, or spend my time as well as hearing the warnings about "men" that she continually chanted in lieu of giving us real information about sex.

"Watch out for any man who tries to be too friendly to you; you never know what's in his mind," was often repeated until we were sick of hearing it and didn't listen anymore. We both had good instincts about people and hated the perpetual lectures when we knew we could spot a con man a long way off. Hell, we lived with her, didn't we?

It was a while before I pieced together the real reason behind my mother's strong reluctance to discussing any information about sex with my sister and me, and by that time I had distanced myself so far from her emotionally that it was possible for me to intellectually understand while keeping my feelings about it locked up safely. I don't think that if I had this information earlier it would have made a difference in my attitude toward her, though. When you feel you are being unjustly imprisoned, all you want is to get out and be free.

I resented her stingy attitude toward giving us other information as well. To the entire family's annoyance, she was always talking to a particular friend named Martina, whom she worked with, on the phone after dinner. Their chats sometimes went on for as long as an hour and my father frequently had to tell her to get off because she'd see her friend the next day at work and he or my sister and I needed to use the phone. When he did that, she'd cut off the conversation quickly and then complain she hadn't wanted to stay on the phone that long. We'd all figuratively roll our eyes at her disclaimer since she had usually been talking animatedly about some incident or other at work. My sister and I usually tried to listen in on these chats since the main phone was in the kitchen where we were usually busy doing the dishes after dinner.

Sometimes, we'd hear enough snippets of the conversation to become active eavesdroppers because it was interesting to get a glimpse into her work life, where we felt a great deal of her real life occurred. We knew, unlike our friend's mothers, she had *always* worked, that was why our Granma Mary had been our real mother figure until she passed away when I was eight and my sister Alice was five. After reacting to that unexpected loss with a near mental breakdown and lingering grief, my mother tried staying home with us until my sister entered first grade the next fall, but that wasn't for her.

She applied for and was accepted as one of the New York City Board of Education's original lunch aides in the newly instituted school lunch program. From her point of view, it was an ideal part-time job, with low pay, but mother's hours of 10:00 am-2:00 pm She traveled on the Sea Beach subway line not far from our home to an elementary school in Coney Island, which was deemed an area where most kids lived in families below the poverty level and qualified for the free lunches offered by the new program. She worked those four hours a day in the cafeteria of a school where the kids were poor, like she had been as a child, and she enjoyed feeding those children, often telling us how she'd sneak a second milk or sandwich to a hungry kid she'd gotten to know. We felt through this job she saw how far she had come in her life.

She always told us how the ladies all took home or gave away the leftover food at the end of the day instead of throwing it away as they were instructed to do.

"How stupid is that—to throw away perfectly good food!" she'd tell us indignantly.

"They hired us to feed the kids and then tell us to throw away the leftover food! What a waste!"

These sentiments of hers were usually expressed to my sister and me as she unloaded the extra sandwich halves wrapped in waxed paper and half-pint cartons of milk from her tote bag and transferred two sandwich halves and a milk container each into brown paper bags for our own lunches the next day. My sister and I *hated* that she insisted we eat the leftover "welfare" food scraps as our own lunches and resented that she had figured out how to choose work over us once again and had also managed to feed us on the scraps she got from that work. My father didn't like it either-he'd tell her that he made enough money at the Navy Yard to afford real food for our lunches, not leftover "government crap." But he didn't make our lunches as he often worked the 4:00 am-12:00 pm shift at the Brooklyn Navy Yard to make extra money for his overnight work when there was a deadline to finish a ship in time to be commissioned, so she won again.

When we complained to her that the other kids asked us where we got the milk in the same containers as the school gave out with snacks, and asked us why our sandwiches (usually surplus American cheese or the hated peanut butter) were on brown, funny-looking, and tasted like day-old whole wheat bread which carried the smell of the school cafeteria in it, she'd glower at us and reply, "Those kids and you were never hungry and besides, they don't pay for your food, Daddy and I do, so tell them to mind their own business."

If we persisted in telling her that we hated the taste of the bread or the peanut butter, and Dad did too, she'd get angry and tell us that we were spoiled and end it by writing our names on the lunches and putting them into our old Kelvinator fridge, which our dad had repaired several times. Then the only thing we could do was hope for another refrigerator breakdown that spoiled all the food, and if that made us spoiled, who cared!

* * *

If my sister and I heard a snippet of conversation between her and any friend from work, usually Martina, we had to behave as if we weren't listening to anything she said, just washing and drying the dishes and pots from dinner while listening to our transistor radio in the background as we worked. By this time, when we were responsible for meals and cleanup, our mother worked at the Brooklyn Army Base (housed at that time below the Brooklyn Queens Expressway in lower Bay

Ridge) as a statistical typist copying long columns of numbers with great accuracy and tallying them with precision using only a manual typewriter, a process that also demanded great mathematical ability in the days before computers, which she also learned to use at age eighty when she still worked part-time at Brooklyn's Fort Hamilton.

This more professional job was now her full-time work and provided her with paid leave and benefits in addition to a good pension, like our father. She was aware this made her his equivalent in earning ability and never felt shy about saying that to him when they argued about a purchase or a vacation, a fact that we knew hurt him (because of the way she said it) even if, for once, she told the truth.

Since I was old enough now to walk my sister to and from school and had even learned a few cooking skills, I was happy to be able to start preparing dinner, with a few suggestions from our father, who had always wanted to become a chef. I felt proud that the quality of our meals improved as I learned to cook. Now free to explore cooking, I went to the library and looked up and copied recipes for meat loaf, fried chicken, and other simple meals that could easily be put together by a beginning cook like me.

Although I didn't think it was fair for me to have to cook and clean up afterward, my sister usually helped and we'd listen to the WMCA

"Good Guys" on the radio as we did the kitchen work; it was almost fun and became even more fun when we could hear part of our mother's phone conversations regarding what went on at her job. A lot of their conversations focused on their immediate supervisor, whom they both loathed.

"If he were a woman he would have been fired years ago... They only keep him on because he's so busy kissing Mr. A's butt and selling A's daughter's Girl Scout cookies," were common complaints that we overheard.

My father said that wasn't true, though, that he couldn't be fired easily at all. He also said her boss was a "typical" civil service worker who got paid for showing up and not messing anything up too badly. When we didn't understand what he meant, he showed us an example of this on an episode of I Love Lucy where Lucy needs to get a passport before a trip to Europe and gets to the office late. The guy behind the counter gives her a hard time because it's close to 5:00 pm, when he goes home, no matter who needs his help. After Lucy begs him to help her, gets her passport approved and is leaving, her friend who had accompanied her plugs in the office clock (that has read two minutes to five for the entire episode) and waves goodbye to the angry and now chagrined clerk. We all laughed and my sister and I understood what our father meant; from then on, we could usually spot a person with that kind of attitude, whether it was in a government office or elsewhere.

Our only question was, if the difficulty of firing the guy was true, why did they have to talk about it and complain almost every night? After thinking about this, I realized they were on the phone about the most important part of their day: their time at work. Little incidents would be rehashed in these conversations and gossip exchanged, and woe to us if my sister or I asked too many questions about their secretly monitored discussions. Even away from it, her work life had the same pull on our mother and her friend that home life had on many of my friend's mothers, who constantly discussed with each other how to get out stains on clothes or where to buy the cheapest chicken cutlets on sale.

It was like a light bulb went on in my brain when I understood that. My mother tried to do the 1960 equivalent of "having it all"—husband, children, house, and career—in reverse order of importance to her. But why was that? Why weren't my father, sister, and I enough for her? To answer that question, I had to get past the lies and dig out the truth. Although I was only a young teenager, I had some of the answers already and would gather the rest as I went along in life I reasoned, not suspecting at that moment in time that some of those answers would be supplied through my first reading of one of my all-time favorite novels, *A Tree Grows in Brooklyn* by Betty Smith.

* * *

The first time I read Betty Smith's most famous work was during that summer of 1960 before I returned to ninth grade in junior high and it wasn't originally for pleasure, but rather as part of a school assignment. I needed to prepare for an oral book report for my English teacher; all the 9SP students would be required to give reports on their summer reading in the first week of school when we returned from vacation. I had chosen the book before school ended in June on the recommendation of my friend, Tina Carcioffi, who had loved the story. Since we usually had similar tastes in books, I impulsively wrote it in on my summer assignment sheet on her say-so.

So, on a rainy day before we left for our family vacation at the Twin Lakes house, I took a walk to the local library with my friend Marissa, who also had to do a summer reading assignment. She had to read science fiction or mystery for her report, which could be written before school resumed since she was a year younger and would only be entering eighth grade at our junior high school in September. I tried to urge her to read some *Sherlock Holmes* stories, but she opted for a *Nancy Drew* mystery, afraid if the book consisted of different stories, it wouldn't be accepted as a novel and she'd have to do a makeup report in the hectic first week or two of school.

"I'm better off safe with *Nancy Drew* than buried with work because the teacher's picky," was her philosophy and I agreed with her logic. No one wanted to start off on the wrong foot with a teacher after you had done the reading assignment, unlike a lot of our classmates who'd rush to Taverna's to buy the *Classics Illustrated* comic book of a novel the day before school resumed and use it to write a crappy one page report to hand in on the first day back.

We got our books and stopped at the pizzeria on the way back to relax and talk and glance through the books before returning home. That was when Marissa told me that she was also leaving for two weeks' vacation at her grandfather's house on Long Island and we both promised to read a bit and tell each other the stories of our novels when we returned. We also agreed to get together to see a movie, hopefully without our little sisters, before school began again. I didn't know it then, but by the time I saw Marissa again, I'd have some of the important puzzle pieces put together and be a lot closer to figuring out the why's of my mother's behavior and also understanding more than I wanted to comprehend, thus joining the Too Much Information Club when it came to my mother.

As usual, I dove into the book as soon as I got home from the library and was immediately caught up in the story of Francie Nolan and her family which, despite taking place in a different Brooklyn neighborhood back in the days of my Granma Mary's youth, had a great many things in common with my own life. Looking back and remembering my love for that book, I believe I decided to try to be a writer partly as a result of reading about the real and yet symbolic Brooklyn tree, the *Ailanthus*, which is also called "The Tree of Heaven," from which the author derived her title.

Although it is denigrated by the National Invasive Species Center (NISC) on their website and is described as a member of an invasive species that "damages pavement and building foundations in urban areas," I admire and respect the *Ailanthus* species, which I think of as the "Jesus" tree. To paraphrase Betty Smith, it pushes itself up through the concrete and insists on living defying any and all efforts to permanently eliminate it. If it is cut, it reasserts itself, regrows even stronger than before and goes on living in even the harshest of city conditions. It provides shade and even hope for the poorest people who know no other greenery. In short, it recapitulates the divine within the human spirit, which will not be crushed by even the worst physical conditions or human dictators.

That book and its tree gave me hope, because Francie Nolan had it worse than I did and still succeeded, but the novel also inadvertently taught me a lot about one of the reasons for my mother's often unfathomable behavior. In one of the chapters, Smith describes how the Nolan family lives on the top floor of a tenement apartment rent-free because the mother, Katie, acts as the super of their multi-family building, keeping the stairs swept and mopped and tending to the garbage for collection in addition to many other backbreaking duties. Their family is poor and in reduced circumstances due to the father's alcoholism and his consequent inability to hold a job, so the mother takes up the slack as best she can, and proudly keeps both her two children and the building clean.

Mama Katie also continues the habit, encouraged by her own mother, Grandma Mary Rommely, of having both children read one page each night from a work by Shakespeare and another page from the Bible as she had done before they were able to read on their own. This reminded me of my mother's practice of reading to my sister and me aloud from a book we chose (that she approved of) in the summer before bed. It was one of the nicest things I remember about her relationship with us and the similarity of these reading experiences endeared this book to me even more.

Although poor, Francie lives in an innocent and safe and mostly loving family, but her world is eventually threatened by the dark presence of a predator in their area of Brooklyn when a rapist/murderer is known to be on the loose in their neighborhood. Although she has just turned fourteen, had begun to menstruate, and knew about the facts of life from her mother, Francie was still innocent of the most brutal aspects of life in a poor city neighborhood.

A rapist is on the prowl but, due to the shame of the neighbors at the nature of his crimes, and the inability of the police to catch him his presence isn't broadcast until an innocent seven year old girl is found assaulted and murdered in the basement of a nearby tenement home. Everyone is terrified and knows he will try to strike again. Since he is away working at night when he can manage to get a job as a singing waiter, Francie's father, Johnny, borrows a gun from his night watchman friend and, warning his family not to ever touch it, saying: "This little cylinder holds death in it for five people."

They listen to him and he keeps it under his bed pillow as a safety precaution and trusts only Katie to know it is there. Time passes and a lot of people forget about the predator, but one day, while her mother takes a break from cleaning and is having an afternoon cup of coffee at home, Francie is attacked by the pedophile while climbing the stairs in the dark vestibule hallway entrance on her way up to her apartment after school. He grabs her around the neck and is choking her into silence while dragging her down the stairs to the basement with his pants already unbuttoned when her mother manages to come down the stairs just in time. She had walked down the stairs to look for Francie and had seen the murderer go for her child. Without thinking, she ran quietly back up to their apartment to get the gun, which she held under her apron with both hands, aimed directly in front of her. When he sees her, the killer reluctantly lets Francie go and tries to slink toward the basement stairs, but Katie shoots him right where his pants are open, leaving "blood ... all over that part of him that had been worm-white" and filling the narrow hallway with smoke.

The shot draws the neighbors out of their apartments, screams are heard and the hallway soon fills with people. Her mother, reacting in terror to what might have happened to her daughter, grabs Francie and pulls her up the steps, taking her up into the safety of their apartment. Still in shock, she asks Francie if he hurt her; she replies he didn't, but says, "it ... touched my leg" and says she can still feel it and she wants her leg cut off. When her father and brother return to the apartment through the fire escape, due to the crowds and police in the hall, and Johnny ascertains Katie has saved Francie with the gun and has "shot him good," Francie cries out to him to please cut off her leg because she can still feel where it touched her. He replies kindly that he'll take care of it and swabs the exact spot on her leg with carbolic acid. Francie welcomes the burning pain and feels "the evil of the man's touch was being seared away" by her beloved father's kind attention and his understanding that drastic measures had to be taken to keep her safe and help sear away the horrifying memory of what occurred.

At that moment, a firm knock on their door and the announcement that it's the police with a doctor interrupts the moment and Johnny lets them in. The Nolan's learn the killer will live and is going to the electric chair for the other little girl's murder and two more that he confessed to the policeman in the ambulance. Katie replies to this information that she's sorry she didn't kill him and says, "I meant to kill him". When the policeman announces he will probably be promoted due to the confession, she replies at least someone will get something good from all of this.

The doctor attends to Francie's chemical burn on her leg and tells her that he's going to give her something to help her sleep and when she wakes up it will be like a bad dream that's over. The next morning, Johnny is there to comfort her and tell her exactly that: it was a bad dream and it's over and she's safe now. Her mother has to attend a hearing and her father is fined five dollars for having a gun without a permit, but afterward, life goes on for them almost as it had before. Francie's only physical reminder is the scar, which fades over time to the size of a dime, along with any fears related to the incident that ended well for her.

For her mother, however, the damage is done: their family's safety is now in question because of where they are forced to live and she feels her husband's inability to support them due to his alcoholism has led the family to a near disaster. She has been forced to save her daughter from a horrible fate and, although she still truly loves him, she can't forgive Francie's father for his weakness and inability to stop drinking. A while after the incident, Katie is paid a visit by Sergeant McShane, a kindly neighborhood police officer who had asked Francie if Katie was her mother after the shooting. He finds her hauling a can full of ashes from their building to the curb and tells her that the local cops have taken up a collection for the Nolan family due to Katie's help in closing the pedophile killer case. She thanks him, but refuses to take the money, knowing it was from him, but thanking him politely. She knows McShane, who is over twenty years her senior, has a wife who is dying of tuberculosis in a sanatorium and she is attracted to him because of his kindness and steady nature in spite of herself. Although she has rebuffed his offer, she calls after him as he leaves to resume his police work: "I hope someday you'll be as happy as you deserve to be, Sergeant." The wish was also for herself.

* * *

When my mother saw my head buried in yet another book, she asked me what I was reading and I explained it was for an oral report on the first day of school. She said if I liked, she would read from it aloud to me and my sister, and I agreed. We enjoyed the novel all together as we had enjoyed *Little Women* and several other books. However, as the reading progressed, and we got to the part about the shooting, something happened. Our mother looked upset, almost like it happened to us instead of being an upsetting scene in a book about a poor girl's life.

She stopped reading and said that was enough for the night, leaving us lying on our side-by-side twin beds, once again not understanding what our mother had done and why. All we knew was our happy time together reading and listening had come to an abrupt end. She had gotten up from her chair between the two beds, kissed us on our foreheads and left our room without a word of explanation. My sister and I looked at each other, shrugged our shoulders, and picked up our comic books and movie star magazines and read by ourselves until we got tired and went to sleep.

The next day, when we got up, I went looking for my book. My sister went right to our mother and asked her what had happened to make her stop reading to us. Our mother looked at her for a long time and said, "Nothing special. I just realized that book wasn't appropriate for you. You're too young to read it."

"But I liked it," Alice protested, "and anyway, Rosemary's older than me and she should at least be allowed to read it."

"She can," our mother said, "but silently and only to herself, certainly not aloud at bedtime when you especially need to have nice things in your heads before you go to sleep."

"But I want to know the story and find out what happened to Francie," she persisted.

"Not yet. Maybe in a year or two. Not now. The discussion is closed."

And that was it. She gave me back the book and made me promise not to tell my sister about it, especially not the part about what happens to Francie in the hallway. I promised I wouldn't and ran off to read it myself, more curious than ever now. She had read other scenes where Francie and her brother, Neely, got into trouble playing with rubber things that her Aunt Sissy gave them and dangling them out the window. I didn't know why, but I knew that scene had to do with sex and she had read it to both of us.

The beginning of the chapter about the shooting even told about an unwed mother and her baby and she had read that part. What was so horrible that we couldn't hear about it before bed, especially my sister, who was prone to nightmares?

After I finished reading, I knew it was a scary scene, but in my twelve-year-old innocence, I didn't understand why Francie had wanted her own leg cut off at first. Although I knew I was skating on thin ice, I resolved to ask my mother. But before I could, I got a phone call from Marissa inviting me to go over to her house for lunch and forgot about it for a while.

When I returned later, my mother was alone in the kitchen cutting up vegetables and I went to the table and started to help her. She immediately asked me if I had read the chapter and I told her I had. She looked at me seriously and said in a low voice, "Then you understand now why I'm always worrying about you and your sister and tell you to be careful around men and won't let you go to sleepovers, right?"

I stared at her, more confused than I had been before.

"Not really," I said in a tiny voice.

She looked at me and said, "So I have to spell it out for you?! What was in that book happened to *me* when I was five years old and Granma Mary was washing the floor and left the front door open. I wandered out in the hall and a man was there and took my hand and walked me up to the stairs near the roof and pulled down my underpants."

She stopped and looked at me, pausing for a moment before going on.

"Granma missed me and ran up the steps and found us before it was too late, but he was *bad*! She screamed when she saw us and kept screaming out loud; he ran up to the roof and disappeared. When she told my father, Grandpa Rocco decided to move us away from that neighborhood. We came to live in Brooklyn, but Grandpa was a lot older than Granma and he couldn't take the strain of the subway steps on his heart. He died six months after we moved. That's why I'm so careful of you and your sister. Understand?"

I didn't, but knew I was supposed to, so I just nodded my head. Then I asked, "I understand, but what does this have to do with sleepovers?"

"If you have to ask me that, you don't understand! There are a lot of bad men out there and they can be anywhere. I'm not letting you go anywhere overnight unless it's with Dad and me."

I knew enough to shut up after that, but my mind and heart were racing. I had to simultaneously process what my mother had just told me and also figure out why this made her so mean when she said she wanted only to protect my sister and me. Did Dad know about all this? Did he agree with her about the way she scared us about men, didn't explain anything, and then told us too much? She said it was to protect us, but we didn't know what it was from.

All I understood from what she said was that her being attacked by this man caused them to move to a safer place and then her father died because of it. Maybe she felt responsible for that or for wandering out of their apartment and letting the man grab her in the first place. I was now the President of the Too Much Information Club and I had to figure it all out on my own.

I did share some of what she told me with my sister, the part about living in a tenement like Francie and being scared in the dark hallway. I didn't want to know the other stuff myself so I certainly wasn't going to share it with my little sister. Of course, she asked my mother about living on the Lower East Side and being scared of the dark hallway. When my mother found out from her question that I had been talking about this with Alice, she glared at me and told her that it wasn't scary at all, just not as nice as where we lived now. This method of coping, to deny the truth and manipulate facts was what had hurt me as it protected her. I learned then that trying to control or change the truth with lies was futile and destructive. Feeling that fiery anger from her stare, I realized my favorite sin was also my mother's.

Chapter 14

The End of the Beginning

A lot of Americans who were of the age of reason on November 22nd, 1963 will tell you that the 1950's ended on that day, when our collective innocence and sense of well-being were shattered by the bullets that assassinated President John F. Kennedy in Dallas, Texas. They symbolically hit us all as they turned that sun-filled day into a long night that cast a shadow not just over our country, but the whole world. The dark events of that day have never completely stopped obscuring our view of the sunlight, making our country and its people a bit more cynical and mistrustful in their wake.

On that morning, I was in the hallway of Lafayette High School, going from one class to another, when I heard people saying someone had shot the President. This rumor unnerved me enough to make me wonder out loud just why and how the president of our school and government, whom I knew personally, could have been singled out for this previously unthinkable violence. None of us had never even heard the words "guns" and "Lafayette High School" used in the same sentence before.

I realized later (after listening to a friend's transistor radio, and understanding everything was even more awful than I had imagined) that my horror and innocent misunderstanding were products of my refusal to give up the last tiny parts of my childhood, which had stubbornly lingered in my soul like unconfessed venial sins. After the teacher in my next class set up a small black and white TV set for us to watch instead of doing our lesson, I finally understood what had occurred and felt a kind of numb fatalism about it.

The horror of the events that would unfold there brought me back to another time when I had reluctantly been pulled out of my childhood by a giant unseen hand, and unwillingly thrust into the land of adulthood, where no one—even those you loved the best—lived forever.

For me, the end of the fifth decade of the twentieth century actually had come on Monday, December 19, 1960. That day was only a month and change after JFK had narrowly defeated Richard Nixon, but before Kennedy had even been inaugurated as President of the United States. The present generation, still clinging to their hanging chads, is mostly ignorant of the fact that the election of 1960 was actually the closest one in American history. Its outcome had been so impossible to predict that my favorite magazine, *Mad*, had published a pre-election issue with two "front" covers, one on the front and one on the back. One read: "Mad Congratulations Richard Nixon!" and the other front cover read: "Mad Congratulations John F. Kennedy!"

To the delight of its mostly adolescent readers, the editors of *Mad* encouraged us to hold up whatever front cover was applicable in the aftermath of this too-close-to call election. The usually gentle but unfailingly truthful comic stance of this wonderful publication went a long way in helping me learn that the increasingly complicated absurdity of life could be a source of laughter as well as frustration, if your angle of perception was correctly skewed.

Brooklyn was already in need of whatever laughter it could muster up on that cold December Monday six days before Christmas. We had already had a significant amount of snow and we all feared it would be an unusually cold and icy winter, thus making life especially hard for my father and my uncle Dom, who had both been working steadily on the almost completed *USS Constellation* at the Brooklyn Naval Shipyard.

With the work on the ship about eighty-five percent done, according to their reckoning, they were at least able to work mostly inside the metal structure during the icy weather, and not outside, exposed to all the elements as they had been during other winters, when I had listened to them exchange stories about the best way to stay warm. Their stories usually included what kinds of foods to eat (spicy) and, how to dress (in a lot of layers with long johns).

My father had a friend at work who was originally from Jamaica in the West Indies, and he swore eating a Bermuda onion raw like an apple would ensure you didn't feel the heat or cold as badly. Dad so far had never tested his friend's advice, but it stuck in my mind as I considered what it must have felt like to be forced to work in conditions so cold or hot that you'd change your diet in an attempt to counteract the weather's effects on your body.

Others had not been so lucky as my father and uncle, who we thought were safe working inside, and away from any dangers related to the cold. On the previous Friday, December 16th, a United Airlines DC-8 carrying seventy-seven passengers and a TWA Constellation carrying fifty-one people had been simultaneously crossing a fog enshrouded New York City, with the TWA plane headed for Cleveland, Ohio. The two planes, which appeared only as blips on the respective radar screens at LaGuardia and Idlewild Airports, had suddenly lost all contact with both the respective airports, whose less sophisticated equipment couldn't accurately register how close the planes were to each other in those last crucial moments before all communication ceased.

We later learned the planes had collided in mid-air, with the DC-8 plowing right into the TWA Constellation and tearing off one of its own wings as a result of the collision. The Constellation then crashed into Miller Army Field on Staten Island, killing everyone on board, but miraculously, not hitting anyone on the ground. The pilot of the DC-8 had tried to guide his crippled plane toward LaGuardia airport, or more likely, to nearby Prospect Park, but only made it as far as Seventh Avenue and Sterling Place in Park Slope before crashing into the street of this densely populated Brooklyn neighborhood.

Sections of the plane and debris fell along the street, destroying cars and businesses, as well as killing eight people on the ground. The resulting fire from the crash also destroyed a church, burning it to the ground and killing its caretaker. We were all shocked to hear of the utter destruction and I was filled with a more sober sense of the bizarre (finely tuned from reading *Mad* magazine) when I learned from the newspaper that the church had been called "The Pillar of Fire." Yet, my contemplation of the comical absurd was abandoned immediately when I learned the only survivor of the 128 passengers on both planes was an eleven-year-old boy. He had been thrown from the plane and was found by a rescue worker lying on the snowy street, screaming and badly burned with both legs broken.

I remember praying for him when I read the story, partly because he was the only survivor, but mostly because he was only eleven, two years younger than me and older than my sister—like a middle step between us—a would-be cousin or brother. On Saturday, when we learned he had died because his lungs had been so damaged by the fire and smoke of the crash, I hoped all the prayers for him had carried him to heaven and I cried for this boy we didn't know who would never grow up now. His untimely death was simultaneously unbelievable and scary; eleven-year-old boys weren't supposed to fall from the sky, thrown out of a plane so badly burned that they couldn't breathe anymore.

No one in my family, except for my father and my uncle, had even been on a plane until their first flights on transport aircraft during World War II. I wondered why this boy was alone on a plane, and how his parents must have felt. Would they have to fly here themselves to get him and bring him home? How would they be able to stand what had happened to him and keep on living? I had no answers for any of my questions, but all of them and more were discussed back and forth with my friends at lunch and even in classes at school that Monday after the planes crashed. Anything our teachers had to teach us shrunk in size compared with the significance of this horrible thing that had happened in Brooklyn, my home borough.

Even though it hadn't occurred in our neighborhood, the horrible photos in the newspapers had shown an area of businesses and buildings that didn't look too terribly different from our own Avenue U, but with an almost fake-looking section of the body of a plane sitting in the middle of the street, like a surrealist painting. There was one photo showing a tree and a lamppost, unharmed by the crash, each of them framing what looked like the wing with the letters "Airliner" painted on it and still readable, although all those people were dead and the buildings destroyed. The photos depicted only the dark side of the story with none of the funny tilt of comic relief, as no sane person could find any humorous twist in this story.

I thought about all of this as I walked home that December Monday after school through even more snow. It was cold and there were about four inches of snow on the ground as I crossed Avenue U and walked down West 5th Street, trudging along with my books in my arms and sullenly dragging my snow boots through what was already on the ground. Even with all the snow, Christmas felt a long way away, a lot longer than the six days that were left before the holiday. I wasn't looking forward to it as much as I usually did, not only because it would occur on a Sunday, thus robbing us of an extra day or two off from school—it didn't feel as joyful as it usually did at this time of year. The snow itself looked black and sooty underfoot, mirroring my dark mood, as I walked down the driveway to the side door of our house. I looked ahead and saw there was a trail of absolutely black and sooty footprints leading to the side door that led to our apartment in my grandfather's house.

I didn't step into those footprints, as I usually would have at other times, because they scared me for no reason I could rationally explain. They were like footprints that might be left after a fire, but they couldn't be that, could they? Fire? Our house looked okay, and they led toward the door, not away from it. Anyway, fire would be quenched by snow, wouldn't it? I stopped walking abruptly as these thoughts and feelings raced through my consciousness and just stared at the footprints between the door and me. I turned around to look behind me and saw they had originated on the sidewalk, where I traced them from there with my eyes back to where our car was parked not far from the house, with a light coating of snow covering the windshield.

Our car? Why was the car even there? How long had it been parked there? Hadn't my father taken it to work much earlier that morning? The footprints formed a dark path from the car behind me to the door ahead of me, like a trail of steps in a horror movie that you knew shouldn't be followed because they would lead to someplace bad. I shook myself out of that thought—this was where I lived, not a horror movie set—and trudged ahead to the door, unlocked it, and went inside. Both my confusion and my sense of reality stretching itself to near the breaking point only increased when I got inside and went up the steps to our kitchen, where I immediately found my father sitting at the table.

He had no shoes on, just his thick winter work socks and he had a glass of milk. *Milk?* He was dressed only in his long johns, top and bottoms under his old bathrobe, not his usual work pants and shirt. I found what he was doing and how he was dressed to be disturbing for no other reason than that it was a Monday afternoon and he should have been at work. I ran to him and hugged him tight, not knowing why, but feeling I needed and wanted to hold onto him. He hugged me back awkwardly, which wasn't how he usually responded to a hug from any of us, and then pulled away quickly and coughed. He made noises like he was clearing his throat and turned abruptly and went into the bathroom and closed the door. What had happened?

Then my mother came out of their bedroom carrying a clean pair of pajamas, a pile of clean handkerchiefs, and my father's slippers. She looked at me and shook her head and put her finger up to her lip to silence me before I had a chance to speak. I knew I'd be told nothing if I started asking questions and pulled off my coat and snow boots and put them by the side door without saying anything. Only then did I notice there were two pairs of work boots on the steps, both covered with a film of what looked like thick black greasy soot—the same kind that has stained the snow in the path of footprints outside.

All I could do then was walk straight to the bedroom I shared with my sister, drop my books on the floor, and sit down on my bed, feeling exhausted and not knowing why. I was also frightened and didn't know exactly why that emotion was so strong either, except that I felt in my gut that my father was in danger. My sister, who had come home from PS 95 earlier than I had because it was closer than my school, came into the room from the front parlor where she had been silently sitting and talked to me in a scared little voice:

"He's gonna be okay. Mommy said so."

"What's going on?" I asked, angry to have to find things out from my younger sister.

"Didn't she tell you? There was a fire on the ship, but he got out."

"On the *Constellation?*" I asked incredulously. "But it was almost finished! When?"

"Today. It's okay. He got out."

Then she started crying and, as I hugged her gently but firmly, and knew I had been right to be frightened.

My sister and I stayed quietly together in the bedroom that we usually shared a lot less amicably until nearly dinnertime, talking occasionally in low voices the way we had after Granma Mary had died, and a part of my mother's sanity and sense of security had died with her. I had pulled out my old copy of *Little Women* to read so I could distract myself and calm down a little and Alice asked me to read it our loud to her, so I obliged her and began at the beginning as though it were the first time we had ever heard the familiar story of the March family, which always comforted us when our mother read it to us, even if it had sad parts. We sat side-by-side on my bed with me reading and finally my mother knocked on the door and came in. She told us that dinner was ready and that Uncle Dom would be eating with us.

Uncle Dom!

My sister and I looked at each other and didn't have to speak our thoughts. We had completely forgotten about him! He had been working on the *Constellation* too! If I hadn't been so permeated by the sense of fear and unreality that had plagued me all day, I would have remembered that and worried about him too.

I put my arm around my sister's shoulder and spoke up for both of us, "Is he okay?"

Our mother didn't answer, just quietly nodded her head and turned around to go out of the door before we could ask her any other questions. We followed her out, went down the hall, and saw our father and Uncle Dom sitting at the kitchen table; each of them had a glass of milk next to their plates, where there would usually have been a glass of wine or a beer to enjoy with dinner. My absurdist inner eye took in the sight of them sitting in their pajamas at the table and told me that they now resembled two giant kids. They had only that morning been grown men, but now looked somehow shrunken—with pajamas that appeared to hang loose on them—and not the same strong adults who had left for work earlier in the day.

We didn't stop to think, my sister and I, but ran to both of them and hugged and kissed them. I was relieved to feel the firmness of their flesh and bones under my touch. I had desperately needed that physical contact with them not only to reassure myself that this was not a bad dream, but more to convince myself that the world I knew hadn't morphed into some strange universe where planes exploded in the sky, throwing children onto the street to die in the snow, and ships turned into walls of flames that consumed the very men who built them. Their hugs had sent all the ghosts and demons back where they belonged and helped me feel my little life had not turned into a modern version of a Greek myth complete with fiery monsters.

For the first time since I'd heard about the collision of the planes in the skies over Brooklyn, I felt real again, like myself, and it was the human touch of the people I loved that had done it. We sat down in our places and waited for my mother to put the food down on the table before we said a word, looking at the two men we loved best in the world and waiting for one of them to speak and break the last thread of the web of fear that had been cast over us. It was my uncle who did that first.

He looked at my sister and me and said, "I know you have a lot of questions about what happened, but let's eat dinner first and then we'll talk about it. Your dad shouldn't talk too much for a couple of hours, but he'll feel a lot better in a while, especially after he has his dinner."

My father looked at us and coughed more gently than he had before, then he smiled; it was a real smile that involved his eyes as well as his mouth, and it was for us, so we picked up our forks and began to eat. I've forgotten what we ate that night, but it was that smile that truly fed us anyway. My mother tried to act normally, as though nothing was going on as she passed the food, but we knew that wasn't how it truly was. My sister and I talked about school and the stupid things that had formerly felt important in our lives, but only to fill in the gaps until we could hear the details.

The details were what would save us. That was what our parents didn't get. They thought telling the details of something terrible would frighten us, and maybe with some children, that was the case, but not for me, and not for my sister. The details were what reassured us, what kept us from imagining things that were even worse. It was the truth, no matter how horrible that truth might be, it would let us sleep at night. That was true for me as a child and it hasn't changed at all for me in adult-hood. Don't lie to me. Give it to me straight, no matter how horrible it is. I can handle it so much better than a lie, especially a lie that was meant to reassure. And the truth is what we eventually got, piece by piece. And as bad as some of it was, there was also a lot of good in it too.

* * *

"They have too many damned fire drills," Uncle Dom began. "Especially when it's cold and the finishing work has to be done and we're behind schedule. This was one of the problems today that made everything worse. There were always little fires breaking out all over the ship all the time, so everybody got called away from what they were working on and had to go out. Then we'd hear that the fire was already out when we got topside, so everybody got dis-gusted and we mostly ignored the false alarms 'cause they turned out to be bullshit most of the time."

My mother gave him a look that told him to watch his language, but just his using that forbidden word made our world feel more normal, so when he said "Sorry" and winked at us, we covered our mouths and snickered despite our mother's admonition.

"Just like the boy who cried wolf!" said my sister, nodding her understanding.

"That's right, honey," Uncle Dom said. "You're an awful lot smarter than the guys who kept calling those damned drills! That's for sure."

My mother let that one pass.

In spite of the seriousness of the discussion, Alice smiled, happy to have been acknowledged for her intelligence.

We were in the living room after dinner and he had explained he was staying over because our mother had insisted she could take care of both our father and him while they recuperated from the effects of smoke inhalation.

"I know better than to argue with her about something like this, especially on a day like today," he had said, shaking his head softly and smiling.

Having him gently criticize our mother was one of the things that especially endeared him to us, and it had made it sound more like normal for us to hear him do that as we cleared the dishes after we had finished dinner. We had all moved to the living room after my sister and I had efficiently washed and dried the dishes together, something we hadn't done happily in a long time.

"Anyway, your dad was going up a few decks for some more insulating material when the fire drill bells went off, so he went all the way up to the main deck to see what was going on. I was working near the same section as him today and most of the guys just cursed when they heard the alarm. We're a little behind on the work and nobody wanted to waste any more time going all the way up and outside into the cold and then coming back in a half hour or an hour later to start again in the same place, especially with the snow. What a waste of time!"

My sister and I sat still listening to every word.

"So, anyway, your father went up and saw smoke and flames and a lot of confusion and realized this was a real fire and came racing back down to tell everybody that it wasn't a drill and to get out ASAP. He hollered into the section where he knew I was working and I heard him and yelled back that I was telling everybody with me and then leaving. Then he went farther down to where a bunch of the guys he knew were working and started yelling:

'*Fire! It's not a drill!*' and telling people to get out.

"A lot of the guys didn't listen the first time, so he yelled to them again what he had seen and then went back up. By that time, there was smoke starting to fill up the hold of the ship and a lot of the guys were scrambling to get up those thin little ladders. They all started to know that it was for real. We all ate a lot of smoke, but we got out—because of him," and he nodded his head at my father.

My father coughed and looked a little embarrassed, but we knew Uncle Dom had told us the truth. Our father had tried to tell everyone about the fire and had probably saved some men's lives because he had gone back down into the ship to warn them. We all got quiet and, finally, he talked.

When he did his voice was raspy, like someone with a bad case of laryngitis: "By the time we all got back up to the deck, the flames were so hot that your lungs felt a little seared from the smoke. The doctors told us all to drink a lot of milk to help coat the mucus membranes."Then he coughed again and looked over at our mother, who looked at him gently and just mouthed, "That's enough."

"Let's put on the TV," she said. "You'll probably be able to see all about it on the news and your father won't have to talk anymore. He needs to rest his voice and his lungs so they can heal."

We switched on the set and watched the news reports that showed scenes of the Navy Yard with the smoke billowing out in a huge plume, practically obscuring the view of the ship. We learned the fire was believed to have started around 9:30 am when a tank with over 500 gallons of fuel in it on the deck of the ship was accidentally hit by a forklift and pierced. This had caused the fuel to leak down into a lower deck inside the body of the ship where it was ignited by the sparks from some welders using their equipment down below.

We looked at each other when we heard this. My sister and I were seated side by side and I instinctively put my arm around her as if to shield her from my thoughts, but I knew she had the same thoughts I had: *Uncle Dom was a welder.*

"Thank God he had been working below and not on the deck where it had first happened."

The report went on to say a lot of extra wooden materials were being stored in a make-shift hangar, also made of wood, on the flight deck of the ship because the ship was close to completion and the materials were to be moved soon.

"Not soon enough," I thought.

As the details had come in, it was revealed they had attempted to fight the fire on the deck with the regular firefighting equipment kept at the shipyard, but when a huge flame shot up from the shed as it completely ignited, the Brooklyn Fire Dept. had been called at 10:30 am.

Not soon enough again, I thought.

The Firemen, who were called from as far away as Nassau County on Long Island and Yonkers in Westchester County, not only had to fight the fire, but also had tried to save the over 4,000 people who worked on the ship. This was all complicated by the fact that the ship had no electrical power of its own.

As my father and Uncle had told us for months before the fire, they were all basically using extension cords for light and power. The ship was not far enough along in its construction that it had self-generated power, so the shipyard workers were always tripping on these extension cords as well as the compressed air hoses that appeared to be everywhere. These air hoses were typically fed through the doors of the ship's labyrinth of compartments and were used to get compressed air into the compartments for the equipment that they needed to do their work. This deadly combination of blocked compartment doors and electrical wires snaked around the entire inside of the ship's intestines and did not allow any compartment to be closed off to contain the fire. We had learned from the Fire Department's visits to our school since we were little that a closed door slows down the spread of fire inside a building, but there had been no doors that could be closed on practically the whole ship.

Also, the fresh paint on the interior of the ship literally melted into a toxic stew with the heat of the fire. One report said the typical breathing apparatus for a firefighter lasted approximately forty-five minutes, but during the fire aboard the *Constellation,* it only lasted for twenty minutes before the air was used up because of the density of the toxic smoke that was produced.

It took the firefighters twelve hours to put out the fire. The miracle of the day was that they saved all but fifty people, most of whom were overcome by the smoke before they could escape, a fact that made my sister and me shudder.

After my mother insisted we switch the channel from the news to something else, we just sat and looked at our father instead of at the TV. He had willingly gone back into that inferno and by doing so, had saved some of those guys he worked with; whoever had listened to his warning when he went back to tell them it wasn't a drill and had gotten out had been saved and had gone home to their families that night, too. Because of him. Uncle Dom was one of those guys and he knew it, too.

I'd never thought of my dad as a hero to anyone in the world except me. He was just a guy who worked hard and took pride in what he did to keep our country strong and manage the best he could to provide for himself and his family. I knew he had been in World War II and had had malaria multiple times while he served in the Philippines, because they had no supplies of the quinine that was used to fight the disease, only the synthetic compound Atabrine, which didn't work as well. The plantations in Java that produced most of the world's supply of the drug (which is extracted from the bark of the *cinchona* tree) were then controlled by Japan, which explains why the American soldiers couldn't get any.

My mother had told us about his repeated bouts of malaria, with its debilitating bouts of fever and chills, which had left him weakened and susceptible to a lot of illnesses when he returned from the service at the end of the war. She said the first winter after he had been discharged after the war and returned to New York, he had been constantly sick and had finally developed a full-blown case of pneumonia. She told us that he then had decided to stop smoking his occasional cigarette and had gone back to work as soon as he was well.

When I asked him about the malaria and how it had weakened him so he got sick when he returned home, he said he had been in the hot climate too long and his blood had "thinned out." He told us that all he had needed to do was to get used to the New York weather again and stop smoking and then he was fine. He always told us that nothing he had done in World War II had been "hero stuff." He had simply tried to survive and stay alive to return home. A lot of guys like him had just "done their duty" as he called it. Then, to change the subject, he told us that he had begun to respect Elvis Presley because when it came time for him to be drafted, he just did what he was supposed to do; he had liked that about him—that and

"Love Me Tender," a song he said his generation could like, too.

When he spoke about his service in World War II, he had made us laugh with his stories about working as a cook in the Philippines and making a sort of crumb cake for the men, to hide the fact that their only store of flour had been infested by tiny insects called boll weevils. He told us that after they managed to get a new shipment of flour (*and hopefully quinine*, I thought), he stopped making the crumb cake because "there was nothing to hide anymore." After a few crumbless weeks, a number of the men in the unit requested he make it again and so he did. However, after they ate it they complained to him that "something was missing." He always laughed with us when he told this story, adding it was sometimes better not to know the recipe.

Like most of the men of his generation who had served in World War II, he never talked about it much unless we asked him questions, except to say he was glad he'd served his time and had a chance to see San Francisco for a few days when he had been discharged after the war. He had liked that city so much he'd even considered moving there—a thought that was quickly extinguished by my mother, a diehard New Yorker.

He had always had a great pride in being able to work with his hands and do the best job he found himself doing at any given moment, whether it was insulating the pipes on the ships by sewing a covering over the raw asbestos that would one day take his life from him too soon, or making an omelette for his children's breakfast. He had wanted to go to school to become a chef when he got out of the Army, but the combination of my birth and the offer of a return to the good steady job at the Brooklyn Navy Yard (where he had worked before the war, until he had been drafted into the Army) had postponed that dream until he found himself cooking only for his family. He was better at it than my mother was, because, unlike her, he loved to cook, and taught us a lot of kitchen skills that girls usually learn from their mothers, but not how to make crumb cake.

When I think of him now, I am reminded of a little needlepoint sign that I picked up in an antique store and still keep on a wall of my home. It says:

"Bloom where you are planted."

My father would have told you that, of course, people don't get to pick where they were born, but that he felt particularly lucky that he had been born in Brooklyn. He also didn't choose to be an Italian-American, but he was proud of his heritage and the fact that his people had contributed a lot to the world in general and America specifically; why, he might even have told you that Caesar Rodney (who, although dying of cancer, traveled from his sickbed to ratify and sign the Declaration of

Independence) was an Italian-American, giving greater emphasis to the word after the hyphen, but proudly speaking the first word.

I think it was this sense of—two feet firmly planted in the ground—common sense that most made an impression on me in the few weekdays left before Christmas after that horrible December day. I would rush home from school for the rest of that week to be sure he was okay; our mother had gone back to work and my sister came home to eat lunch with him and check on how he was doing. I'd still find the piles of dirty handkerchiefs by the washing machine stained with a mixture of soot and sputum that he continued to cough up for another week or more. He was always okay, and once I even found him reading my latest issue of *Mad* magazine.

To my surprise, he told me he liked the way they looked at life; I promised to share the magazine with him whenever I bought a copy. In the future, the Spy vs. Spy cartoon stories created by Antonio Prohias became a favorite of his, just as the Sunday comics used to be for me when I was little and he read them to me. He especially liked the fact that Prohias had escaped from the totalitarian Castro regime just in time to find success in America. It felt right to him, he told me, that our country would always be a place of hope for people from all over the world—like the guys he worked with at the Navy Yard.

He still drank milk until Christmas arrived and then he told my mother that he thought it was making him produce more mucus and he was going back to my grandfather's home-made red wine and pasta *Aglio e Olio* to cure himself. He and my Uncle Dom were going to the doctor the next week to be checked out so they could return to work right after the holidays. Although none of us felt good about this, we knew it would have to be. It was the right thing that should happen in the next part of our lives.

The *USS Constellation* was finally finished in October 1961. It would be the third ship in the US Navy to bear this name and was known affectionately as *"the Connie"* by her crewmen. She was named for the constellation of stars on the flag of the United States of America. The *Constellation* eventually saw service in Viet Nam and other parts of the world. The ship was eventually decommissioned in 2003 and at last report was retired to Puget Sound Naval Shipyard in Washington State.

My father and Uncle Dom were both deemed okay to resume work and did go back to the Navy Yard, where they continued building and repairing other ships until the Brooklyn Naval shipyard was closed by then Secretary of Defense Robert McNamara in 1966—the same cabinet member who contributed to our country's disastrous experience in Viet Nam.

In all the losses of the future, both personal and collective, I have always remembered the fact that our family continued to go on and on after a tragedy. Perhaps they didn't take enough time to heal or to mourn, but because of the way they faced up to their hardships, I learned from my family that our city, our country, and that precious family would continue to survive. I know I can never repay them for this important lesson, except by living it and passing it on.

As my father would say:
"La vita deve continuare!"
"Life must go on!"

November 9, 2011
Rosemary Neri Villanella

CPSIA information can be obtained
at www.ICGtesting.com
Printed in the USA
FFOW05n0106260417